Evan Dickson

MR FIVE PER CENT

By the same author

COUNT FOLKE BERNADOTTE

RALPH HEWINS

Mr Five Per Cent

THE STORY OF

CALOUSTE GULBENKIAN

RINEHART & COMPANY, INC.
New York

To

MY MOTHER

who made this book possible

FIRST PUBLISHED IN THE UNITED STATES IN FEBRUARY, 1958

CONTENTS

PREVIEW

A BRIEF entry in *Who's Who*, 1955, reads: 'Gulbenkian, Calouste
Sarkis . . . has pursued a commercial and industrial career;
recreations art and gardening.'

That must be one of the biggest understatements and most misleading self-exposures in a monumental reference book.

What garden? For the first sixty-five of his eighty-six years—in
Turkey, Russia, London and Paris—he never cultivated an acre of
garden. For the last twelve years of his life he lived almost entirely in a
Lisbon hotel. His interest in flowers began at the florist and ended with
the smile of his current lady friend. His fondness for vegetables did
not go beyond the dishes prepared by his chef. He is never known to
have soiled his hands with manual labour, in the potting-shed or the
herbaceous border.

True, he built a fantastic £25,000 "winter garden", which took
three years to lay out on his Paris rooftop in the 1920s and nearly
drove his wife out of her wits. But he did not supervise the construction
and only very rarely visited it to dictate letters in hot weather.

There was also the "Gulbenkian Folly" six miles outside Deauville.
This was 150 acres on which he spent hundreds of thousands of
pounds from the late 1930s onwards. It was laid out by the celebrated
French landscape gardener Duchene, who was responsible for Blen-
heim Palace gardens, and would have been an international showpiece
if ever the public had been admitted. There were trees from all over
the world, including many exquisite Japanese pines. There were also
exotic oriental birds, including peacocks and Japanese pheasants.
Sixty gardeners were employed and the superintendent had a fine house.
But Gulbenkian never built a house for himself on the estate, not even
a summerhouse. On his rare visits—for a week or two in June and in
September (out of season)—he preferred to stay at the Hotel
Normandie. There were not even comfortable seats, just a couple of
occasional chairs on which he used to spend most of his time working
at his papers.

The only soil he ever really cultivated was the desert of the Middle
East and the tropical wastes of South America which produce the
liquid gold to make the modern world go round.

For sixty years little, five-feet-eight, "Mr Five Per Cent"—as he

vi

was called with a suggestion of mingled awe and contempt from his holding in the Iraq Petroleum Company—bestrode the oil world on both sides of the Atlantic, like a small colossus. In the process he also became known as "The Richest Man in the World", which was probably not much of an exaggeration, until the Texas oil magnates outstripped him towards the end of his life. If his estate could have been realized, when he died in 1955, he would have been worth something in the neighbourhood of £150,000,000.

He was also known as the "Mystery Millionaire", because he did not seek fame and set no store by personal publicity. 'The most precious thing money can buy is privacy,' he said.

After publishing a technical book on oil as a youth, and a few magazine articles, he never again broke into print. He addressed no annual general meetings of shareholders, gave no Press interviews, was seldom mentioned in the gossip columns, even more rarely photographed. He carried self-effacement to the extreme of his *Who's Who* entry.

It is possible to reconstruct a full and intimate account of his long, involved and hidden life only thanks to the co-operation of his son, Mr Nubar Sarkis Gulbenkian, to whom I am deeply indebted.

Nubar Gulbenkian says: 'Father consulted me about everything and, although we sometimes quarrelled seriously—possibly because we were so much alike—I was the apple of his eye. I had real affection and respect for him, despite the fact that he always terrified me.

'He was not a saint and I don't want a whitewashed biography of him. I want an objective account, showing him as he really was, with all his faults, as well as his virtues. That is why I am helping you. I want the book to be accurate.'

That is how Nubar has come to spare many hours during the eighteen months since his father died, giving me 15,000 words of closely condensed notes.

He has also helped me to obtain access to the *Memoirs* written by his father in September 1945, 'with particular reference to the origins and foundation of the Iraq Petroleum Company Limited.'

These *Memoirs* are unique and indispensable material, without which the momentous ramifications of the present oil situation in general, and of the I.P.C. in particular, cannot be understood, even by the modern chairmen of the great petroleum companies. For forty-five years Gulbenkian was an active and leading director on the inside of the growing oil industry, a record which nobody else has approached.

He says in his Introductory Note: 'This memorandum . . . has been drafted to acquaint my representatives in London, and also my lawyers, with the outline of the Iraq Petroleum Company's evolution, since its inception.

'It is a frank exposé of my work and activities in connection with the oil developments of Mesopotamia. . . . I have not hesitated, for the sake of accuracy, to make this memorandum as open as possible, even at the risk of displeasing the interested parties, but my only preoccupation has been throughout to respect the truth. . . .

'I shall be exclusively guided by the objectivity of facts I have known for certain. I know that truth is not always palatable in many quarters, but that will not perturb me.'

He does not disappoint his privileged readers. It is a detailed document, often hard-hitting and sometimes surprisingly humorous, which builds up into drama and will cause some blushes in the fastnesses of several boardrooms.

With the aid of Nubar Gulbenkian and the *Memoirs*, it is possible to compose an imaginary, but frank and true, *Who's Who* entry for 1955, thus:

'Gulbenkian, Calouste Sarkis: financier, industrialist, diplomat, churchman, philanthropist, connoisseur and Casanova. Creator of the Iraq Petroleum Company Limited. Founder of the international charitable Gulbenkian Foundation.

b. 23rd March, 1869. At Scutari, near Constantinople, of Armenian parentage, but Ottoman Turkish nationality. Eldest of three surviving sons of Sarkis Gulbenkian (kerosene exporter and one-time Prefect (*Vali*) of Trebizond) and Dirouhi, of Constantinople and Baku, Azerbaijan.

Educ. Constantinople, Marseilles and King's College, London. First in Civil Engineering. Hon. Fellow and oldest surviving engineering graduate of King's, 1952.

1888, entered father's oil business in Baku. 1891, published in Paris a technical book on oil and magazine articles. 1893–4, oil research for the Ottoman Government in Mesopotamia. 1896, London representative of Russian oil interests and first contact with leading British oil companies and financiers.

1897–8, obtained Persian oil concession for £15,000 and offered it to Royal Dutch-Shell, who rejected it as "too speculative". 1902, naturalized British subject.

1902–3, brought the Russians into the new Royal Dutch-Shell merger, thus consolidating it against Standard Oil competition.

1907, arranged American finance for the Royal Dutch-Shell to break into the American market, thus laying the foundations of the present main British dollar asset.

1910, Financial and Economic Adviser to the Turkish Embassies in London and Paris. 1910, Technical Adviser to Sir Ernest Cassel's Financial Mission to Constantinople and Executive Director of the resulting all-British National Bank of Turkey, which was to merge successively into African and Eastern Concessions Ltd. (1911), the Turkish Petroleum Co. Ltd. (1912) and the Iraq Petroleum Co. Ltd. (1929). Original shareholding in the Bank 40 per cent, whereof 25 per cent surrendered in order to introduce the Royal Dutch-Shell in 1911.

1912, Senior Financial Adviser to the Turkish Government. 1913, surrendered another 10 per cent in the Turkish Petroleum Co. in order to introduce the British Government's Anglo-Persian Oil Co., thus reducing shareholding to 5 per cent. March 1914, Foreign Office agreement, signed by Britain, Germany, Turkey and the Royal Dutch-Shell and the Anglo-Persian Oil Co., the companies each providing a 2 ½ per cent share in the Company for the Gulbenkian interest. 28th June, 1914, the Grand Vizier, Said Halim, confirmed the concession in writing.

1915, introduced Royal Dutch-Shell to 65 per cent of the Aranguren Oil Concession, Venezuela, thus promoting the Company's half-share in the world's second largest oil-producing and largest oil-exporting country. 1918, introduced Royal Dutch-Shell to the Mexican Eagle oilfields, thus again consolidating the Company's world-wide interests against competition.

1916–20, organized French entry into Turkish Petroleum Co., instead of the Germans: ratified at San Remo Treaty, thus founding the French oil production industry. 1918, Gulbenkian oil interests in Russia confiscated by the Soviets. 1921–8, organized American entry into Turkish Petroleum Co. Definitive "Red Line" Agreement bound the partners to collaborate in all aspects of the petroleum industry within the borders of the former Ottoman Empire, thus shaping Middle East oil development for twenty years.

1921–24, invited to represent the Armenian people at the Peace Conference. Refused. President of the Armenian International Benevolent Union.

1922, built and endowed the Armenian Church of St Sarkis, Iverna Gardens, London, W. 1934, built the Armenian Library, Jerusalem.

1931, was offered Saudi Arabian oil concession for £20,000 gold, but frustrated by the British Government, thus letting the Americans into the second biggest oil reserves in the world.

1933, obtained Qatar concession by means of the "Red Line" Agreement.

1940–3, in "Vichy" France: 5 per cent Iraq Petroleum Co. interest confiscated by the British Custodian of Enemy Property: declared an "Enemy under the Act": assumed Persian citizenship, having been a Persian Commercial Counsellor for twenty years: on Persia entering the war on the Allied side, took up residence in neutral Portugal. 1945–8, obtained back-payment for 5 per cent Iraq Petroleum Co. oil confiscated during and after the war. 1948–54, the "Stroke 54 Documents", absolved the American partners from "Red Line" restrictions, thus letting them into Saudi Arabia; and, in return, permitting the Iraq Petroleum Co. greatly to increase production (34,000,000 tons in 1955), making Iraq the sixth oil country of the world.

1945, advised Mr Harold Ickes of the United States Government to admit Soviet oil interests into the Middle East, in exchange for compensation for expropriated Western interests and fresh rights, as being a basic solution for the area. Rejected.

1951, advised Persian Government not to attempt to nationalize the Anglo-Persian Oil Co.: position as Persian Commercial Counsellor terminated.

Art Collections include paintings by Rembrandt, Reynolds, Lawrence, Gainsborough and Fragonard: Houdon's sculptured figure of Diana, commissioned by Catherine the Great: Marie Antoinette's table: the late J. P. Morgan's collection of Ancient Greek gold coins: the Yeates-Thompson Collection of Manuscripts: the Ancient Egyptian obsidian head of "The King of Kings": Old French Silver and Gold by Germain; Vermeil; jade; ceramics and Persian carpets. Loan exhibitions at the National Galleries, London and Washington, D.C., the British Museum, and National Museum, Lisbon.

Hobbies: negotiating, walking and women. Decorations: none.

M., 1892, Nevarte Essayan. One s., one d.

Address: 51 Avenue d'Iéna, Paris, and Hotel Aviz, Lisbon.

(Died, 20th July, 1955, Lisbon, leaving $70,000,000 cash, £5,000,000-a-year—rising to £10,000,000-a-year—and the art collections to an international charitable Gulbenkian Foundation to be headquartered in Portugal.)'

PHASE I

1869-1914

OCCUPATIONAL RISK

WHEN Calouste Sarkis Gulbenkian was born at Scutari, on the Asiatic shore of the Bosporus, in 1869, he qualified technically as an Oriental, although his father had by then opened an office on the European side of the water in Constantinople. Spiritually he was always an Oriental—in business and in private.

At the age of seven he was given a Turkish five-shilling piece (a silver *medgedeh*) and took it straight to the bazaar—not to invest in a sticky mess of Turkish delight, but in an old coin. On his return home, he showed it to his father, who scolded: 'If that's the way you're going to use your money, you'll end up in the gutter.' Or so Mr Five Per Cent liked to tell his children. That is the earliest recorded deal of "The Richest Man in the World".

The few survivors from the family circle of his youth relate also how, as an adolescent, he used to come home and pull out his trouser pockets to show they were empty and proclaim: 'Now I've made a packet or I'm bust.'

He was by instinct a speculator, but he lost all his money in his early twenties. The shock and humiliation were so great that for ever afterwards he curbed this weakness. He followed a "hunch", but he was not a gambler. When he settled in London as a youth, he took the advice of the cleverest and most successful speculator of the day, Horatio Bottomley. With Bottomley's help he made a small fortune on the Stock Exchange and they parted before the First World War. So Bottomley's subsequent conviction for fraud did no harm to Gulbenkian's reputation.

He respected money and expected his family to respect it too. He was not extravagant and wanted value for his money. Until he was over seventy he never owned a big limousine but preferred to use an inconspicuous runabout. Not only did it suit his furtive way of life, but it was an economy. Even when his son talked him into a discreet black Rolls-Royce, he seldom used it and stuck to a smaller car. He liked the sea for a change, but he never owned a yacht. He reckoned it was less wasteful to charter a boat when he needed it at £100 a day.

His wife and children could have what they wanted in lump sums for specific purposes, but he was always reluctant to provide fixed allowances lest they should squander them. He also enjoyed the power which money gives over people. Mr Five Per Cent's overweening pride of possession extended over his personal relationships as well as his business organization and art collections.

The mere amassing of money was a secondary consideration for Mr Five Per Cent, although no man ever defended his own rights more stoutly, against more terrific odds. He was not a miser who gloated over money for its own sake. What made him tick was his intrinsic interest in his work, amounting to dedication and almost mania.

He was so uninterested in the results—apart from what he regarded as a fair share of the profits—that he himself seldom bothered to sign an agreement. He would leave that to his son or another of his representatives. He rarely attended a board meeting although he was always "around" on important occasions and knew exactly what was happening. He took little interest in the routine of the great enterprises which he brought into existence. He was too busy planning another coup from the comfort and seclusion of his own room. Honours, titles and kudos—fame itself—held no attraction for him. Compromise was his business and he never had regrets about how much more money he might have made if circumstances had been different. He was interested in facts and realities, not "ifs".

His son says: 'Father kept his brain clear of unnecessary detail so that he would always be able to see the wood for the trees. He didn't want to develop a technician's outlook and lose his vision.'

Everybody who knew Mr Five Per Cent agrees that he was a terrific worker. Not that he often went to an office. It was mainly done by thought from his own armchair, personal contacts and conscientious reading of reports from his associates and subordinates all over the world.

One of his advantages was excellent health, which did not desert him until he was eighty-three.

*　　　*　　　*　　　*　　　*

His elder brother died in infancy and Calouste was a small, sickly baby, who was accordingly coddled by his parents and nurse. Later he coddled himself.

Says Nubar: 'He insisted on the finest French cooking and wines, at home and in restaurants. But he ate and drank sparingly. He never let himself get comatose with heavy food or drowsy with drink when he was on business, although he would sometimes celebrate liberally after bringing off a deal.

'Because he "hated people", he evaded big dinners and receptions unless he thought he might be able to buttonhole somebody useful or pick up an interesting new acquaintance. But these outings became very much less frequent as he got older and his select circle of gifted friends became more firmly established. The time came when he reckoned he had the best people in the world working for him and he did not need to go in search of fresh contacts.

'He did not believe in expending social energy indiscriminately and refused to take part in most of my mother's more gregarious activities. He avoided everything which he regarded as unnecessary.

'His moderation, in diet and entertainment, was really a means of conserving energy for his main purpose in life, his work. He looked after himself so carefully and took such pains to keep fit that sometimes he was thought to be a hypochondriac.

'There was the daily massage and Swedish drill and the twice-daily constitutional. He surrounded himself with a battery of patent medicine bottles. He even employed two independent sets of doctors, checking one against the other to be on the safe side.

'Throughout his life he never took any violent physical exercise, nor played any competitive games. He considered they were either dangerous or a waste of time or both. When I went to Harrow he forbade me to play games on the pretext that I had a weak heart and when I started riding to hounds up at Cambridge, he protested: "I sent you to be educated, not to kill yourself."

'All these measures he regarded as ordinary, rational precautions for keeping his health and self-preservation. He was not really seriously worried about himself. He seldom went to bed before midnight.

'As he repeatedly pointed out, his grandfather lived to 106 in a less hygienic age, before the development of modern science. He firmly believed he would break that record and acted accordingly.'

The one blemish which did worry Mr Five Per Cent was his prematurely bald head. His brother-in-law, Atvarte Essayan, says: 'Anybody who could put another hair on Calouste's scalp could get something out of him: and he didn't part with much lightly! He scoured the world for new hair lotions and was always experimenting with new barbers. But nothing seemed to help. He was very sensitive about it and for that reason usually wore a hat. His baldness also partly explains why he so seldom allowed himself to be photographed. Although he prided himself on his virility, he never seems to have heard of the comforting theory that bald men are supposed to be good lovers. An obsession over being small would have been understandable, but that never seemed to worry him.'

*   *   *   *   *

His father and mother, Sarkis and Dirouhi Gulbenkian, were Armenians, sprung from a race with which the word "massacre" has been associated for centuries. Calouste was therefore born to a tradition of danger and horror. No wonder he was wary and suspicious, even of his own kith and kin. Only the craftiest Armenians survived.

They were persecuted for three reasons. Their historical homeland was in the eastern half of modern Turkey and spilled across into Russian Transcaucasia and North-west Persia: at the crossroads of East and West: on the highway of great invasions and migrations, with hostile cultures on every side. The Armenians were the first nation on earth to adopt Christianity as their state religion: in A.D. 303, ten years before Constantine the Great proclaimed it from Byzantium through the Roman Empire.

Ever since they have had to fight and scheme to preserve their faith, against Zoroastrian Persians, Mohammedan Seljuks, Osmanlis and Arabs and, latterly, atheist Soviets. Thirdly they are "the intellectual cream of the Middle East", as Lord Cromer, the creator of Modern Egypt, put it. Their clear minds, administrative ability and commercial genius earned them great positions and enormous wealth: but their very qualifications aroused the jealousy, envy and fear of their overlords and the mob—with dire consequences.

During the century since Mr Gladstone first alerted the British public to the plight of the Christian Armenians under the Ottoman Turks in 1853, three out of four of the 2,000,000 Armenians in Turkey have been exterminated. Today, according to Vazgen I, the Catholicos (Primate) of the Armenian Church, there are 1,400,000 in their Soviet Republic, another 1,500,000 scattered throughout the Soviet Union. Altogether there are probably not more than 5,000,000 Armenians in the world. At their zenith, under Tigranes the Great, the "King of Kings" and mightiest monarch in Asia (94 to 56 B.C.), they numbered at least 30,000,000.

The miracle is that they survived at all—let alone prospered. When Sarkis and Dirouhi were young, a Mohammedan was entitled to stop an Armenian or any other Christian in the street and cut his head off—just to test the quality of his sword. An Armenian was obliged by law to carry a special handkerchief to wipe the dust off any Muslim's shoes. To carry or possess arms was a legal offence for an Armenian and punishable by death. They were not even allowed to have knives beyond a certain length.

These things were not at all in Calouste Gulbenkian's line and he left Turkey behind as soon as possible—only returning briefly, at long intervals, when necessary and then only with safe-conduct. He last visited the Middle East in 1934.

Gulbenkian *père* was one of the select few Armenians who triumphed over adversity. His son notes at the start of his *Memoirs*: 'My uncle and father were large importers of Russian oil.' In fact, Mr Five Per Cent was born with liquid gold in his veins. He was never the traditional "Armenian rug merchant", although the *Daily Express* repeated this myth as recently as 5th August, 1955, under the headline: 'When Mr Five Per Cent sold carpets at the Savoy.'

'My father,' wrote Calouste, 'besides being a petroleum importer, was also entrusted, through his agents, with the collection of the revenues of the *Liste Civile* (the Sultan's Privy Purse) in Mesopotamia.' In this Sarkis was following a profitable and dangerous Armenian tradition.

Lord Radcliffe, who was Mr Five Per Cent's lawyer and confidant for twenty-five years, adds yet another fact to the scanty knowledge of the Gulbenkians' rise to riches. Sarkis was also Prefect (*Vali*) of Trebizond for a time. From surviving relatives we also know that Sarkis and Dirouhi originated as petty merchants in Caesarea (Kaisaria) of Cappadocia, the sheep-raising and carpet-weaving province in the heart of Anatolia.

The Gulbenkians belonged to one of three distinct types of Armenian. They were not from the active and courageous type, tall, good-looking and sharp-faced, who held out in semi-independence in the fastnesses of the Taurus and Anti-Taurus Mountains until 1916. Nor were they the sort found in the Armenian Republic and scattered round the world, who are usually descended from Aryan and Semitic ancestors, deported or emigrated when the Arabs and Seljuk Turks swept forward in the Middle Ages. The Gulbenkians belong to the stocky, coarse-featured group, with thick, straight, black hair and the hooked nose of Semitic peoples. Such are the sturdy, frugal, industrious and intelligent Armenian peasants, who still form the backbone of this incredibly hardy race; intensely conservative in faith, manners and customs, but still ambitious and progressive, with a passion for education.

Mr Five Per Cent's most notable features were his bushy black eyebrows, and in early middle age he grew a black beard in deference to the Edwardian cult. His son's apostolic blue-rinsed beard is the joy of contemporary Press photographers.

Neither could ever have been accused of looking Aryan. Sarkis
Gulbenkian and his brother came of peasant stock and, as young men,
move into Caesarea, hawking the traditional carpets, and set up a
booth in the bazaar. Caesarea is a market town and communications
centre of about 50,000 inhabitants today and apparently the brothers
soon branched out into general merchandise, including kerosene or
lamp oil.

The modern petroleum industry was not born until 27th August,
1859, when Colonel Edwin L. Drake, in stove-pipe hat and tailcoat,
struck oil by means of mechanical drilling at sixty-nine feet in Titusville,
Pennsylvania. In 1873 the new technique was first used successfully
in Russia (when Calouste was four years old) and his father was one
of the Turkish pioneers in obtaining kerosene from the great new
supplies thus opened up. Sarkis and his brother moved to
Constantinople about this time. Through the inevitable Armenian,
who was Keeper of the Privy Purse, they obtained contracts to supply
kerosene to the Sultan and his sprawling dictatorship in Europe and
Asia. Thus the family fortune was founded.

For his services to the Sublime Porte, Sarkis was rewarded with
the governorship of Trebizond, a Black Sea port 100 miles from Batum,
the outlet for the great oilfields of Baku on the Caspian shore of the
land bridge between Russia and Asia Minor. Soon Sarkis was growing
richer from his expanding imports of Baku oil and the perquisites of
his Prefecture. From this quick rise to affluence it was a short step to
banking, since the Armenians were the usurers and financiers of the
Middle East, and the Sultan's economy was largely in their hands.
Sarkis Gulbenkian founded a merchant banking house, which lent
money and financed business all over the Ottoman Empire.

By the 1880s the Gulbenkians had graduated into the cosmopolitan
plutocracy of Constantinople, which then ranked with London, Paris,
Vienna and St Petersburg as one of the five great capitals of Europe.
But it took years before the family was accepted in high Levantine
Society. As Nubar Gulbenkian puts it: 'We were considered to be
rather provincial, as my father found out when he wanted to get
married. The Gulbenkians were only merchant bankers and were
considered to be on a lower grade than the pukka financial banks which
handled "real money".'

This is how Mr Five Per Cent's brother-in-law, Atvarte Essayan,
describes society in the Sublime Porte:

'Family life in upper-class Levantine Society, in which my sister
and I were brought up, was formal and patriarchal. Father was an
autocrat. When he entered the room, we stood up, put our heels

together, bowed and waited for him to open the conversation. When he beckoned us to sit, we sat up straight, kept our knees together—never crossed—and called him "Sir".

'In company, women did not express opinions, although they wielded great influence behind the scenes.

'The men wore formal morning coats, stiff butterfly collars—never soft collars—and they carried gloves and canes. The red fez was universal. The women wore gorgeous gowns, often from Paris, right down to their ankles. They were heavily perfumed and jewelled. Marriages were "arranged", like royal alliances, and the husband's word was law. The wives connived at their husbands' mistresses and in return were treated with courtesy, respect and often generosity.

'The men did not smoke inside the house—not even Turkish cigarettes or the hookah. If they wished to do so they had to hide in the garden. I remember my nephew, Kvork Essayan, telling me how my father asked, "What's that?" when confronted, as an old man, with a box of cigars in the office.

'Our home was one of the mansions overlooking the Bosporus in the select residential district occupied by the Pashas, wealthy Greeks, Jews and other Armenians, and the diplomats. The poorer minority groups—Jews, Greeks and Armenians—lived in their own distinct quarters.

'We had two chefs and three butlers and hordes of other servants and entertained on an almost royal scale. It was not easy. The Turkish Ministers and Pashas, being Mohammedans, were always difficult to fit in because their women were kept in the veiled seclusion of the harem.

'We got on quite well with our rich fellow-Christians, the Greeks, but not so well with our Hebrew business rivals.

'Europeans and people from the Embassies eked out our company and provided a refreshing change. We spoke Armenian in the family, but French, English, German, Greek, Turkish and some Russian and Persian were in common use: very little Arabic, because the Arabs were then subject peoples.

'It was a polished, sophisticated and well-informed society, full of gossip and intrigue, and stimulating against the decayed background of the Imperial system.'

*   *   *   *   *

Nubar Gulbenkian and Atvarte Essayan both have theories of how their elders survived, winkled their way into the Sultan's system, made themselves indispensable and enriched themselves.

Nubar says: 'It was like pruning the rose tree. Only the fittest survived and blossomed. . . .

'The Old Turk was in a way like the English country gentleman of fifty years ago. He wouldn't soil his hands with commerce. He had remained a nomadic soldier by nature ever since the fifteenth century, when he swept from the highlands of Central Asia and through Asia Minor into Europe, right down to the twentieth century, when his caste disintegrated. He lived by exploitation of his subject peoples. The administration and finance of his domain were repugnant to his nature and beyond his capacity. Somebody had to do the dirty work, which was where the able foreigner came in.

'It was always dangerous for us, although the massacres were localized and spasmodic. One developed the know-how of survival. The Sultan's self-interest and Armenian intelligence ensured a measure of safety. One struck a balance between getting richer and being useful to the régime. Friends at Court warned us when trouble was brewing. If one wasn't tipped-off, it was just too bad! Constantinople was usually all right. We did not go in daily fear of our lives. Nor were we armed or accompanied by bodyguards. In the remote and inaccessible Armenian provinces of Anatolia the risks were greater.'

Atvarte Essayan says: 'The Sultan and his Pashas lived off the Armenians, Jews, Greeks and other foreigners. It was Imperial policy to slap down the upper-class Turks, who might form an opposition and alternative régime, and at the same time to be tolerant towards the upper-class foreigners, while slapping down the masses among the minorities, who might harbour ideas of independence.

'Abdul Hamid also wanted to introduce a veneer of Western civilization. So, in some ways, we foreigners were respected—in addition to being remunerative.

'The Armenian grapevine and the instinctive wariness of our race told us when trouble was in store and our upper-class Turkish friends were usually able to confirm or deny our suspicions.'

Atvarte gives this picture of how the Ottoman Government functioned and how the Gulbenkians and Essayans operated: 'The Ministries, around the Imperial Palace on the heights of Pera, worked about three days a week from 10 a.m. to 3 p.m. Each Ministry had a courtyard, thronged with seekers after favour from the Minister and his Secretary. Each official had his price, from the top right down to the doorkeepers. More than a score of people might have to be bribed. If the baksheesh was too much, the upper hierarchy would conclude that the suppliant was rooking the state excessively and inviting the Sultan's revenge. If the baksheesh was too little, the recipient all along the line would be insulted and there was the additional risk of a competitor muscling in with the right amount. It was also fatal to tip an underling too much because his superiors would hear of it and their dignity would be affronted.

'Calouste Gulbenkian's success was due to his never making a mistake with the baksheesh. His inside knowledge of each man's precise position in the price chain to the top was uncanny.

'He also knew the exact state of each Minister's health and frame of mind and the most propitious moment to see him. He found out by bribery exactly whether the Minister had enjoyed a satisfactory session with the lady of his choice from the harem (or with one of his boys, who were often more prized than the women), whether the Pasha had eaten well or had a stomach ache. Calouste seemed even to know when the Pasha was going to belch or break wind!

'At the right moment the visitor shuffled forward, never looking at the Minister, keeping his knees together, bowing and scraping. Then, with hands crossed across the breast, he would ask after the Pasha's health, mention the business in hand, receive a nod and be swept with a wave of the hand towards the Secretary.

'The serious business then started. What was the Minister's cut on the contract to be? How much was the Secretary to get? When the price was fixed it might be three times as much as the contract was really worth. The state, the officials and the trader each had to be satisfied under conditions which were understood by all parties, but nevertheless the negotiations were extremely difficult and tedious to carry out.

'Calouste had a genius for this technique. One of his favourite sayings was the Arab proverb: "The hand you dare not bite, kiss it." Compromise was in his blood.

'It was also a nerve-racking procedure for the Ministers. Their lunch arrived daily at the office, straight from the Sultan's kitchen, on trays, under white napkins. And it had to be eaten. It was supposed to be a compliment to be fed by His Sublime Majesty and an insult not to leave a clean plate.

'In reality it was the Sultan's method of securing his Minister's loyalty. A dose of poison could so easily be concealed in the highly spiced dishes or the sickly Turkish delight. Spies saw that the food was not refused or thrown away. And if the Minister jibbed, it was taken to mean that he had a guilty conscience, perhaps over accepting excessive bribes.

'Each Government deal was therefore worse than tricky. It was a matter of life and death. Such was the exacting business school in which Calouste and our two families were conditioned.'

2

PRODIGY

FOR generations the Gulbenkians have been intermarrying. This has been due to the isolation and scarcity of the Armenian communities in Asia Minor; their distinct racial and religious characteristics; close ties in the face of constant persecution; and the urge 'to keep the money in the family'. There was nothing therefore unusual in Sarkis Gulbenkian marrying his distant cousin, Dirouhi Gulbenkian, from the flea-bitten suburb, Talas, in Caesarea.

The result of their inbreeding was shown in their four children. The first son died in infancy; the second was the infant prodigy, Calouste, and then there were his very ordinary brothers, Karnig and Vahan.

Sarkis and Dirouhi seem to have spotted Calouste's quality at an early age. They shared the Armenian passion for education and spared none of the available opportunities of giving him his chance. It is on record that 'Sarkis Gulbenkian led a life devoted to abnegation and constant concern for the education of his three boys. He had a horror of haughtiness or showing-off. Winter and summer he went on foot to the office, eating a democratic lunch at his desk of bread, cheese and grapes.'

In common with other successful Armenians in Constantinople, Sarkis had English and French tutors for the boys when they were of preparatory school age. They were also brought up to speak Armenian in the home, since the parents knew no other language, except Turkish, and anyway Armenian was useful for conspiratorial purposes, since it had its distinctive characters and was not widely understood. Furthermore, the Armenian tongue stirred pride in the historic achievements of the race and inculcated the Christian virtues (particularly thrift). All his life Calouste spoke Armenian in the family circle.

He was not, however, an accomplished linguist by Armenian standards. After Turkish, French was his best acquired language. His English always sounded guttural. His German remained a smattering and did not enable him to read the newspapers. Nor did he ever master a word of Russian, Azerbaijani, Persian, Arabic or Portuguese, although he lived or worked among those languages for considerable periods at one time or another.

Calouste obviously shared his parents' ambition for him. He made the best of his educational opportunities. While Karnig and Vahan were out playing the fool with other Armenian boys or swimming in the adjacent Bosporus, Calouste would be poring over his books, sticking close to the tutors and, whenever possible, listening-in to his father and other grown-ups. His thirst for knowledge seemed insatiable. He was old for his years and patronized his flippant brothers. They were never friends and he showed his contempt for them to the last by leaving their widows a mere pound a day in his will. That was about what he thought their deserts.

The two existing Armenian schools in Constantinople—the Berberian and Guetronaguan—were not good enough for Calouste, in his father's estimation. It had to be the modern new American school, Robert College (the Roumeli-Hissar). Entry was by selection and attendance there carried considerable prestige—both for boy and parent. It served as an introduction to the great world outside the effete Ottoman Empire. It also threw Calouste into the companionship of bright boys from the leading Levantine and Turkish families who had their mansions on the European side of the Bosporus.

Schoolfellows made fun of little Calouste, calling him "spotty face" because his surname literally meant "rose (gul) pimple (benk)". In order to escape he used to lose himself in the bazaars, listening to the bargaining and sometimes doing a small deal himself. He was not popular and was glad to return with his father to Scutari in the afternoon. Besides, he was the son of a rich Armenian and there was always the danger that he would be kidnapped and held to ransom.

Robert College gave him one consuming ambition—to continue his education in England, like one of his contemporaries, Vahan Essayan, who went to Harrow. With that end in view, Calouste swotted harder than ever, showing great promise at mathematics, and he was encouraged by his father.

The Essayans were self-made, like the Gulbenkians, and also came from Caesarea. But they were several steps up the social ladder, being big bankers and shipowners.

Moreover, the Essayan brothers, Ohannes and Meguerditch ("The Baptist"), who was Vahan's father, lived in two of the finest mansions on the fashionable and exclusive European side of the Bosporus. These minor palaces were built of timber in order to provide an even interior temperature winter and summer alike, and had magnificent pillared balconies overlooking the water. Each house was three stories high, with private access to the water-front, and about a quarter of a mile of wild garden behind, running up the cliffs.

The Gulbenkians, being mere kerosene importers and merchant bankers, lived suburbanly in comparison. Their stone house had no grand balcony and was almost uninhabitably stuffy in summer, because of the hot winds blazing through from the arid Anatolian highlands.

Such snobbisms bothered "Spotty Face" Gulbenkian and his ambitious father, who were determined not to be outdone by Vahan Essayan. There was, therefore, terrible disappointment when Calouste's comparative weakness in French and English rendered it impossible for him to enter an English public school. When Vahan went off proudly to conquer the world from Harrow, Calouste was taken away from Robert College at the age of fifteen and sent to Marseilles to perfect his French.

From his fifteenth year onwards for seven decades, work became Gulbenkian's preoccupation. Everything else was secondary—his own family, his foibles and even money, which he regarded merely as a token of reward for his own industry. Hence his contempt for his ineffective brothers and his arrogance towards persons to whom he became indebted. He stood or fell by his own efforts.

In the autumn of 1884 these efforts were recognized. He was admitted to King's College, London, as one of five hundred and seventeen Matriculated Students, when he was still only sixteen and a half years old and at least a year ahead of his age group, even allowing for the fact that boys went to college younger then than they usually do now.

'He must have been very advanced, especially as he was a foreigner,' say authorities at King's College today. The normal course for a boy of sixteen would have been to join five hundred Juniors in what is now King's College School, Wimbledon, or the five hundred part-time Juniors.

To revert to Calouste: in 1887, when he was still only nineteen and a half he graduated as an Associate of King's College with a First Class in Civil Engineering and won medals in Science and Engineering. In 1952 he was created an Honorary Fellow, because he was the oldest surviving graduate of the Civil Engineering School—this was the only honour which he ever accepted.

His graduation thesis dealt with mining-engineering, with particular reference to the dawning petroleum industry, as one might have expected from the son of a major kerosene importer, and a boy who had watched cisterns of oil passing through the Turkish Straits from the Caucasus to the West since childhood. (The first oil-tanker was not built until 1884.)

His thesis is still recalled in oil circles as one of the most searching and prophetic assessments of its kind, and marked him as a pioneer among the budding breed of modern technocrats.

Yet he pretended to be no technician—except on very rare occasions when it suited him to parade some knowledge. In his *Memoirs* he perpetuates the fiction, saying: 'Oil technology has always been my weak side. . . .' He was in fact shrewd enough to keep his rivals guessing. It also suited him to include his son, Nubar, in certain negotiations. Thus the *Memoirs* concede: 'My son was sufficiently acquainted with the technical side of the oil business and I asked for his assistance.'

Calouste Gulbenkian's academic precocity was paralleled by his son and his grandson, Mikael Essayan.

In Nubar's case there was no inbreeding. His father and mother were not even distantly related. So there seems to be an hereditary streak of brilliance in the family.

Having alternated between London and Paris as a child and been looked after by French nurses and English governesses until he was fourteen, Nubar entered Sir Arthur F. Hort's House, Newlands, Harrow, as a scholar in the summer of 1910. At last the Gulbenkians were all square with the Essayans.

Nubar stayed only three years. But he reached the top of the school, winning four open prizes (including the Gold Medal in 1912), given by the National Society of French Masters in 1911.

Those were happy days, despite his father's ban on competitive sports because of his son's alleged weak heart and despite the fact that he was "no good at games anyway". Nubar says today: 'Loyalty to the Old School is the strongest attachment I have had for fifty years. I always attend the three-yearly reunion dinners where I sing the school songs until the tears run down my beard.' Recently he was purring over his portrait—(beard, monocle, cigar, orchid and all) on view as the centrepiece at an exhibition of Old Harrovians in a London gallery.

Having extracted full value from Harrow within three years, Nubar went to Bonn University to learn German which his father was never able to master.

It is no use asking him today how many languages he speaks. Somebody once told him: 'You speak as many languages as a good head waiter, but not so many as an efficient hall porter.'

From Bonn Nubar went to Trinity College, Cambridge, in 1914, and took an excellent Degree (LL.B., 1917 and M.A., 1928). He was considered to have a better brain than his father, who was by this time being talked about as a "financial wizard".

Mr Five Per Cent's only grandchild, Mikael Essayan, is inbred,

according to the Gulbenkian family tradition. In the third generation he
fully lives up to the academic precocity of the three remarkable families
from whom he descended. He took a Double First, in Classics, at
Balliol College, Oxford, and has since been called to the Bar. He
has not been left a millionaire by his grandfather and he will need
all his erudition to extract something from the financial tangle left
behind. Before he married at the age of twenty-eight, Mikael also
became a gourmet and was writing expert articles for *The Good Food
Guide*.

Nubar explains the recurring triumphs of his family at English
universities in these words: 'Armenians are often a year or two ahead
of their Western contemporaries. Being Orientals, they grow up quicker
—like tropical flowers—and therefore have an advantage when they go
to British or Continental schools and colleges. It doesn't necessarily
mean that Armenians have better brains, although that may sometimes
be so.'

NOTE.—At King's College, London, Gulbenkian was befriended
by the late Professor William Thompson (later Lord Kelvin), who
suggested that he should go on to the Ecole Normale Superieure in
Paris to study astrophysics. Gulbenkian wrote to his father saying he
was set on becoming a professor of physics, instead of a businessman.
but was overruled. The father called the idea "academic nonsense",
but in later life Gulbenkian referred to his earlier project with a
certain longing.

3

BUILD-UP

1. Suitor

GULBENKIAN was rising twenty when he returned from London to Constantinople towards the end of 1887 with an excellent degree, a fashionable Victorian beard and a good opinion of himself.

From his own writing during the next two years it is clear that he had decided to make a career in the rapidly expanding oil industry: not merely following in father's footsteps on a parochial scale, but in the world at large.

He was already an expert on the geology, exploitation and marketing of the oil companies in England, France and the United States. Obviously he had acquired an insight into the industry going far deeper than anything he could have picked up by hearsay in the family circle in Constantinople or by casual reading in London. He quotes from the most recondite technical and historical sources on both sides of the Atlantic. There can be little doubt, too, that he had already made contacts in the British oil industry, although he does not mention them either in his early publications or his *Memoirs*. His mastery of his subject and the maturity of his views were far beyond the compass of an ordinary youth of his age. He must have slaved at his research.

But this priggish and dedicated young man was still human. He was vain enough to gloat over the shame to which his fine beard put his brothers' mere moustaches. He was also conceited enough to look up his fellow-Armenian, Old Harrovian Vahan Essayan, in order to talk big about 'varsity life in England.

Once more Vahan was a jump ahead. He had won the hand of one of the great heiresses of the Armenian world, none other than Anna Karakechia, daughter of Abraham Pasha of Egypt, who was brother-in-law of the great Nubar Pasha, Prime Minister to the Khedive Tewfik and his four predecessors. Abraham Pasha was immensely wealthy, the owner of the ex-Empress Eugénie's famous pink diamond, which had to be sold after the deposition of Napoleon III in 1870. Nubar Pasha was even wealthier and had been for forty years a statesman of world repute. The brothers were the pioneers in reclaiming and developing the desert of what is now Heliopolis, the millionaires' suburb outside Cairo. From the point of view of prestige and money, Vahan had made the best catch available to an Armenian. The match crowned the Essayans' status as the greatest Armenian family in Constantinople.

Calouste was shaken. The Essayans had stolen a march again. Socially they were now a further grade ahead of the Gulbenkians. But his instinct for one-up-manship came to the rescue. If he succeeded in marrying the Essayan heiress—Vahan's eldest cousin—he would be all-square.

He remembered Nevarte Essayan as an attractive child of ten, when he had set forth for Marseilles and London nearly four years earlier. The fact that she was still only thirteen did not deter him. Girls ripen early in the Orient. Besides, her beautiful mother, Virginie Hovassapian, had married Ohannes Essayan, the head of the family, when she was fourteen.

Calouste therefore strolled next door — from Meguerditch Essayan's big white house, where Vahan lived with his father, to the formidable mansion occupied by the senior branch of the family. Ostensibly it was a courtesy call.

Ohannes and Virginie received him ceremoniously, with the bowing and scraping formality which was the Levantine fashion of the period, and with the native suspicion of the Armenian race.

Host and hostess were of such humble origin that they could not even speak Armenian correctly, let alone French or English. They were most at ease in Turkish, which educated Armenians despised almost as much as Arabic. They were therefore on their guard against the cocksure little graduate from an English university.

Ohannes also had a shrewd idea that Gulbenkian had an eye to the main chance. When business cropped up during the conversation, as it inevitably does before long amongst Armenians, Ohannes was sceptical. Young Gulbenkian evidently had great ideas, but the fact of the matter was that he had no job. Nor was there any certainty that his austere father, Sarkis Gulbenkian, had a good position waiting for him. It was a discouraging interview.

But on his way out he caught a glimpse of Nevarte. Her sister, Madame Anna Frenkian, says today: 'Without doubt Calouste fell in love with her on the spot.'

It was no gawky schoolgirl nor demure debutante who met Calouste Gulbenkian's penetrating eye. He saw a petite, well-moulded dark young woman, with a natural peach complexion and great big

brown dancing eyes. She oozed vitality, gaiety and charm. It was
scarcely credible that the vision was no more than a child. She had
to be his.

He wooed her with all his persistence, persuasion and cunning
for the next six months. He was a constant caller at the adjoining
Essayan mansions on different pretexts, but he could never see enough
of her. Courting was done in the family circle in those days and they
were never alone. The two lovely gardens, full of flowering shrubs,
ran invitingly up the rocks at the back and the limpid shores of the
Bosporus beckoned to the front. Yet he dared not guide her out of
sight of unseen eyes prying from behind the shutters. Nor did she
respond. 'It was never exactly a love match on my sister's part,' says
Madame Frenkian. 'Marriages were usually arranged in the Armenian
circles of my girlhood.'

Nevarte's parents also opposed Calouste. Difficulties were put in
the way of their meeting. But he continued to besiege her secretly
with smuggled letters and flowers, books and poems.

The trouble was not only her youth and his future. Ohannes had
come up from nothing the hard way and had great ambitions for his
delightful first-born.

Says her youngest brother, Atvarte Essayan: 'The Essayans became
the greatest, richest and most influential Armenians in the Ottoman
Empire. When Calouste eventually married my sister he went up in
the world, as he undoubtedly realized, although he did his damnedest
not to show it.

'The fortune was founded by my father, Ohannes, who started as
a small trader in mixed merchandise in the provincial Anatolian town
of Caesarea. Ohannes broke through as a very young man. Besides
trading in rugs, in the true Armenian tradition, he also dealt in metal
scrap. He and his brother, Meguerditch, worked up the business until
they dared to put in a tender for the supply of copper to the Ministry
of Marine in Constantinople. This was of two qualities—one good and
one bad. The clerk at the Ministry mixed up the two prices, making
the better copper cheaper and the inferior sort three times more
expensive. And the Ministry signed for the latter! By mistake or through
bribery, history does not relate. But for five years my father and uncle
were paid three times the proper price.

'From this amazing deal my father never looked back. Nor did
my Uncle Meguerditch, although he played second fiddle in the
partnership. They branched into shipping and owned a line which
sailed the Black Sea and Eastern Mediterranean. They built the famous
Pera Palace Hotel and eventually sold it to Wagons-Lits, who had a

twenty-five-year option on it: and it was not bettered until the Park
Hotel was built before the Second World War and the Hilton
afterwards.

'My father bought land and made another fortune building along
the Bosporous for millionaires and for the Turkish Government. He
founded and owned the leading bank in Constantinople.

'When he died he was a multi-millionaire and is still remembered
as one of the great benefactors of the Armenian race. He built the
Armenian Church in Constantinople and the largest Armenian school.
In comparison Calouste Gulbenkian's benefactions to Armenian causes
were trifling and he is not considered to have been a good Armenian
from the point of view of charity.

'My sister, Nevarte, being the eldest child, was therefore an
heiress and one of the biggest catches in Constantinople. But father
being an autocrat we children could not marry as we pleased. When my
second brother, Yervante, married an alleged Jewess, it was considered
to be a scandal and, until he died, our parents never admitted that he
was married at all.

'We were supposed to marry Armenians, if possible from Caesarea,
because father insisted that "the best Armenians always come from
there". That was the one advantage which Calouste had when he was
courting.'

Calouste therefore had to prove his worth.

2. *Traveller*

'On my return to Constantinople, my father sent me to Baku to
gain experience and contact his business friends there,' writes
Gulbenkian in his *Memoirs*.

He sailed in 1888 as a first-class passenger on the Messageries
Maritimes steamship *Niemen* from Constantinople, with a horde of
riff-raff exposed to the four winds on the lower deck. As the beauties
of the Golden Horn receded into the distance he reflected on the
architectural horrors of the German Embassy on the heights of Pera,
"with a nest of rapacious eagles perched on the architecture."

First stop on the three-day voyage through the Black Sea was
Samsoun, which he noted was the point of departure for caravans
to Cappadocia, the province of the Gulbenkians' and Essayans' origin.
It was a town of 10,000 inhabitants, leading down the Kyzil and Irmak

river valleys to Mosul, Baghdad and Basra. Samsoun was also the
mailing point for Mesopotamia and beyond. He therefore recommended that a modern road should be built southwards—especially
as the imports of Caucasian oil were growing.

He did not think much of Trebizond, the next port of call, where his
father had been Prefect. The streets were full of camels and snarling
dogs and the roadstead was worse than Samsoun, although the town
had 45,000 inhabitants.

Disembarking at Batum on the third day, he found a filthy mush-
room town of single-storey buildings, where the population had
increased from 2,000 in 1878, when this new oil port was only a
fishing village, to 18,000, excluding 1,000 Russian soldiers on a war
footing. The far-distant Tsarist Government in St Petersburg seemed
to be interested only in the strategic importance of the place. The water
stank of oil and drains and the inhabitants seemed to exist almost
entirely by smuggling. Apart from fishing, the only local industry
was manufacturing wooden barrels and tin tanks for oil transport.
Indolent Customs official kept Gulbenkian waiting for hours, so that
he nearly missed the solitary train leaving each day. He could not think
why the Government did nothing to improve the sanitation and
smarten up the Customs in the interests of public health and the
economy. He also foresaw that the construction of a pipeline from the
Baku oilfields across the isthmus to Batum would increase petroleum
exports from 450,000 tons in 1888 to 1,200,000 tons in 1890.

The time-table facing him on the two-year-old Transcaucasian
Railway was depressing: Dep. Batum 3 a.m., arr. Kutais 2 p.m.,
arr. Tiflis 10 p.m., arr. Baku 5 a.m.: twenty-four hours for 400 miles.
He decided to break his journey and do some sightseeing.

At the stops to Kutais he noted the exotic birds and vegetation
and the majestic scenery, the handsome Georgian men in their colourful
national costumes and their homely women, the easy-going Ossetians,
who atone for adultery with the gift of a pig, and the remarkable
bargaining powers of the teeming peasants on each platform. 'But,' he
discovered, 'by waiting to the very last moment it was possible to
"Jew down" the vendors to 20 per cent of their original demands and
to buy a turkey for a shilling and a chicken for threepence.'

In Kutais he was surprised to find that St Petersburg was engaged
in a policy of "Russification" in the schools and administration.
Although the Russians were supposed to be the traditional friends of
Armenians, he found that the Turks, being less preoccupied with
politics, were more tolerant. Troublesome Armenians were being sent
to Siberia.

Since the last King of Georgia, George XIII, had "presented" his domain to Tsar Alexander 'to insure happiness, present and future, for my subjects' and privileges had been abolished, Gulbenkian found to his amazement that he was being waited on by Princes and Highnesses. The railway porter, the valet and the hotel cook were all titled and were still receiving feudal dues in the form of vegetables and poultry from their ex-vassals. 'Happy people, who remain so faithful to their traditions!' he reflected and tipped his princely porter ninepence.

He sampled the wine of neighbouring Gori, which was famous for its bacchanalian orgies, and regretted that it travelled badly. He also noted that the solitary telegraph line between Great Britain and the Indian Empire passed through Kutais, and that the famous Swedish engineer, Ludwig Nobel, was employing 2,000 men day and night to construct a tunnel to improve the gradient for oil transport from Baku.

In Tiflis, the capital of Transcaucasia and centre of the Russian administration, he chanced upon 'a joyous and spectacular popular reception of the Tsar'. From the third floor of the Hotel Berlin he saw the Tsar pass by, escorted by the newly formed Georgian, Armenian and Tartar regiments, which had been trained since the introduction of conscription three years previously. A Cossack regiment followed. Russian relations with the people seemed good, but 'excessive police zeal forbade the crowds to raise their hands and the procession passed in respectful silence.' The fireworks afterwards outdid the Thousand and One Nights.

Gulbenkian so enjoyed himself that he stayed two and a half weeks. He found that the bazaar on the right bank of the river, near the Sion Cathedral and the fashionable quarter, was dominated by Armenians. On the left bank the Persians were in control, but were accommodated in filth and muddy squalor, so foul that it was a menace to public health and cried out for extinction at the hand of the authorities.

He also found a flourishing colony of 4,000 German emigrants, most of them from Württemburg, who had left home in search of religious toleration. They seemed wedded to the Fatherland, with their own schools, culture and customs, and were so young and energetic that they were making a good living. In a few years these Germans were to be regarded as a sinister "fifth column", planted among the riches of the Caucasus as an adjunct for the Kaiser's imperial dream of a Berlin-Baghdad Railway, and a menace to British aspirations in Persia and Mesopotamia.

Gulbenkian found that the population of Tiflis was 100,000, composed of 40,000 Armenians, 30,000 Georgians, 12,000 Persians and Tartars and 18,000 "others".

It was nearing 11 o'clock at night when the time came for young Calouste to press on to his objective, the fabulous oil-fields of Baku. '*Au revoir*, Tiflis, *au revoir!*' he sighed sentimentally; '*Au revoir*' to the friends he would always value and remember; '*Au revoir*' to the kind hospitality and precious sources of information, which persuaded him to break his journey. In reality it was "Good-bye". He never returned.

3. Prophet

At 4 p.m. he reached the big new railway station at Baku and found it 'contrasted violently and disagreeably with the eternal silence of the desert'. Meeting him was another young man, a son of Ludwig Nobel. Sarkis Gulbenkian could not have provided a better introduction.

The Nobels were probably the most inventive family of all time and at the same time leading industrialists and financiers with world-wide interests. The father, Emmanuel, invented torpedo-boats. His sons, Ludwig and Robert, built the St Petersburg Dockyards on the River Neva. Alfred, the donor of the Nobel Prizes for Peace, Literature, Physics, Chemistry and Medicine or Physiology, was the inventor of dynamite. All of them were multi-millionaires and their wealth was incalculable. Each of them was a pioneer.

Robert Nobel was the pioneer in the Caucasian oilfields. But he and his family always co-operated and, one way or another, the brothers were all interested in Baku. Hence the presence of Ludwig's son.

Calouste learned that Robert had seized the chance of breaking into the Russian petroleum industry in 1875, three years after the monopoly held by the Armenian Brothers, Mirzoieff, was suppressed. Between 1840 and 1871, crude oil production in the Baku area had only been increased from 3,500 to 24,000 tons. But by the time of Gulbenkian's arrival in 1888, the annual production had been raised to 2,500,000 tons: thanks largely to the imagination and efficiency of the Nobels. This was fast approaching half the total United States production, which was declining. The Nobels owned 266 of the 408 Baku wells.

Gulbenkian divided the history of the Caucasian oilfields into two epochs, pre-Nobel and post-Nobel. Before the arrival of the Swedes, the oil was transported in barrels, which wasted time, money and labour, and anyway did not always reach their destination. The precious fuel was even channelled in open troughs and delivered by force of gravity to loading points.

The Nobels introduced pipelines, on the American model, from the wells to their reservoirs which could hold 4,000,000 gallons each. They also introduced the large tin cisterns, each marked with the owner's name in large letters, which were loaded on their 1,500 railway tank-cars at the reservoirs for transport to the Caspian or Black Sea. When Gulbenkian was in Baku the Nobels were busy with thousands of workmen blasting a tunnel with Alfred's dynamite so that trainloads could be increased. Ludwig had already built the first experimental oil tanker at the Motala Works, Sweden, in 1884, and by 1889 had 53 tankers plying with a total capacity of 40,000 tons.

The colossal wastage of the Baku oilfields shocked Gulbenkian's intelligence. Although it was fifteen years since astonishing reserves of petroleum had first been revealed by mechanical drilling in the Caucasus, vast gushers were often allowed to run into the sands. It was not unusual for a new well to burst 300 feet into the air and send 60,000 gallons of precious petroleum flying each day for a month on end. Two million gallons might be lost in this way before the pressure subsided and made it comparatively easy for owners to tap the supply. Gulbenkian himself got caught in a shower of petroleum. He was soaked with oil, but he noted that it was 'fine and consistent' and therefore not unpleasant. With the untrapped gushers came a hail of stones, which peppered him. The desert was literally caked with petroleum, which solidified into asphalt on which no vegetation could grow. The soil for the little park in the middle of Baku had to be shipped, on empty oil boats, all the way from Astrakhan, near the mouth of the Volga. The Caspian was black with wasted crude oil. Often there were fires, which were a menace to shipping and to the workers' miserable barracks on land. Sometimes the conflagrations spread to the wells and further millions of gallons went up in smoke.

Nobel Brothers were the only owners who bothered to cap their wells properly in the American manner, thus obtaining the maximum quantities from their properties and conserving their resources. Other owners were merely interested in getting rich quickly and could not have cared less about conservation. Gulbenkian estimated that efficient capping in the Nobel style would have doubled Baku oil profits.

The Nobels also led the way in economical distillation of the crude oil for the production of kerosene and benzine. Otherwise the valuable by-products were burned off or passed into the Caspian. Gulbenkian considered that 'the manufacture of by-products such as vaseline, benzine, sulphur, varnish and substances which go into aniline dyes was still much neglected'. He was also looking far ahead in deploring the wastage of 100,000 square miles of natural gas each day from the Baku wells.

He observed: 'I should like to instil into some French engineers the idea of going to this land of petrol, where they would find it easy to improve the drilling and exploitation of wells in many ways, as well as the refining. Products which are worth their weight in gold today are dumped in the sea. Then the rivalry between Baku petrol and the United States product will be only a memory.'

Gulbenkian was full of praise for the pioneer work by the Nobel brothers in providing amenities for their staff: 'Of all the refineries the Nobels' is the vastest and the best organized. It is not a factory, but a town of 4,000 souls. In this "Petrolia Village", flats are provided for the executives and proper quarters for the workers. There is a hospital and school at which treatment and education are provided free of charge.' Again he was looking many years ahead when great new oilfields in South America and Asia Minor would provide work for thousands more people who had been living for centuries in medieval poverty. In the 1880's such humanitarian ideas were confined to pioneers.

He was critical of the Caucasian oil marketing system, whereby owners parted with their product for a certificate, which became a negotiable asset and subject to speculation all over the world. Thus the owners were robbed of much of the profit. He recommended that owners should pump their surplus into a pool, thus regulating the price and avoiding the costly fluctuations of the world's stock exchanges.

For all his criticisms, Gulbenkian was immensely impressed with what he saw with his own eyes and what he was told on the spot 'by the highest authorities on the subject', notably Nobel Bros. Boyhood hearsay of the industry and three years' intensive bookwork suddenly became real. The future began to take shape in his mind.

His conclusions were that Baku oil was the best in the New or Old World, but that this was no use if it remained the least well known; that the most urgent need was for more well-trained engineers; that the "flash-point" of Baku petrol was lower than its American rival; and that when the Apcheron Peninsula's full 1,200 square miles were exploited, instead of a mere fifth of the area, Baku petrol would have nothing to fear from American competition and would put British oil interests in the shade. British hopes in Burma seemed to him greatly exaggerated.

He saw such a mighty future for the Transcaucasian oil industry that he was bound to consider the political implications. Thus we catch the first glimpse of Gulbenkian in his future capacity as the leading oil diplomat of the world.

He admired the way Britain was 'armed to the teeth for the economic conquest of Persia with public works, road-building, canal-cutting, shipping, banking and policing the Persian Gulf—all aiming north-wards at the Caspian'. He saw that Persia was threatened by Russian aspirations and could never resist an invasion from the north. It was 'the persistent imbecility of English diplomats' to believe anything to the contrary.

'The day when accord between Britain and Russia comes about, the tranquillity of the Orient would be established on an indestructible basis,' he recorded, adding: 'It is petrol which would contribute most powerfully to that happy result.' Prophetic words, which might have been referring to the current Suez Crisis, and a theme to which Mr Five Per Cent was to return to the end of his life.

Nor was he far wrong, in assessing the potentialities of Russia, when he anticipated the "Russification" of Asia and the reduction of the British Empire in India to 'a few enclaves like Pondichéry'. He already thought that one day we should be talking of 'The Russias of Europe and Asia', or, in modern phraseology, 'The Soviet Bloc'. One of the main reasons, which he cited, was Russian preponderance round the Caspian. The Russians were absorbing the bulk of Persian exports, because this was natural, with the Volga and its canals leading straight from the Caspian as far as St Petersburg.

He noted, too, that the French were quietly seeking by diplomatic means to realize Napoleon's dream of establishing a link with India, from the Mediterranean across the Levant. Having been Francophile ever since his studies in Marseilles, he was pleased to observe that amicable relations were being established between Paris and St Peters-burg, which would greatly contribute to the development of trade between the two countries. Years later he was to prove one of the best foreign friends France ever had.

The McKinley Bill, shutting European oil out of the United States, had not yet come into full effect. But he thought the European govern-ments would in turn refuse to accept United States oil, with the result that the demand for Baku products would double.

Briefly, everything concurred to convince him that 'the definite triumph of Russian oil was imminent'. He was on his way.

Rather than expose himself to 'the rigours of the Transcaucasian winter and the terrible storms of the Black Sea', Gulbenkian started home. He only passed two nights in Baku, where 'there was nothing to see'. The rest of his visit he had spent in the oilfields beyond the town, which had no theatre, concerts, water supply or vegetation, although it had mushroomed into a metropolis of 100,000 inhabitants and was a busier port than Odessa or any of the Russian harbours on the Baltic.

Again he said "au revoir" from the bottom of his heart, uttering 'a promise and hope of returning one day to come'. He never did.

4. Author

One of the "terrible tempests", which he had tried to avoid, turned Gulbenkian's three-day return voyage from Batum to Constantinople into a nightmare fortnight. The *Armenie* was delayed five days off the 'detestable ports' of Trebizond and Samsoun and he was relieved to reach 'the enchanting skies of Constantinople'.

The next problem was to turn his remarkable trip to account. He decided to try his hand at writing. So there came into existence the only detailed account of his many travels.

He aimed high: at the eminent *Revue des Deux Mondes,* for whom he wrote a series of articles entitled *"La Péninsule d'Apchéron et la Pétrole Russe"*, which were accepted—an achievement in itself for a foreign youth of twenty. Next year, in 1891, he expanded the articles into a book of 336 pages, entitled *La Transcaucasie et la Péninsule d'Apchéron: Souvenirs de Voyage*, which was published by Librairie Hachette et Cie, Paris, in grey calf and gilt, with maps and engravings: a de luxe production. He was an author in the leading language of the civilized world before he was of age.

His object, he wrote, was not merely to describe the wonderful Caucasian scenery, nor the legends of the cradle of humanity, but to present a study of the little understood industrial revival which was transforming the weird Apcheron Peninsula. The research must have been prodigious and the glimpses of his findings in the previous section do no more than indicate the detail which he wove into his text. In its day it would have served as an admirable tourist guide to Transcaucasia, although the style is too Ciceronian, with its crowded conjunctions and elaborate cadences, for modern taste. The chapters on the economics and technology of the petroleum industry were more than readable. They were the most expert and up to date assessment of Baku oil which had yet been compiled, and they made his name.

That was what he wanted—prestige. For once it was neither money nor power. There was no direct financial profit from the book.

Numerous spare copies of it are still stacked away in obscure corners of the Gulbenkian family's shelves.

The family believes that the ulterior motives of his literary labours were five in number:

(*a*) to convince his close-fisted father, Sarkis, that he was no longer a callow youth but a serious oil man, worthy of a responsible post and a good allowance;

(*b*) to impress Ohannes Essayan that he was a man of the world, with a future in oil, and worthy of consideration for his daughter's hand;

(*c*) to interest Nevarte in his abilities and to make up for his insignificant personal appearance;

(*d*) to provide himself with the necessary knowledge and documentation for bearding the officials of the Sultan's administration, with a view to doing business; and

(*e*) to furnish himself with impressive credentials when the time came to strike out on his own in the capitals of Western Europe.

For each special public he introduced passages calculated to make a personal appeal. For Sarkis, the former rug merchant, there was a separate chapter on the history, technique and art of weaving Oriental carpets. For Ohannes, the head of the Armenian community in Constantinople, there were the repeated eulogies of Armenian character and achievement in the Caucasus. For romantic young Nevarte there were moving legends of damsels throwing themselves from tall towers and virgins being pursued by shining knights through sacred groves. For the Turkish despots, there were allusions to their "tolerance" in comparison with the stern "Russification" of the Tsarist Government. For the insular British, at the peak of their Industrial Revolution, there were prophecies of oil replacing coke in furnaces and oil supplanting steam in the mercantile marine. For the French, who were well behind in the oil race, there were openings for engineers and other technicians to cash in. For the high-handed Americans, there were warnings that they had better look out. Baku oil—and, by inference, a young man in a hurry, named Calouste Sarkis Gulbenkian—was on the march.

Eventually the book served all its hidden purposes. His *Memoirs* say: 'I was very much struck by what I saw in the Apcheron Peninsula and, on my return, I wrote articles on petroleum, one of which, particularly in the *Revue des Deux Mondes,* a leading French review, made its mark. I also published a book on petroleum, in Paris, now

out of print. I am making these references because they have been
conducive to unexpected developments which will be explained.'

The first "unexpected development" was an invitation to call on
one of the most powerful, trusted and inaccessible officials in the
whole sprawling Ottoman Empire: the guardian of Sultan Abdul
Hamid's private finances. The *Memoirs* say: 'My publication attracted
the attention of the Minister of the *Liste Civile*, Hagop Pasha, who was
a great friend of my father, and of the Minister of Mines, Selim
Effendi. . . .'

There was no baksheesh, endless waiting in courtyards and humiliating bowing and scraping on this occasion. Calouste's travelogue
had made such an impression on his father and Turkish officialdom
that he walked straight in at the top at the first attempt: an unheard-of
feat in the formal indolence of the Sublime Porte in the days of Sultan
"Abdul the Damned".

The *Memoirs* explain why the Ministers wished to see him: 'Round
about 1890–2, German interests were most anxious to obtain mining
and oil concessions for the Anatolian Railway. (Actually the Deutsche
Bank had secured a concession in 1888.) On the other hand, the Sultan's
private Minister of the *Liste Civile* was very keen on acquiring concessions for the Crown in order to realize on these later by granting them
on account of the Imperial Treasury, instead of the Turkish Government.

'Hagop Pasha and Selim Effendi asked me to gather all the information I could get on the oil prospects of Mesopotamia. . . . I elaborated
a comprehensive report which was nothing else than a compilation
of various travellers' books, principally of reports made by Colonel
Chesney on his East India missions, and particularly from what I had
heard from different engineers of the Anatolia Railway who had been
in Mesopotamia.'

It was an historic interview. It was the origin of the mighty Iraq
Petroleum Company of today. It was the beginning of intense Anglo-
German rivalry, focusing on the oil rights and strategic importance of
the Kaiser's plan for a Berlin-Baghdad Railway, which blew up into
the First World War and had its counterpart in Hitler's dash for the
Caucasus in 1941. It was the germ of the oil rivalry between the Great
Powers, which was to dominate the subsequent history of the Middle
East, right up to the Suez Crisis of 1956–7.

The *Memoirs* continue: 'Whatever its value, there is no doubt that
my report prompted the Minister of the Liste Civile to obtain possession for the Sultan of immense tracts of land in different provinces of
Mesopotamia. Telegrams were sent to the Governors from the Palace
for that purpose. Very little money passed for the purchase of these

territories. The owners ceded when they were told that the Governors
were sending numerous Tapous (official certificates of land ownership)
transferring Government lands to the Liste Civile without any
payment.'

Henry VIII's seizure of the Monasteries was (materially speaking)
a trifle compared with the Sultan's giant land grab in 1890 and its
completion in 1899. The astonishing fact is that it was precipitated by a
pint-sized youth of twenty-one, who had stirred the cupidity of his
Turkish masters, either with information gleaned from books (without
ever setting foot in Mesopotamia) or by hearsay from the Germans
(his supreme rivals). I might add that he never visited Iraq once during
his remaining sixty-five years, although the Mesopotamian oilfields
were his lifework. His son Nubar says: 'It was only towards the end of
his life that he perhaps began to pride himself on never having seen the
land of his riches. It amused him to hear his associates saying "No
other man has made a million in oil, never having seen an oilfield for
more than half a century and knowing so little about the technique of
the industry!" '

Mr Five Per Cent's *Memoirs* point out: 'This part of the history
should be carefully noted because, later on, the heirs of the Sultan,
even after the conquest of Mesopotamia, came forth to claim these
territories (now being exploited by the Iraq Petroleum Company) as
being private properties belonging to their father.

'The Minister of the *Liste Civile* thanked me profusely for the
services which I had rendered in making the report and I shall not
forget what he told me at the time: "My boy, you ought to be very
proud because you served the Treasury of His Majesty, and to serve
His Majesty's Treasury is to serve your conscience!" With the exception of this kudos, I had no remuneration of any kind, directly or
indirectly, for all the trouble I had taken.'

But the book had not been wasted. He had earned his father's
confidence and was on the inside track on the way to the wealth which
the Sultan's Ministries sometimes offered useful Armenians.

     *   *   *   *   *

Not that the young author and Government adviser got much
change out of the disdainful Essayans, father or daughter. Towards
the end of 1891 they departed for London in order to send Nevarte's
brothers, Hrand and Yervante, to school. Anna (Madame Frenkian),
the second youngest daughter, who was the fourth child and yet only
four years younger than Nevarte, also accompanied them.

4

MARRIAGE

IN recognition of his London degree and his book, his work for
the Sultan's Privy Purse, and his twenty-first birthday, Calouste
received the then very considerable sum of £30,000 from his
father in order to set up in business on his own. To that extent it
can never be said that Mr Five Per Cent was an entirely self-made
man. He was diminutive and not very prepossessing. He belonged
to an unpopular race; and he was not sociable. But he started with the
great advantages besides brains and determination and a first-class
education: money and useful connections.

With this capital he set off early in 1892 to resume his siege of
the youthful Nevarte on whom he had set his heart and staked his
future. Perseverance was perhaps his outstanding characteristic.

He calculated that he had two new advantages to commend him
to the Essayans, besides being a Caesarean Armenian by extraction,
an expert on Baku and the consultant of Ministers. He had money.
He would also have a scarcity value in London, since the massacres
had not yet reached their height and the great dispersion of Armenians
was yet to take place. Before the Second World War there were not
more than about 500 of his race in England, mostly in Manchester;
in 1892 there cannot have been more than a handful. It was not therefore too much to hope that Nevarte might find him more attractive
in her strange new surroundings than at home. She would not have
had time to make new friends. She was reaching a more marriageable
age. In short, she and her parents might look upon him with less
jaundiced eyes.

Having failed with the conventional courting tactics, he employed
a new technique. He wooed father! This worked.

Nevarte's sister, Madame Frenkian, describes the performance:
'Calouste took a medium-sized apartment in respectable Cromwell
Road, Kensington. It was within easy distance, across the Park, of
our large house at 11, Hyde Park Terrace, Bayswater, which was then
fashionable. Whether he hoped to lure Nevarte to trysts in the Park,
I don't know. Although we all knew that he wanted to marry my
sister, he seemed to pay strangely little attention to her.

'He always seemed to be with my father, who was at that time just fifty years of age and suffering from consumption. Calouste was perpetually crouching on the edge of the oriental divan on which my father rested, talking business, business, business.

'Father disapproved of dancing and night life and Calouste was obviously trying to impress him. As Father did not speak English, Calouste was also useful to him in keeping him up to date about events and people. We entertained on almost the same scale as in Constantinople and my father felt rather out of it.

'Calouste hid in corners at parties, but he managed to be around when Father wanted help or information. We girls did not take part in men's talk in those days, so I don't know exactly what they discussed. But clearly Calouste eventually succeeded in making himself almost indispensable to my father and impressing him with being a man-of-the world—somebody who had achieved a genuine success in getting a serious book published in French, which had even attracted the attention of the Sultan's closest advisers.

'Nevarte, too, began to see something in him. There was no denying he had personality. He talked well of all he had seen. He was full of confidence about his own future. And he loved beautiful things, especially pictures and flowers. But the final word did not rest with Nevarte.

'The decisive moment in getting Father's consent seems to have been when they were strolling past a Bayswater house even larger than our own. Calouste stopped, looked hard, and remarked: "That's where I'm going to live." Father thought it was a joke. But Calouste was so serious that he convinced my father he meant what he said. The marriage was arranged. And my father's hunch proved right. In four years' time Calouste and Nevarte moved into that very same house—38 Hyde Park Gardens—and kept it for thirty years afterwards.'

They were engaged for six months and married, according to the rites of the Armenian Church, at the Metropole, then one of the leading hotels in London.

It was a smart wedding. The couple had their pictures taken by Queen Victoria's court photographer. Slender, shapely and radiant, with full red lips and her superb complexion, Nevarte still looks lovely in photographs. Being petite, she did not make Calouste look grotesquely small. With his bright eye, fine moustache and a thatch of hair, he looked presentable. Among several hundred guests was a sprinkling of the banking and shipping friends, with whom the Essayans did business; a number of Calouste's and Vahan's university and public school friends; and a cross-section of diplomats with links in the Constantinople Embassies. Calouste and Nevarte were launched in style into moneyed, cosmopolitan Society.

The honeymoon was spent in Paris, which Calouste loved and Nevarte did not yet know. They spent much time in the art galleries. But there is no record of his even buying her a new hat or a piece of jewellery. He never gave much away freely, even to his family or closest friends.

They also looked up some of his friends. One was M. Georges Perrot, Directeur de l'Ecole Supérieure, to whom Calouste had dedicated his fateful book 'with the homage of profound respect and affectionate acknowledgements'.

More exciting, for gay and sociable seventeen-year-old Nevarte, was an up-and-coming young hotelier named César Ritz. Nubar Gulbenkian says: 'Our family has always enjoyed favoured hotel and restaurant service. Mr Five Per Cent is still remembered as one of the fathers of the modern catering industry, not because he was a multi-millionaire, nor because he tipped more lavishly than other guests. He made a practice of *not* over-tipping. Yet, in spite of his trying whims, he was accepted by generation after generation of staff from the capitals of Europe down to quite humble provincial hotels as the benefactor who saved César Ritz.

'He and Ritz became friends when they were young and comparatively unknown in Paris. When Ritz and his associates were building the Hotel Ritz in London in 1906 and blazing the trail in providing exclusive accommodation and meals for the aristocracy and new plutocracy, they ran into financial and legal difficulties. Papa saved the day by putting up several thousand pounds, for which he accepted a block of shares. Thus the luxury hotel business came to London and a lucrative new form of employment was created. Papa hung on to the Ritz shares for the rest of his life: not for profit, but to keep his reputation as the friend and benefactor of César Ritz alive—and to ensure his own comfort in London, Paris, and elsewhere.'

Nevarte received no allowance from her domineering little husband. Her son Nubar relates: 'Mother *never* had any money, which she could call her own. If she wanted cars, furs or jewels, she could always have them. But she had to ask, which was invidious. Of course she had a banking account, but it was not the same as having a proper allowance and she never knew exactly where she was. Not that she was worried about bills and that sort of thing. My father always paid up. In the sense that he never denied her anything, he was generous.

But he kept a financial hold on her. She was not exactly kept "on a shoe string"—it was a golden thread.

'She was never quite happy about it. Father was very difficult and it was not easy to ask for money, even though she knew she would not be refused. He was aware of her diffidence and made use of it. It was one of his Oriental ways of showing that he was the head of the household: the boss.'

Atvarte Essayan does not agree that his brother-in-law was the real boss: only that he tried to convince himself that he was.

'Calouste Gulbenkian's success was due ninety-five per cent to his wife,' says Atvarte. 'I want you to promise to put that in your book, because it is the truth—not because she was my sister. She was a most remarkable woman by any standards—a queen. Many famous men have been inspired or helped along by their wives and that was true of Calouste. He knew it, too. That was why he so often made life unpleasant for her. Subconsciously he was always trying to prove to himself (and to her) that he was as good as she was (or better). He had an inferiority complex, although it was the last thing he would have admitted.

'Nevarte was a thoroughly sound and decent woman, whereas Calouste—even by Oriental standards—was not very nice to know. What he would have become if he had married a bad woman, goodness knows. He respected her and was superficially courteous. His counter-attacks were designed to bolster up his own ego and were not primarily meant to humiliate her. Nevarte sensed this. If he wanted to play the part of a patriarchal autocrat, like our father, it was all right by her. She had a sense of humour and put up with it. But his act deceived nobody in our two families, except himself. Psychologically Nevarte was the boss.'

Nor was Nevarte merely a moral support. Atvarte and Nevarte's son, Nubar, agree that her beauty and social graces helped him enormously. Says Atvarte: 'Calouste hated parties and people *en masse*. But my sister provided a social background for him which was of the utmost importance to his career. Although he used to say before her parties began, "I'll turn up later" and then, when he did arrive, sulk in the background, a cultured and civilized atmosphere grew up around him: thanks entirely to Nevarte. This inspired confidence.

'She collected a rich, cultivated and influential set around her, not only because she herself loved people, but in order to try and spread the belief that her husband might be human after all. Her plans to break into high Society were deliberate. From the start—when she and Calouste were still living in the Cromwell Road—she realized that it would be impossible for newcomers from the Levant to meet the real British aristocracy in their homes immediately. So she concentrated on the Jewish nobility, who, with the patronage of the Heir Apparent, Edward, Prince of Wales (later Edward VII), were getting everywhere. She realized that the Jews are in the West what the Armenians are in Russia and the Middle East: essential financiers and captains of commerce without whom a nation cannot long manage. These were the people with whom her husband had to do business and so, in his interest, she pocketed her Armenian dislike of Jews, and set out to climb the social ladder on their backs.

'Being a daughter of one of the great Christian houses of Constantinople, where her parents entertained diplomats regularly, she also had the *entrée* to many London Embassies. She brushed up these contacts and, with the help of the Jews, soon build up a *salon* where the British aristocracy were not ashamed to appear. From 1900 to 1925, her mansion at 38 Hyde Park Gardens became a centre of London social life.

'People did not come to her home just because she was rich and hospitable. Nor because she was intellectual. She took little interest in painting, literature or music. The arts were one of her weak spots and that (again subconsciously) may have been a reason why Calouste trained himself to become a connoisseur and collector: to show her up and emphasize his own supposed superiority. He planted his collections on her, ostensibly to adorn her home, in reality to educate her (against her will) and, in the process, turned the house into a museum.

'Her attractions were her wit, vitality and charm—and, in her youth, her beauty. In middle age she got plump and in later life deaf. Old and young, rich and poor, insignificant people and V.I.P.s, all interested her and she was adored. She always wanted to know how her friends were getting on and remembered what they had said at the next meeting: like royalty. She had extraordinary sympathy: a real genius for people and a flair for entertainment. Her own family and children worshipped her. Our young mother, Virginie, could not keep away from her and had to pay her a long visit every six months. Nevarte was always outwardly gay, although Calouste often made her sad and sometimes angry But he never succeeded in breaking her spirit or her good humour

'The inferiority complex, which she gave him, developed—in the familiar paradox—into a megalomania by over-compensation. Having been brought up in a patriarchal society, he became, as he grew older and realized he could never subdue Nevarte, a dictator.'

Atvarte remembers several examples of this mania. . . . At Hyde

Park Gardens he would order rare tropical fruit and exotic dishes for himself and—even in the presence of relations—keep them all to himself: just to show who was master in the house. This so annoyed Atvarte that he used to walk round to Calouste's end of the table and, helping himself, pass some of the delicacies on to Nevarte's plate. When Calouste understood his brother-in-law's intention of showing a spirit of independence, he would help himself liberally, before Atvarte could seize the dish, and then pass it, to indicate that the rest of the family was getting the scraps, as a sort of dispensation from on high.

When Mr Five Per Cent hired a steam yacht to take a girl friend on a Mediterranean cruise and—after a protest from Nevarte—was obliged to take his daughter, Rita, instead, he ate in solitary state on the sundeck, just to show his displeasure. Rita, his doctor, the captain and officers were confined below deck to feed off canned food, while fresh peaches and fish straight from the sea were sent up specially for him alone. When he was in Lisbon after the Second World War he demanded weekly catering accounts (down to the last chop) from Nevarte in Paris. If the food or wine was too good (in his estimation) for the guests, she was promptly reprimanded.

Nevarte and the rest of the family were kept perpetually on the end of the telephone. He would say, 'I may have something important to tell you at noon or after tea.' So nobody could ever settle down to anything for long or get away with a carefree feeling. Mr Five Per Cent was always in remote control, operating them like marionettes.

It was the same on holiday. Nevarte, Nubar or Rita would want to go away. Calouste would say, 'Where do you want to go?' or 'I know a good hotel,' and add, 'I'll arrange it.' *He* would make the reservation. *He* would arrange to pay the bill. He would also specify a series of fixed telephone calls, which the members of the family would be expected to take, if necessary.

In his own homes he organized an intelligence system to keep him informed of what the family were doing when he was absent. In London and Paris, the servants were spying for him; also his social secretary, Elize Soulas, who was also Nevarte's secretary. Armenian employees and six curators who were responsible for his art treasures, were also in his home espionage system. Frequent checks were taken to see that nothing of value "walked" out of the house. Even his suits and shoes were numbered.

Thus, although after 1925, when they moved from London to Paris and he usually slept at the Ritz, he rarely shared a double room with Nevarte, he knew exactly what was going on at home day and night. The atmosphere of suspicion, in which both families were brought up in the Constantinople of the Terrible Turk, was perpetuated in their Western life.

It was years before any of the family dared rebel. The heroine was Nubar's second wife, Doré who was on the stage before their marriage in 1928, after which she took up hunting and golf at Nubar's suggestion. She recalls: 'Soon after our wedding we went to see father-in-law in Paris and he tried to keep us on the end of a string. Nubar and I were golf-mad at the time and liked to play three rounds a day. But we were always being hauled back from Chantilly by telephone on one pretext or another and asked to accept calls at the club-house at such-and-such a time. I refused. Those calls quite spoilt our day. And, much to our surprise, we got away with it. Mr Five Per cent seemed to appreciate people who stood up to him.

'He also took a house for us in the Rue Emile Menier at Passy, so as to inveigle us into moving from London to Paris, where he could keep a better eye on us. Again we flatly refused and got away with it. When he knew he had lost a battle, Mr Five Per Cent seemed to make the best of it and bore no malice.

'It was the same over our marriage. I only met him once before the ceremony and he was charming and polite. But we did not have the courage to tell him we had arranged to go to Prince's Row Register Office to become man and wife. We only broke the news a fortnight later when we were honeymooning in Paris. Much to our surprise he accepted me immediately as a daughter-in-law and seemed to grow quite fond of me. In many ways he was quite sweet.'

Nevarte also came to terms with Mr Five Per Cent. When she died, three years before him, he mourned her grievously. He was never the same man again. In his own peculiar way he may have been "quite sweet" to her, too—a long way beneath the surface.

5

DOWRY

MILLIONAIRES are not popular as a class. 'A millionaire seldom laughs,' as Andrew Carnegie observed. They are secretive and the public often finds the only interesting thing about them is their money. They are also suspected of having skeletons in their cupboards. Mr Five Per Cent conformed to type.

When he and his lovely, rich, young bride moved back to Constantinople, soon after their marriage, they kept her parents' big house of the Bosporus warm while the rest of her family remained in London. Her brother, Hrand, was going up to London University to become a Civil Engineer. Her second brother, Yervante, was going up to Oxford, where he eventually took his M.A. Anna stayed at home to be a comfort to her mother, Virginie, and ailing father, Ohannes. Thus English became her first language.

Once he was installed in Ohannes's mansion, having achieved his ambition to marry the Essayan heiress, the first signs began to show of those illusions of grandeur, which were to cause trouble later. Calouste felt he owned the place. He looked with some contempt from the big balcony, across the narrow waters to suburban Scutari, where his own parents still lived.

This ostentation would not have been dangerous if some money had been coming in. But, as he had noted with pain, he received 'no remuneration of any kind, except kudos', for his services to the Sultan. Besides the Germans, there were others showing an interest in the possibilities of Mesopotamian oil, notably a M. de Morgan and A. F. Stahl. The Turks, awakening to the importance of their hitherto barely suspected assets, adopted their classical attitude of "playing hard to get". So began Gulbenkian's years of lobbying in the sultry courtyards of the Sultan's officials.

As the *Financial Times* said in his obituary notice: 'The question of how to extract the fuel would not have been solved for at least a generation had it not been for his uncanny powers as a negotiator. He possessed a remarkable capacity for obtaining decisions from Ottoman officials and their vassals in the Arab lands, in whose natures vacillation reigned supreme. A patient man, indeed, was required to deal with these timeless pashas and beys.'

These negotiations all involved baksheesh and the remains of his
£30,000, after his marriage trip to London, began to dwindle fast.
He could see the day approaching when he could no longer play the
grand seigneur in the Essayan mansion and would have to go cap in
hand to his parsimonious father, Sarkis. The prospect was humiliating.

He took a chance. He dabbled in stocks and shares: and lost. He
also humbled himself to go into a partnership in carpets with his
despised brothers, Karnig and Vahan, each of whom had also received
£30,000 from Sarkis to start off in business. An average of 120,000
hand-made Oriental carpets were sold every year in Constantinople
in the 1890s and it was a highly expert, competitive trade. Again, he
lost. Karnig and Vahan lost their money and were for ever afterwards
out of favour with their father.

But Calouste had one way out. He appropriated Nevarte's £9,500
dowry.

Legally, of course, the money was his. But even under the Victorian
code, Nevarte had some ethical claims to it. He did not recognize them.
Nor, according to his brother-in-law, Atvarte, did he come to the
rescue of his brothers. 'Partly because he did not believe in throwing
good money after bad: more cogently because he calculated that the
disaster would disgrace them in their father's eyes and improve his
own chances, as eldest son, of benefiting under his father's will.'

In the sense that Nevarte's £9,500 was a quarter of their joint
capital when they married and their whole capital after his own
£30,000 had disappeared, Atvarte's claim that, financially, as well as
psychologically, his sister was the most important influence in
Calouste's life, does not seem exaggerated. Her son, Nubar, agrees
with that verdict: so strongly that he quarrelled with his father on the
subject. Nubar relates that in 1943–4 his mother fell seriously ill in
Portugal, whither she and her husband had fled from Vichy France,
and expressed a wish to make a will. Mr Five Per Cent at first declined
to help her do so and finally forbade it, saying, 'It's quite unnecessary.
Tell me what you want and I will see that it's done.'

Knowing only too well how her husband liked to control his
family's finances, and that he stubbornly refused to face death, Nevarte
decided on her own, when she was better, to put his promise in writing.

So she wrote a long letter to her brother in Nice, not only recording
the promise, but recalling that she had brought the dowry of nearly
£10,000 into the marriage in 1892 and that her husband had appropriated it in order to finance his business.

She went on to estimate that her money must have multiplied in
value many times over during the intervening years and asked that it

should be devoted to the foundation and endowment of an Armenian
orphanage after her death. Besides numerous bequests to relatives
and friends, she included some outspoken phrases about a woman
with whom her husband was on affectionate terms.

First, the brother died. Then, when Nevarte died in 1952, Nubar
came across a copy of the letter in her filing cabinet in Paris. She had
written such unpleasant things about the woman and the whole
letter was so painful that Nubar decided it would be unnecessary and
unwise to show the document to his father. There was argument, but
Nubar flatly refused to let Mr Five Per Cent see it and 'this went
down very badly'.

Moreover, Nubar was determined that his mother's dying wishes
should be carried out. He estimated that the dowry must have been
at least a tenth of his father's capital in 1892 and that Nevarte was
therefore entitled to at least a tenth of his father's fortune in 1952.
He demanded that the tenth should be devoted to the foundation of
the proposed orphanage forthwith and Mr Five Per Cent was 'very
upset at the suggestion'.

Next year Mr Five Per Cent altered his will, made in 1950, and
"cut off" Nubar with a mere 1,000,000 dollars in cash and another
1,500,000 in trust to be administered by Lord Radcliffe, the son-in-law
Kvork Essayan, and the Portuguese lawyer, Azeredo Perdigao. More
wounding still was the suggestion in the new will that Nubar 'might
be considered by the trustees as a possible co-trustee, if that should be
thought wise'.

As he says: 'Father may have been prepared to carry out Mother's
wishes in his own time. But he wasn't going to take it from me.' There
was no mention of the orphanage in Calouste's will. Funds for the
orphanage were not provided until nearly two years after his death—
under pressure from Nubar.

Family differences over the will have not yet been composed. Nubar
and his brother-in-law, Kvork Essayan, have issued writs against each
other regarding their respective powers under the Will. The skeleton
is still rattling.

*   *   *   *   *

The justification for seizing the dowry was that he needed every
penny for the realization of his ambition to extract a Mesopotamian
oil concession from the Turks. The *Financial Times* records that: 'He
was one of the first to see the infinite possibilities of oil' and wrote 'a
masterly paper on its future, which he circulated to eminent but
unbelieving capitalists'. Competition for the Turk's favour was

increasing rapidly and he had to have the baksheesh to clinch a deal.

Stephen Hemsley Longrigg says in his authoritative *Oil in the Middle East*: 'Gulbenkian watched every tendency and did business with both British and Russian interests.'

Time was running out. Gulbenkian's local knowledge was becoming common property. His *Memoirs* say: 'The German interests were very anxious to enlarge the (1888) concessions of the Baghdad Railway. But two main reasons militated against their attaining their aim.

'First, they had obtained the concession from the *Government* and it was not possible, at that time, to obtain mining rights in the same region concurrently from the *Liste Civile*. Further, to press the Government to grant concessions on lands that were in the possession of the *Liste Civile* was not advisable.'

(Any Minister, who was so tactless as to grant them, was liable to find a dose of poison in his Imperial luncheon.)

'Secondly, the German interests were not financially strong enough to tackle, at the same time, the railway and the mining enterprises. They thought that the best policy was to mark time and, meanwhile, not to let another nation obtain any concessions.'

Not that the Germans remained idle. The *Memoirs* add: 'As an alternative to direct concessions the German interests strengthened their position by obtaining from the Government a *"Lettre Vizirielle"* (in 1888) by which they were promised preferential treament regarding mining rights. This should be noted as it will later be seen to become of great utility.'

Briefly, the Mesopotamian oil situation up to 1895 was this: Gulbenkian's French magazine articles in 1889 (expanded into book form in 1891) had alerted the Sultan to the possibilities of petroleum: his report on Mesopotamia had confirmed the Sultan's hopes of development in that area: the Germans were first in the field, but their railway-minerals concession from the Turkish Government was invalidated when the oil-bearing territories were appropriated by the Privy Purse: German interests were protected only vaguely by the *Lettre Vizirielle* promising "preferential treatment"; an effective concession could only be granted by the Sultan's personal representatives; and Gulbenkian was on the inside track through his friendships with the Keeper of the Privy Purse, Hagop Pasha, and the Minister of Mines, Selim Effendi.

The British and Dutch were also in the offing. It was a tedious and expensive time for Gulbenkian. He needed every penny of the dowry.

6

MASSACRE

WHAT Mr Gladstone had to say was said for the last time in public at Chester on 5th August, 1895, when he was eighty-two. It referred back to his forty-two-year old theme—the plight of Christians in the Ottoman Empire. His biographer, John Morley, calls it 'one more vehement protest against the abominations of Turkish rule, this time in Armenia'. In effect it demanded Armenian independence. It was well meant but ill-conceived. Armenians still regard it as the death knell of their race.

Since the Gulbenkians and Essayans were caught in the consequences of Mr Gladstone's folly and the Cyprus question is bound up with it to this day, an historical sketch is necessary.

In October 1853, six months before the Crimean War, Mr Gladstone, as Chancellor of the Exchequer, first brought the Armenian cause to the notice of the British electorate. But his emotions and power politics became inextricably confused.

He recognized the need for maintaining the integrity of the Ottoman Empire, in order to preserve the balance of power in Europe. The absorption of the outlying provinces of the Ottoman Empire by Russia, which would have followed the collapse of Turkey, would have been dangerous to the peace of the world. It was the duty of England, at whatever cost, to set herself against such a result.

But the maintenance of the Ottoman Empire was incompatible with Mr Gladstone's liberal and humanitarian ideals. It implied acquiescence in the barbaric rule of the Mohammedan Sultan over twelve million Christians.

Mr Gladstone wanted it both ways. The result, says John Morley, was that the Middle East 'has been subject every few years since we were born to European discussions'. Another result was the Crimean War, in which the plight of the oppressed Christians served as cover for the imperialism of both sides.

The Treaty of Paris, which ended the Crimean War, was regarded by Disraeli as 'on the whole satisfactory', because, according to his biographer, G. E. Buckle, it stopped the precipitate solution of the Eastern Question, which Russia had attempted to force; gave Turkey respite and breathing time, and, theoretically, 'afforded the Christian races an opportunity of showing whether they possessed the vitality to win the independence of both their would-be protectors'.

This last theory was a blatant piece of hyprocrisy. Actually the Turks were given a free hand to continue massacring defenceless Christians for another forty years.

Armenian hopes rose briefly in 1877, when Turkey lost her war with Russia. Besides freeing Bulgaria, the Treaty of San Stefano stipulated in Article 16 that Turkey should 'carry into effect, without delay, the improvements and reforms demanded by local requirements in the provinces inhabited by Armenians in Asia Minor'. Russian troops were to occupy Turkish Armenia until those reforms were carried out—a clause which brought British humanitarianism (and diplomacy) to the boil. Once in, how were the Russians to be got out?

A solution, comparable to the partition of Berlin in 1945, was reached at the Treaty of Berlin in 1878. Russian troops were to be withdrawn from Armenia, *before reform started*, and were to be replaced by troops from the West.

The betrayal of the Armenians was completed, behind the backs of the other Western Powers, by Britain concluding the Secret Cyprus Convention with Turkey in the same year. The Turks merely 'promised to introduce the necessary reforms for the protection of Christians and other subjects in Asia Minor'. In return for this worthless promise, which could not be enforced and which relieved Turkey of any internal supervision, Cyprus was ceded to Britain. In return for Armenian lives, Britain obtained an outpost against Russia at the eastern end of the Mediterranean. It is fair to say that British statesmen were not so cynical as deliberately to compound the Turkish felony; but, in effect, this was the cost of the Cyprus deal. At the time the deal was regarded as a rebuff to Russia and a diplomatic triumph for England.

In reality it obliged the Armenians and other minorities under the Turkish yoke to look to Russia (instead of Britain and France) for protection. This increased Russia's scope, which she has ever since turned to account. From the Black Sea to the Persian Gulf, Russia is regarded to this day as the true protector of the weak Middle East masses against "imperialism". That was the background to Mr Gladstone's disastrous last speech.

The Sultan, understandably, fastened on Gladstone's speech. He wasted no time in setting about the Armenians, whose existence seemed to be inviting a fresh attack by one of the Great Powers. He was taking no risks. The immediate result was the massacres at Mush, Trebizond and Erzeroum, where at least 50,000 Armenians perished before the end of the year.

Worse was to follow. In 1896 a raid took place on the national Ottoman Bank in Constantinople. Rightly or wrongly, it was attributed to revengeful Armenians, egged on by a hostile foreign power. The Sultan's bodyguard, successors of the Janissaries, was called out.

This famous body of men had no loyalty except to the Sultan. All squeamishness had been knocked out of them. They were as tough as nails and highly efficient. Their quarry hardly had a chance.

Often these Janissaries were recruited by professional kidnappers who roamed the Ottoman Empire in quest of healthy little boys and tore them from their parents, never to be seen again.

One reason for the profound loyalty of the Greeks to their Church today is the memory of the Janissaries' kidnapping expeditions. The priests used to save small boys by hiding them in remote churches and monasteries in the mountains. The people have ever since remained grateful and regarded the priesthood as protectors against foreign oppressors. Hence the loyalty which a Makarios commands among Greek Cypriots today against the British overlords. The fear of the Turk in the Greek Cypriots' midst and less than a hundred miles away on the mainland is very real.

Such was the ruthless machine which Mr Gladstone loosed upon the Armenians in 1895–6.

The Gladstone speech of 1895 sounded the alarm for all Armenians in the Ottoman Empire. Those who could get away fled abroad. But the Turks were reluctant to grant exit visas. Any mass exodus would have reflected on the stability of the country. Any substantial flight of capital might have rocked the Imperial finances. So the majority of Armenians were caught.

Among those who succeeded in escaping overseas was Ohannes Essayan, who not only had the necessary graft but was so ill with tuberculosis that he also had health grounds for a visa. His youngest daughter, Anna, accompanied him to Egypt, where they had their influential connections, Abraham Pasha and Nubar Pasha. The boys, Hrand and Yervante, were still in England.

But Virginie could not go with her husband, because her beloved elder daughter, Nevarte, was expecting her first baby. Moreover, Calouste's business was at such a crucial stage that, anyway, he had to stay behind. They continued to live at the big house beside the Bosporus, taking comfort from the limitation of the 1895 massacres to the Anatolian mainland, and from the fact that so far the Sultan had been chary of disgracing the Sublime Porte with liquidations under the eyes of the world.

The Ottoman Bank robbery upset this wishful thinking. It was obvious that there was trouble in store for the Armenians in Constantinople as well as in the provinces: even for such rich and influential families as the Essayans and Gulbenkians. High Turkish officials, among Calouste's contacts, confirmed the danger. The Armenian grapevine removed the last doubt. At about midsummer the Gulbenkians and in-laws decided to escape. By then they were again mobile. Nevarte had given birth to a son at Kadiköy, near Scutari.

One evening in August the two families collected furtively in the Essayan mansion, Sarkis, Dirouhi and the two younger boys slipping across the Bosporus from Scutari, trying to look natural. Whether Calouste and his father managed to obtain exit visas by graft is uncertain. But Anna, Atvarte, who was four at the time, and Nubar, who was three months old, piece together the following account of the flight, as told by their parents.

Sultan Abdul Hamid declared: 'The only way of ending the Armenian problem is to put an end to the Armenians.' This was his personal policy and early on 26th August, 1896, the troops and mob set about carrying it out. They were put into civilian clothes, to fool the Diplomatic Corps, and armed with clubs with which they broke into the rich Armenians' homes along the Bosporus and into the crowded poor Armenian quarter.

Fifty thousand Armenians were clubbed to death in the capital and their homes, shops and offices robbed.

As they were on the outskirts of Constantinople, the Gulbenkian party received warning in the nick of time. The men disguised themselves as poor rug merchants, wrapping Atvarte and Nevarte's infant up in carpets to hide them from the murderers and kidnappers, and made off for the Golden Horn in groups. The party nearly came to grief when Nevarte's mother, Virginie, panicked. At the last moment she kept insisting: 'We can't go. The washing hasn't come back.' But they reached the Essayan steamship, which was waiting to sail for Egypt in the ordinary course of business.

And so they escaped the notorious Constantinople Massacre, which shocked the world. Simultaneously massacres took place in the provinces at Van, Egin and Niksar. At least 150,000 Armenians were butchered in 1896, probably 300,000. Between Gladstone's first championship of the Armenian cause in 1853 and the deposition of Abdul Hamid by the Young Turks in 1908, at least 1,500,000 Armenians perished at the hands of the Janissaries and the mob.

The Erzeroum and Constantinople Massacres of 1895–6 gave birth to the Armenian Independence Movement. Secret societies, such as the Dashnaktsutioum and Hunchakist, were formed and spread over the Russo-Turkish frontier at Mount Ararat into the Caucasus.

The Georgian, Stalin, and the Armenian, Anastas Mikoyan, graduated as Bolsheviks in those societies and succeeded in mobilizing the local workers against the "White Intervention" after the First World War. Thus the Red Revolution was forced upon Transcaucasia; the great oilfields were lost to the Western world; the ascendancy of Stalin was made possible. Incidentally, Mr Gladstone came within an ace of forfeiting Calouste Gulbenkian's life and depriving Britain of the Iraq oilfields as well.

This moment of escape marked Calouste Gulbenkian's lowest ebb. But, as the boat put out of the Golden Horn to safety, a huge hulk of a man shambled on board. He turned the tide.

7

FACTOTUM

CALOUSTE GULBENKIAN had not previously met the giant late arrival, who stumbled aboard the Essayan mercy ship. But he knew instantly who it was—none other than the fabulous Alexander Mantachoff, one of the three Armenian multi-millionaires in Baku oil.

Everybody in kerosene, like the Gulbenkians, had heard of Mantachoff. Judged even by the rugged standards of the wild Apcheron Peninsular, where a Russian proverb said, 'Whoever lives a year among the oil owners of Baku can never be a decent person again,' Mantachoff was rough. He had been born and raised there.

Little Gulbenkian seemed a mouse beside this six-foot-three character, broad and corpulent, loud-mouthed, coarse and vulgar.

Mantachoff had started even more inauspiciously than his Armenian contemporaries, Sarkis Gulbenkian, the ex-rug merchant, and Ohannes and Meguerditch Essayan, the ex-scrap metal pedlars.

He was a humble peasant with no prospects, but he was thrifty. When he had saved a little money, he bought a tiny plot of land with some vines near Baku.

Next he became a servant in the Baku office of General Zakhari Mdvani, one of the Tsar's twelve permanent A.D.C.s, a minor oil magnate and father of the five much publicized "Marrying Mdvanis" of the inter-war years.

Princess Nina Mdvani (Mrs Denis Conan-Doyle, widow of Sir Arthur Conan-Doyle's elder son) remembers her father telling how Mantachoff always seemed to be slouching idly over a high stool at the office, like a permanent fixture, until one day he did not turn up. He was going to be fired. But the general never got the chance. Oil was struck in Mantachoff's little garden. Overnight he became worth $400,000.

It was said that among the two hundred Baku oil magnates ten were honest: one Armenian, one Swede (Ludwig Nobel) and eight Mohammedans.

They were up to such tricks as digging a false oil well, filling it with petroleum and then selling it as a concession even to such shrewd operators as the Rothschilds; or tapping their rivals' oil reservoirs secretly with a pirate underground pipe. There were enormous conflagrations, costing millions of gallons of oil, for which rival oil millionaires were sometimes blamed.

Desert Baku, waterless and entirely lacking in public amenities, was worse than Gulbenkian cared to depict it in his book. The dominant building was a huge prison. Thousands of labourers of different nationality lived three to a cot in wooden barracks, in comparison with which the Nobel Brothers' flats were palaces. They worked sixteen hours a day under frightful conditions and were usually paid in kind, often no more than bread and water. Married workmen were discharged.

Murder, racial and religious rioting, and robbery were everyday occurrences. Every man took his life in his hands. Baku was probably the worst place on earth. There Stalin and Mikoyan were to find fertile soil for Bolshevism, and it was just the sort of hell where a great bull of man like Mantachoff was in his element.

The oil owners built bizarre palaces outside the wicked city. One millionaire modelled his mansion on a house of playing cards and would not install a lavatory because he thought such a humble room would disgrace him. Another millionaire built a palace of gold plate, which was inevitably plundered in a beggars' riot.

The hated owners each protected themselves with fierce bodyguards of *kotschis* or dispossessed Georgian "princes" with a few retainers, armed to the teeth. These thugs might be "princes" tracing their lineage back to Alexander the Great, leaders of one of the teeming religious sects, successful robbers, younger sons of transient modern dynasties in the area or indeed anybody who had attained a position of some authority and attracted a following. The apotheosis of a *kotschi* was a Mehemet Ali, the Albanian who carved a throne for himself in Egypt, or a Riza Khan in Persia.

It was a sort of early feudal society at its worst, with Oriental barbarity added. At the top were the oil magnates, the "barons", owing nominal subservience to a shadowy monarch away in St Petersburg. The *kotschis* might be likened to the "knights" (anything but gentle), who swore allegiance to their oil lords. At the bottom of the scale were the swarming workers, the "serfs", who were exploited mercilessly. This was the element from which Mantachoff sprang and flourished. It was also the origin of the Duschnaktjutjun, the "expropriators", who ultimately brought Russian Armenia into the Soviet Union.

An honest Armenian was Gregor Martinovich Arafelian, who

eventually became by far the richest of all the Transcaucasian oil kings. His seventh and last-surviving son out of eight, Martin Arafelian, is now seventy-eight and lives in Paris as an antique dealer. He is one of the few people who still remember Mantachoff and those fantastic days of the Baku oil boom. He relates:

'Soon after oil was found on his land Mantachoff became so rich that he insisted on distilling his kerosene in platinum cisterns.

'Unlike my father and the other Armenian oil Croesus, Aramiantz, who were misers, Mantachoff needed what he imagined to be *la belle vie*. He was an extrovert. He would delight in going personally to the reservoirs where the oil owners sold their supplies for gold roubles. Then he would drive back in state, with wonderful horses, and hold Arabian Nights parties in his palace. There would be retinues of the most beautiful women from all over Eastern Europe and Asiatic Russia, troupes of Oriental dancers and acrobats, vast meals and unlimited wine and spirits. Sometimes there would be fights, but Mantachoff could hold his own.

'Attempts were made to murder him by all manner of means, poison, daggers and rival bands of *kotschis*. But he was a match for anybody, so strong that he could lift two grown men off the ground by the shoulders with his outstretched arms.

'Later in life Mantachoff mastered foreign languages and loved to swagger round the great hotels of Europe, buying art treasures and endowing Armenian charities. He built the Armenian church off the Champs-Elysées. He was also a contractor for the Siberian Railway.

Nubar Gulbenkian recalls how, when Mantachoff, Mr Five Per Cent, and Frederick Lane, the stage-manager of the famous Royal Dutch-Shell merger, were signing an agreement bringing Russian oil into the ring in 1903, Mantachoff kept repeating in Armenian, which Lane did not understand: 'I'll rape your mother, I'll rape your mother. . . .' Mr Five Per Cent kept translating this to Lane as 'All right, all right. . . .' To which Lane kept replying, 'Thank you very much, thank you very much. . . .'

Atvarte Essayan says: 'At one time Mantachoff could not read a French menu. So he used to sit by the kitchen door in the leading hotel restaurants in London, Paris, and Cairo when he was alone so that he could see what other guests were getting and order it for himself.'

That was the amazing figure to whom Calouste Gulbenkian attached himself like a small limpet from the moment their ship left the Constantinople Massacre behind.

Since Mantachoff was a Russian subject—and the Tsar was

favouring Armenians, in order to show up the Turks by contrast and to curry favour with oppressed minorities in general—he was not a refugee.

Calouste—being on an Essayan ship—had influence with the captain and so was able to be of use to Mantachoff. Though Nevarte was nursing her child, she was turned out of her cabin for Mantachoff, for whom nothing on board was too good. From the first moment, Calouste had obviously decided to ingratiate himself with his formidable fellow passenger, even at the expense of his wife.

Atvarte says: 'The meeting with this former peasant, who was also a multi-millionaire, gave Calouste a big chance. On the boat and later in exile in Egypt, Calouste made himself indispensable, as a sort of general factotum, a secretary-cum-butler. He would organize parties for Mantachoff, fetch a doctor for him, vet the newspapers, letters and balance sheets, and order his meals. Gulbenkian also handled Mantachoff's business correspondence and some of his investments. In a very short time he learned many of the tycoon's secrets and such a lot about the inside of the Russian oil industry that Mantachoff dared not part with him.

'He was paid a small retainer. More important, he was able to invest Nevarte's dowry profitably and scrounge so much from Mantachoff that very soon he was rich again by his previous, impecunious standards.'

Mr Five Per Cent's *Memoirs* do not mention Mantachoff by name. The only reference to him is: 'I got established in London and had the representation of Russian oil producers, who exported kerosene in cases to the Near East and India.'

It was a momentous contact.

Oil rights within the former Ottoman Empire as defined by
C. S. Gulbenkian in the Red Line Agreement of 1928

8

ENTRÉE

T HE flight from Constantinople brought Gulbenkian a second
stroke of luck. He found refuge with the great Nubar Pasha,
to whom he was related by marriage through Nevarte's cousin,
Vahan. The Pasha ruled Egypt for twenty years, as Foreign Minister
or President of the Khedive's Council of Ministers. Statues of him
stand in Cairo and Alexandria to this day. A suburb of Cairo is named
after him: so is a breed of cotton.

To Armenians in Turkey, Russia and in exile he was known as
"The Little Father", since he subscribed generously to Armenian
causes and, as a world statesman, did much to rouse sympathy for the
Armenian plight.

Gulbenkian was not one to ignore such an influential connection.
He stuck as closely to the Pasha as he did to Mantachoff, wasting no
time. Nubar Pasha was already an old man in retirement. A year later
he was dead.

Calouste Gulbenkian spent three months with the elder statesman,
who became more to him than a "Little Father". He became "Uncle"
and also godfather to the Gulbenkian firstborn, who was christened
Nubar in his honour.

The young Gulbenkians—Calouste, who was twenty-seven, and
Nevarte, now twenty-two—became members of the Pasha's family.
'That was one of the reasons why we survived and prospered. We were
well connected,' says Nubar Gulbenkian to this day.

Calouste was so proud of acquiring the great man as godfather
that for ever afterwards the name Nubar was reserved for his
son.

Through the family connection with Nubar Pasha, Gulbenkian
obtained a new status. He did not have to approach great financiers
in the West merely as some thrusting Levantine upstart. He was the
friend, protégé and "nephew" of the world-famous statesman.

When he needed an introduction to the Prince of Wales's multi-
millionaire financial adviser, Sir Ernest Cassel, Calouste found Nubar
Pasha a name to conjure with: the Prince and the Pasha had been
friends since the Royal visit to Cairo, and since Sir Samuel Baker's

anti-slavery expedition to Central Africa in 1869, which had been inspired by Nubar, a pioneer in the suppression of Egypt's slave trade in the Sudan and Central Africa.

Through Sir Evelyn Baring, Nubar Pasha had long-standing links with Baring Brothers, the famous City of London merchant bankers. They were to play a vital part in the rise of Mr Five Per Cent.

The Pasha was on equally useful terms with leaders of French diplomacy and finance; for France had been as active in Egypt as Britain since Napoleonic days. Since the Pasha had been educated in France and French was his first language, he was able to introduce Calouste to the most influential people in Paris, including the Rothschilds—another link in the rise of Mr Five Per Cent.

Now that he had learned at first hand in Egypt the strength and enlightenment of British and French diplomacy in the Middle East, it seems that this was the period when Gulbenkian decided to throw in his lot with the two great Western Powers and became pro-British and pro-French. Long talks with the Pasha also seem to have matured Gulbenkian's precocious diplomatic talents.

In Cairo he met another prominent Armenian of the future—the Pasha's son, Boghos Nubar Pasha—then a well-known architect, busy developing Heliopolis for his father and uncle, Abraham Pasha. Boghos was to be leader of the emigré Armenians at the Peace Conference after the First World War and to disagree with his "god-brother".

Any expectations Calouste may have had of his son's benefiting under Nubar Pasha's will came to nought. The Pasha left his millions to Armenian charities.

By the end of 1896 Calouste had the entrée everywhere.

9

ARRIVAL

A T the end of 1896, when he was twenty-seven, the preparatory phase of Calouste Gulbenkian's long, fighting life finished. The time had come to tie the threads together.

While the rest of the Gulbenkians and Essayans either stayed in Egypt or moved to Algeria (where brother Vahan settled), Calouste, Nevarte and their infant son, Nubar, made for London.

Massacres of lowly Armenians continued at short intervals and Constantinople was too hot for the majority of even the most favoured members of the race. But a handful of expert Armenian officials remained indispensible to the régime and through them Calouste was kept on the inside track of business and diplomatic developments in the Ottoman Empire. Outside the Empire he also had influential Armenian contacts in Persia, where oil deposits had been attracting the attention of such adventurers as the naturalized Briton, Baron Julius de Reuter, since 1872. Through the Gulbenkian kerosene interests, the Essayan shipping and banking business and his own travels and studies, Calouste had mastered the ins and outs of the booming Baku oil industry and the potentialities of Mesopotamia. He was *persona grata* with the Nobels, the most progressive Baku oil magnates, and, above all, he now had behind him the wealth and backing of his powerful new Russian-Armenian friend, Alexander Mantachoff. "Uncle" Nubar Pasha had given him the *entrée* to the highest diplomatic and financial circles in Western Europe.

Nevarte's dowry was paying dividends; he was on Mantachoff's payroll. There was real money in his pocket and his recent impoverishment seemed but a distant nightmare.

It is fair to say that if Calouste Gulbenkian had not existed, the European oil magnates would have had to invent him. He alone combined the local knowledge and languages of Asia Minor, the contacts and influence, the scientific and engineering skill, the business acumen and foresight, which could knit the oil interests of Europe and the Near East together and initiate great developments.

*   *   *   *   *

There now began what Gulbenkian called 'the prolonged and arduous diplomatic and economic negotiations' from which a 'unique company' was born.

'Before going into further details of the history of the Iraq Petroleum Company,' his *Memoirs* say, 'it will be useful at this juncture to make short references to the state of the British oil industry at this stage. The reader will thus be able to correlate better the subsequent phases of the oil industry in connection with Mesopotamia; in particular these references will explain how my connections with the Royal Dutch-Shell combine started.'

The Royal Dutch Company for the Working of Petroleum in the Dutch East Indies had been founded in 1890; and the Shell Transport and Trading Company was founded by the Samuel brothers, with the help of the Rothschilds, in London early in 1897.

The *Memoirs* continue: 'Up to 1895, British oil interests were limited to small petroleum distributing concerns (not wholly British) and weak exploitation and exploration concerns in different parts of the world.

'The period between 1895 and 1900 can be considered the most interesting period of development of these interests. It constituted the foundation stone of the present world-wide ramifications of the British oil industry.

'Previously, the whole of the world oil industry was controlled practically exclusively by the American interests, headed by the Standard Oil Company, then a most powerful trust. Later, its dangerous power obliged American legislators to disintegrate the Standard Oil into thirty-two independent concerns.

'The American oil interests were all-powerful, overbearing and never allowed any competitor to live. Bur fortunately they became over-confident and acted sometimes very harshly against competitors; at other times they did not appreciate the position and unintelligently let dangerous activities grow, for example the Royal Dutch-Shell combine and the Anglo-Persian.'

We now come to Mr Five Per Cent's assessment of the budding European oil companies and their chiefs, whom he was to bring together, as representative in London of Russian oil producers and kerosene exporters:

'Owing to these connections, I came into contact with a very eminent commercial genius and organizer, Mr Frederick Lane, who represented the important oil interests of Messrs Rothschild of Paris and was also in charge of the Consolidated Petroleum Company, a distributing concern in Britain, controlled by Messrs Rothschild. We became friends although we were competitors.

'The Dutch interests (under Mr J. B. August Kessler, the head of the Royal Dutch) were labouring very poorly in the rich oil lands of the Dutch Indies.

'Close by, Mr Marcus Samuel (later Viscount Bearsted of the Shell Company) in Borneo, was a weak producer and small trader in oil with Japan owing to his connection with the Japanese import and export trade.

'These two concerns were not only very weak but were also competing with each other, thereby becoming still weaker.

'On top of this uneconomic competition there was the Russian competition, because Baku oil was very cheap and competed advantageously with the above concerns and American oil, in the Near East and many parts of the East. Russian producers also competed not only with the foreign producers but fiercely between themselves.'

Mr Five Per Cent assigns the credit for rationalizing that suicidal state of affairs to Frederick Lane, second place to himself and third place to Henri Deterding, in these words:

'It would take a great many pages to trace the ingenious conceptions of Mr Frederick Lane to consolidate and to mould together the conflicting interests. He must be considered, without any doubt, the father of the British oil industry. The present magnates appropriate to themselves the kudos of many things, but the initial development is due to that modest man who never coveted any honours or fame. He was a great Empire builder.

'In a nutshell, Mr Frederick Lane co-ordinated by agreements and amalgamations the Dutch, Russian and English interests. It is particularly due to him that the Royal Dutch-Shell combine came into existence and that the two corporations were put on their feet.

'Mr Lane asked me to collaborate with him to complete the architecture by bringing into line important Russian interests indispensable for the solidarity of the ring. Mr Lane was on the executive of the Royal Dutch and also of the Shell companies, and thus my connections with the combine began.

'The concerns and interests which I had to co-ordinate were most difficult; however I succeeded. Once the architecture was completed, the concerns mentioned above began to make huge profits and all of us, myself included, realized very handsome material compensations.

'I became intimately connected with the Royal Dutch-Shell and contributed in a very large measure to its development by bringing in big corporations from other parts of the world.'

In 1956, the Royal Dutch-Shell was the sole European oil company with a world-wide exploration-production-refining-marketing organization. Its sales were worth £2,321 million. Its costs were £1,511 million and its taxes £486 million. It spent £388 million on new concessions, exploration and development. The Treasury's 900,000 shares were valued at 155 million dollars and were Britain's biggest single dollar asset.

Those figures show the sort of stakes with which Gulbenkian, Frederick Lane, Marcus Samuel and soon Henri Deterding were playing.

Gulbenkian shows a welcome strain of generosity in according the third place of honour in the creation of the Royal Dutch-Shell combine to his friend, rival and eventual enemy, Deterding. The flamboyant and egocentric Dutchman was not so just when he came to publish his own memoirs. While paying grudging tribute to Lane, he claimed most of the credit for himself and wiped the little Armenian clean out of his recollection. Deterding seems to have convinced himself, his wife and the world at large, that he was *par excellence* the architect of the Royal Dutch-Shell. Any rival claims have so far gone largely by default.

Lady Deterding told me in Paris this year: 'My husband used to tell me Gulbenkian was an unimportant little man, who had been paid £100 a year by Mantachoff and had married a rich woman! It was, of course, my husband who really created the Royal Dutch-Shell Company. That was what he always told me.'

Gulbenkian's *Memoirs* concede this much: 'The official chief (of the Royal Dutch-Shell), and a brilliant commercial man, was Henri Deterding. We worked most harmoniously for over twenty years, but, as has very often been the case in the oil business, personal jealousies and divergences of opinion separated us later. I shall not go into these details here because they are irrelevant.'

As to his 'very handsome material compensations' Gulbenkian explains: 'On very few occasions were my personal activities remunerated by fixed emoluments. As a rule, my policy was to keep myself entirely free, although intimately connected with the combine, and practically having joint activities—but without actual directorial or executive obligations.

'I created a particular position for myself which later excited great jealousies.

'In this way, I participated by taking my share of the risks in the businesses which were introduced through my channel and of which several happened to lead to important developments.

'It was the kind of partnership which worked very well for a time, but afterwards, clashing interests created intricate consequences, chief among which were the serious divergences in the Venezuelan Oil Concessions.'

He adds: 'The prosperity of the Royal Dutch-Shell combine whetted many appetites and oil enterprises became more and more popular. British capital began to explore and exploit oil concessions in different parts of the world.'

In particular he was thinking of the Anglo-Persian concession. But before going on to that drama, it is only fair to give Deterding's one-sided version of the start of the Royal Dutch-Shell combine and the foundation of Britain's world-wide oil interests, which were to prove a matter of life and death in the Suez Crisis of 1956–7.

*   *   *   *   *

In his autobiography, *An International Oil Man,* Henri Deterding says: 'I joined the Royal Dutch Company on 15th May, 1896—a memorable date for me since it marked my beginning in the oil trade. I knew next to nothing of oil.' Previously he had been an official in the Netherlands Trading Society, a merchant banking company in the Dutch East Indies.

On the other hand, Gulbenkian, who was three years the younger, had by this time spent twelve years dedicated to oil. Deterding did not even become managing director of the weak Royal Dutch Company until 1900.

Deterding's public silence about Gulbenkian and his private ridicule are preposterous. He writes: 'In 1903 I managed to complete what was freely stated at the time to be the most gigantic working agreement the oil trade had so far known; the contracting parties being our Royal Dutch Company and the two largest companies (apart from Standard Oil) competing against us—the Paris Rothschilds, whose oilfields were in Russia, and the English corporation, backed by the same famous Rothschilds, which we know today as Shell.

'We had to form a separate company with a capital of about £2,000,000 and called the Asiatic Petroleum Company.

'In China, for instance, although Standard Oil and others were in the field against us, we managed to secure a fair share of the trade. But, so fierce was the opposition, that prices shot up and down as senselessly as a monkey on a stick. Faced by such infernal fluctuations, even the cleverest and most experienced oil traders often couldn't tell whether they were selling at a profit or a loss. Could price madness go further?

'I decided I must see Mr Frederick Lane, representative of the

Rothschilds in London, who was chiefly responsible for the formation
of the Europaische Petroleum Union, merging the various marketing
interests of the Rothschilds, Nobel and the Deutsche Oil groups in
Germany.

'A company so diversified as Shell, which transported oil and
traded in it as well as owning its own oilfields in Borneo and constantly
acquiring or absorbing subsidiary oil businesses, would soon reap the
benefit of price stabilization.

'Under the guidance of Sir Marcus Samuel the Shell Transport
and Trading Company probably covered a wider range of activities
than any other oil company of that day, apart from Standard Oil.

'Mr Lane said incredulously: "You don't mean to tell me that
customers hold off from buying oil because we are selling it to them
cheap?"

'I answered: "That is precisely what I do mean." To prove my
point, I took my pencil and across half a sheet of notepaper I drew a
straight line. I told him: "That line represents our price level, firm
and steady as it should be among all sound and decent oil traders."
Then, rushing my pencil up and down—sometimes above the line,
but more often below it, I said: "That represents prices as they are
today, constantly shooting up and down, so that nobody knows where
he is.

' "Since every small Chinese dealer is a speculator by nature, he
keeps his stocks deliberately low because he always fancies prices may
not have touched rock bottom. He would buy infinitely larger quantities
if prices were kept level.

' "Should we continue these cut-throat methods for another twenty
years, those who survive—even the most powerful—will be in much
the same impasse as we are today. The consumption we lose this way,
by being out of stock, is lost for all time and we can never overtake it.
Now let us agree on a price which allows every producer at least to
live and we shall all benefit from the first moment we fix it."

'I urged that some form of mutual trading agreement between us
was essential: unified control as to placing production, transport and
selling at agreed prices when circumstances so required: serving each
market whenever practical from the nearest source of supply.

'Those two points still comprise the first guiding principle of all
successful oil trading. This elimination of waste and overlapping has
since become known as "rationalization", which would be better
understood if it were called "simplification".'

This pooling of oil resources and joint marketing was precisely
what Gulbenkian had recommended five years previously in his book

and magazine articles, after studying the Baku oil industry on the spot—before Deterding had ever given a thought to petroleum.

The argument convinced Shell, which merged in June 1903 with the Royal Dutch. These together formed the Asiatic Petroleum Company.

Deterding implies that the Rothschilds (with whom he links the Deutsche Bank groups in Germany and Sweden's Nobel, with their oilfields in Russia) also came in at his instigation.

In point of fact, as Gulbenkian correctly states in his *Memoirs*, those important Russian interests (which were vital to the solidarity of the ring) were brought in by him.

The Asiatic Petroleum Company therefore represented all the leading European oil operators and was in time to prove a match for the Americans. The capital was held in three equal parts by the Royal Dutch, Shell and the Rothschilds. Deterding was appointed managing director and took up the reins in London, although he also remained in active control of the Royal Dutch Company at The Hague. Gulbenkian recouped himself from a share in the new company's Russian oil trade, which he had integrated in the combine.

As he said, he created a 'particular position for himself,' accepting the risks but not the routine obligations of a directorship, thus giving rise to later jealousies.

He had arrived.

10

THE GIANT MERGER

THE amalgamation of the British, Dutch, German, Russian, Swedish, Rothschild and Gulbenkian-Mantachoff oil interests in 1902–3 did not stop ruinous American competition at a blow.

World-wide American price-cutting had become crucial for the comparatively small and hitherto decentralized European companies, competing not only against Standard Oil, but against each other, all wasting time and money on unnecessarily roundabout delivery routes and duplicated marketing organizations. There had to be further co-operation between the European companies to reduce costs, fight a way into new markets, retain existing markets and secure fresh resources for the expanding and increasingly competitive trade.

Gulbenkian's *Memoirs* say: 'I must emphasize that my functions, during this period in connection with the combine, were to make financial arrangements for large amounts of capital wherever money could be borrowed advantageously or shares placed, because, as we went on, huge outlays of capital were required.

'We were not content at the time to limit our developments to Europe, Russia or the East, but Lane and Deterding conceived that it would be grand strategy if we could manage to get into the United States, so as to bring more pressure on the Standard Oil group.

'The task of finding finance for such audacious conceptions was left to me. At the time the reputation of the combine was beginning to become world wide and the novel idea occurred to me to try and find finance in New York, and with American capital to establish ourselves in America and compete with the American corporations.

'Although such schemes may appear hazardous, if conducted with skill and energy, they help understandings elsewhere and impose more respect and consideration on the competitors.

'In this way we laid down the foundations of British-controlled oil corporations in America.'

These were valued in December 1956 as a half to a third of Britain's total dollar securities and were pledged to save the pound during the run on sterling caused by the Suez Crisis—a debt to Gulbenkian, Lane and Deterding which has yet to be acknowledged.

No mention is made in Deterding's autobiography of the leading part taken by Gulbenkian in the British breach of the formidable oil monopoly in the United States.

Again in fairness to Deterding, his version of this tremendous development must be reproduced.

His autobiography says:

'The hurdle we had to cross in 1896 was price-cutting, if we were not to be put out of business. It was not competition but annihilation. A giant called Standard Oil was then rearing his head in direct onslaughts on us. None of us dared to stand up to this big competitor's supremacy. That was never Mr Kessler's view—nor mine.[1]

' "Co-operation gives power" runs an old Dutch proverb and this sound piece of national wisdom Mr Kessler had firmly embodied into his commercial creed. We were both convinced that we could soon clear the price-cutting hurdle and any other barrier our financially more powerful competitor might choose to erect against us, if only we could persuade all the other smaller companies in the same dilemma to combine.

'So it was that we of the Royal Dutch became probably the first oil company in the world to determine that henceforth, whenever and wherever possible, a definite system of co-operation with smaller trade rivals must be an essential part of our general business policy; in fact our main working plank.

'Behind this definite working plan there lay a second guiding principle from which we built up what may be termed "our policy of the straight line". The job of an oil man is to bring the oil from the earth, where it has lain hidden through the ages, to the man in whose life it has become indispensable: to find and follow the straightest possible line between, let us say, the oil well and the petrol tank of your motor car.

'Therefore I urged the installation of huge storage tanks in places like Hong Kong, Calcutta, Madras, Bombay and Bangkok, so that delivery of supplies would never be left to chance. In this I laid down the keystone of what is now reflected in Royal Dutch-Shell policy everywhere.

'Had we restricted our trading purely within certain areas, our competitors could easily have smashed us by relying on the profits they were making in other countries to undercut us in price.

'So we had to invade other countries: eventually Roumania, Russia, Egypt, the U.S.A., Mexico, Venezuela and the Argentine.

[1] J. B. August Kessler was Managing-Director and creator of the Royal Dutch Co. He died at sea off Naples, killed by overwork, in 1900 and was succeeded by Deterding.

'This wider world programme would never have been possible unless we had consolidated our finances. . . .

'Until we started trading in America, our American competitors controlled world prices—because they could always charge up their losses in undercutting us in other countries against business at home where they had a monopoly.'

This is the natural point at which Deterding might have mentioned Gulbenkian's part in raising the capital for the Royal Dutch-Shell Company to break the internal American oil monopoly and frustrate American price-cutting. But Deterding is silent.

He continues:

'In 1912 we accordingly purchased five small producing companies, incorporating them into the Roxana Company, which later developed into the well-known Shell Union, comprising all our American interests.

'With the purchase of Californian Oilfields Ltd., in 1913, we went full steam ahead as really big retailers on the other side of the Atlantic. To compete successfully in price, a big world trader must obviously have entry into all world markets. This is now freely recognized by most American traders.'

The truth emerges, after nearly half a century, that the idea of a European break-through into the American market was Lane's and Deterding's; the execution Gulbenkian's.

Deterding adds the following warning: 'It must be remembered, that if too many try to do this, regardless of competitors, there is created an enormous duplication of facilities and terrible overheads. So there *must* be co-operation.'

On that Gulbenkian and Deterding were agreed. It remained the basis of their collaboration until Deterding read "dictation" for "co-operation" and they parted.

*   *   *   *   *

They also agreed on the extravagant incompetence of the early oil industry. Deterding's findings in the Far East were similar to those of Gulbenkian in the Near East ten years earlier.

Deterding's autobiography recalls: 'Suddenly, in 1898, when certain of our competitors had already tried those drastic price-cutting tactics and we had chartered more tankers to convey our increasing output, came calamity; our most productive field, at Telega Said, began to yield salt water. After thinking hard, I got a telegraph working and contracted, not too profitlessly, for enough oil from companies operating in Russia to fill our tankers for the whole of our future trade.'

Besides giving him an early lesson in the interdependence of the oil companies, the incident led Deterding to urge the Royal Dutch to cease relying on "old timers"—the dictatorial, rough-neck oil-drillers in their characteristic blue shirts, riveted trousers and bowler hats. Trained geologists as well as highly qualified chemists and engineers were engaged, who did not "rely on a hunch". The technique of production soon changed completely from that of the old bonanza days into scientific methods of prospecting, exploitation and distribution, corresponding with Gulbenkian's advanced ideas.

The infantile condition of the oil industry sixty years ago is sketched by Deterding thus:

'To us of the older generation, that year, 1896, seems comparatively recent. Yet it shrinks back into the Dark Ages when we suddenly recall that automobiles and a thousand and one other mechanical contraptions, now forming part of our daily lives, were then in so embryonic a state as to make gasoline and the other oil products, now essential to motors, a negligible quantity. Motor cars had then hardly come into being. Around this time, the first reliability trials in motoring history were held. Some forty cars assembled for races between Paris and Rouen and Paris and Bordeaux. Next day English newspapers told an astonished world of how marvellously the different cars stood the strain. In one race it was said "more than half completed the journey without a breakdown and at an average speed nearly equal to that of any horse-drawn vehicle".'

Deterding continues: 'The oil world in 1896 was of course unrecognizable from the oil world of today. I have only to cast my mind back to the first visit I paid, shortly after joining the Royal Dutch Company, to Pankelan Brandon, where the refinery connecting the only oilfield of any consequence was owned by the Company. Hours before reaching this lonely spot in Northern Sumatra, I could see from the deck of the small steamer vast masses of smoke belching into the sky. This came from the refinery daily. It signified the burning of gasoline, now one of the staple products of the oil industry, as everybody knows.

'The oil we then produced contained 48 to 50 per cent kerosene —or to use a more homely term, lamp oil. This alone was saleable. The remainder—which would yield us today gasoline, benzine, fuel oil, lubrication oil and so on—was then treated as waste!' This was just what had struck Gulbenkian in Baku.

*   *   *   *   *

The outcome of this meeting of minds—Frederick Lane, the great business architect, Calouste Gulbenkian, the financial wizard, Henri

Deterding, the commercial genius, and astute Marcus Samuel of Shell —was the consolidation of the Asiatic Petroleum Company in 1907.

Royal Dutch, the Rothschilds and Shell combined to form two new companies—Bataafsche Petroleum Maatschappij (B.P.M.) at the Hague for production and the Anglo-Saxon Petroleum Company in London for transport, storage, distribution and subsidiary businesses: on a basis of three-fifths Dutch and two-fifths British ownership. This arrangement completed the Royal Dutch-Shell merger, which has ever since linked British and Dutch oil interests.

The combined capital of this giant merger was £21,369,862—one of the "large amounts of capital", to which Gulbenkian's *Memoirs* refer—a sum to which he contributed and thus helped the concern to compete with the Americans everywhere, including cutting in on their own ground.

As usual he worked parallel to the concern, running equivalent risks and taking the profits from the businesses which he introduced. 'The reader should bear in mind,' he writes, 'that all these developments and evolutions happened during the period 1895–1910, when solid foundations were laid for keeping prices high and assuring big profits to the Trusts and all those connected with the combinations.'

He adds, with a hint of self-satisfaction: 'The American interests discovered too late that they had let competitors grow whom they could no longer smash and immediately their policy was changed into making understandings, instead of high-handed competition.'

In 1907 the much desired lull in price-cutting came about.

Deterding maintained that there were certain conditions for a profitable merging of big business interests. 'You must keep two points ever in view: first the human element must never be disregarded and no party to an amalgamation should be left with the idea that he has made a bad bargain. Instead of squeezing him out, take him as a partner: in short make him your friend.

'Secondly, definite money value is the only iron test you can apply as to whether an amalgamation is likely to prove worth while. No man can make a success of merging businesses if he fails to compute accurately beforehand the actual worth of each part of the different economic concerns about to be merged. . . . At the time of our Royal Dutch-Shell merger, I knew just where Shell was losing money and I preferred to leave these activities alone. Not unnaturally Lord Bearsted referred to this reproachfully: "I notice that you have deleted from our inventory certain sections of our business although I put them in at very little and I think you should take them over."

'I replied: "I am sorry to disagree with you, but those particular sections are not making money. A thing which has no earning power is no good to me."

'In slower-moving days it may have been possible to run business on the old-fashioned averaging-out principle, but today you endanger profits if you remain tied to the fetish known as "running the good with the bad".'

It was a tough school which Gulbenkian had entered. But it suited him. There was no one tougher. There were two more of Deterding's conditions which he was destined to fight all the way.

'Personally, I have the bad habit of always insisting that I must look after any money I put into a business,' wrote Deterding. 'I make clear at the first interview that I never put money into a business without a deciding voice in the management.'

The essence of Gulbenkian's technique was to split the "deciding voice"—to operate by compromise and at nobody's dictation.

Secondly, Deterding stipulated: 'I am certain as I look back over the years that our Royal Dutch-Shell operations would never have succeeded as they did if we had tried to keep our part of our general working policy secret. Year after year, in our annual reports to our shareholders, I have always taken good care to explain each stage of our development and to announce just where we were expanding in many different parts of the world.'

That was contradictory to the Gulbenkian technique. Being a naturally conspiratorial Armenian—an introvert rather than an extrovert like Deterding—Mr Five Per Cent thought that oil diplomacy (like any other diplomacy) should be conducted secretly. He was no subscriber to the theory of "open covenants, openly arrived at". He regarded such methods as the reverse of true diplomacy.

The crux of 1902–7 was not, however, the dormant differences between Gulbenkian and Deterding on principles but their agreement in practice.

THE GREAT MISTAKE

BEFORE continuing with the theme which Gulbenkian made the main object of his *Memoirs*—'the various stages and circumstances which marked the entry of the present groups into the Iraq Petroleum Company'—I shall follow his chronology and deal with his part in the Persian oil concession. This was where he made his great mistake. It rankled all his life. It had a bearing upon his Iraq concession and loomed up again at the end of his life.

As an Armenian Gulbenkian had all the political and geological intricacies of the rich and strategic frontier district of Northern Persia at his finger tips. In his book he had noted the important place held by Persians, indigenous and emigrant, in Transcaucasian society. The natural oil seepages of Western Persia had been attracting the attention of Western observers since before the 1880s; back in 1872 the Shah had granted petroleum rights to Baron Julius de Reuter. He and Hotz and Company of Bushire had both sunk wells, but unsuccessfully. Moreover, Gulbenkian had Armenian contacts at the Shah's court.

There is therefore no pleading that Gulbenkian was ignorant of the locality. On the contrary, one must assume that such a thorough man must have read all there was to read on Persian oil deposits and cross-examined everybody available who had special knowledge.

He writes: 'Between 1895 and 1900 the concession which afterwards came into the possession of the Anglo-Persian Oil Company was a drag on the market.

'An Armenian, Mr Kitabdji,[1] the Director of Persian Customs, had the concession for which he wanted £15,000. I knew Kitabdji very intimately myself and I submitted this business to my friend Lane —also, I believe, to Deterding. But we all thought it was a wild-cat scheme and it looked so speculative that we thought it was a business for a gambler and not at all for our trio.

'It was on my refusal that Mr D'Arcy, a great speculator in mining businesses in Australia and elsewhere, interested himself and succeeded in forming a syndicate—I believe with the help of Scottish concerns.

---

[1] Nubar Gulbenkian believes another Armenian, Mr Haladjian, also had a share in the offer.

'Today Mr D'Arcy is considered a great pioneer of the oil industry, but to tell the truth, he was a great gambler and his success was due to sheer luck, rather than to any industrial or economic foresight.'

After all those years, Gulbenkian's version sounds suspiciously like sour grapes.

Lane and Deterding must have been guided solely by him, since he alone had the necessary local knowledge to reach a decision, and the blame for this monumental mistake cannot be spread.

Nor is it right to pass William Knox D'Arcy off as a mere "gambler" and "wildcatter". He had made a fortune in the Queensland gold rush and presumably knew something about geology. Moreover, he went to great trouble to explore the area of the concession before signing up. Moreover oil was not struck in commercial quantities until 26th May, 1908, seven years after the signing of the concession, when the Company's funds were exhausted and orders had been drafted to stop all further drilling. It was an historic day and proved just how wrong Gulbenkian could be.

Afterwards, says his son, Nubar, one of Gulbenkian's principles became 'never give up an oil concession'.

In extenuation of his father, Nubar adds: 'You must remember that Pa was then less than thirty years of age. Also Persia was, of course, outside the Ottoman Empire, in which he was mainly interested at the time, and where he had his most influential contacts.' It is also true to add that mining in Persia at that time was a perilous adventure: security was low, justice dubious and commercial morality at its nadir.

Somewhat vindictively, the *Memoirs* add: 'D'Arcy's group started explorations, but, until 1920, Anglo-Persian production was under the control of the Royal Dutch-Shell combine, as a result of distribution arrangements. After that period, the Anglo-Persian started on its own to follow the systems of development laid down by Mr Lane.'

Mr Five Per Cent evidently felt D'Arcy's success was a slight on his own reputation. He did not usually bear malice. His son, Nubar, says: 'Father hated *people*, it's true, but he never hated an *individual*. His practice was to try and sort out differences of opinion. He was not fundamentally vindictive.'

The great discovery at Masjid-i-Sulaiman, near an ancient fire-temple, at 1,180 feet, solved D'Arcy's pressing financial difficulties and led to the formation in 1909 of the Anglo-Persian Oil Company, with an initial capital of £2,000,000. Development proceeded apace.

A refinery was completed on Abadan Island between 1910 and 1913 and by 1912 a pipeline was bringing shiploads of oil to the wharves. Persia thus became one of the world's great oil-producing countries.

Output was 43,000 tons in 1912, 80,000 in 1913 and 273,000 in 1914. At the pre-crisis peak in 1950, output was 31,750,000 tons.

Comparable world figures were 48,000,000, 53,000,000, and 56,000,000 tons in 1912–14, and 518,000,000 tons in 1950, when Persia was the sixth oil-producing country in the world.

Gulbenkian had certainly rejected a liquid gold-mine. Not that his connection with the Anglo-Persian Oil Company ceased when he let D'Arcy in: he retained an interest through his parallel activities with Royal Dutch-Shell, which controlled Persian distribution. The Anglo-Persian Oil Company was to become a partner in his own Iraq Petroleum Company; and in due course Calouste himself was to become a trusted adviser of the Persian Government.

Incidentally, Deterding, in his autobiography, fails to make any mention of his lost opportunity in Persia.

12

HURDLER

1. Start: Baghdad Railway Line-up

IN 1910, when Gulbenkian was forty-one, there came the formative stage of the Iraq Petroleum Company, the project he had conceived and nursed for twenty years: ever since his Mesopotamian oil report had stimulated the cupidity of the Sultan and induced the transfer of Ottoman oil rights from Government to Privy Purse in 1890 and 1899.

It was touch and go. There were four competitors in the field.

Firstly there were the Germans. The Deutsche Bank's Ottoman Railway Company of Anatolia retained its priority to oil rights in 1900 on the basis of promises made in 1888. In 1898 the Kaiser paid a state visit to Constantinople; pro-German feeling reached a peak; and the Sultan was adroit in playing his favourite game of using one Great Power as a foil against another (in this case Britain) in order to prevent the partition of his ramshackle Empire. With the British in Egypt as well as Cyprus, over both of which he claimed suzerainty, and the British pressing forward in the Sudan (another nominal feoff) and neighbouring Persia—not to mention espousing the Armenians— Abdul Hamid found it was time to foster new friendships. In 1903 he confirmed his personal ownership of Ottoman oil properties, and the Turkish-German Railway Convention (with oil rights 20 kilometres each side) was signed. In 1904 a definite option was granted to the Deutsche Bank's Anatolian Railway Company for a year's exploration at Baghdad and Mosul. If oil were struck, a forty-year concession was promised. A strong German exploration party visited Mesopotamia and reported favourably. But the option was not taken up (for lack of funds) and the Ministry of the Privy Purse claimed that it had expired. The Germans claimed £20,000 for exploration expenses, which was refused. But they managed to renew their option annually until 1907, when it was officially stated to have lapsed. Nevertheless the Germans continued to press their claims.

Secondly there was William Knox D'Arcy, whose exploration party forced a way, *via* Baghdad, to Persia in 1901. He also had his eye on Mesopotamia. He sent his assistant, A. L. Marriot, to Constantinople with large funds in 1901 in order to obtain a Baghdad and Mosul concession from the Turks. After eighteen months, Marriot was replaced by H. E. Nichols (later managing-director of the Turkish Petroleum Company, predecessor of the Iraq Petroleum Company, and a director of the Anglo-Persian Oil Company). Nichols was also provided with plenty of money and he claimed to have obtained a letter from the Ottoman Government promising a concession to his newly formed Ottoman Petroleum Syndicate. In 1909 Nichols was again in Constantinople, pressing the claims of the newly formed Anglo-Persian Oil Company. But German persistence and Turkish lethargy frustrated his efforts. The Germans held the whip hand.

Thirdly the Americans began to wake up in the face of Royal Dutch-Shell resistance and also sent a candidate to Constantinople. This was Rear-Admiral Colby Chester, who was sponsored by the New York Chamber of Commerce and had useful contacts from a term of service in Turkey ten years previously. He arrived in 1908. A concession granting him oil rights throughout the Empire was drafted for his Ottoman-American Development Corporation by the Ministry of Mines in 1909 and was ready for approval by the Turkish Parliament in 1911. American rivals followed in his wake.

The fourth competitor was Calouste Gulbenkian, who, in alarm, persuaded his friends, the Samuel brothers of Shell, to open a Constantinople office in 1907—ostensibly to deal with oil shipments from Russia for the new Royal Dutch-Shell combine. In reality, Gulbenkian, who was in charge, used the office as cover for his own intrigues with officials of the Privy Purse and the Ministries. He spent large sums of his own money on *baksheesh* and followed every move. But it was not until 1910 that Nichols and the D'Arcy group became aware of his competition.

The great Persian oil strike of May 1908 alerted the oil companies of the world. But there was more to it than that. The seeds of the First World War were being sown. Visions of the Kaiser's notorious Berlin-Baghdad Railway chilled the hearts of Empire-builders in England, where the threat to Imperial communications with India, the Far East and Australasia was suddenly realized.

Britain awoke to the real meaning of German policy and penetration of the Near East during the preceding twenty-five years.

From about 1910 onwards, Mesopotamian oil ceased to be merely a matter of tremendous commercial importance but also became a symbol round which the imperialism of the Great Powers was fought to a temporary conclusion in the First World War. Henceforth Gulbenkian had to be a diplomat as well as a financier.

2. First Fence: Rocking the Bank

Mr Five Per Cent's own bedside story of the birth of the Iraq Petroleum Company can hardly be bettered. As he says in the introduction to his *Memoirs*: 'I am now the only person who has acted without interruption as a Director.' He was writing in 1945 and he had no reason to change his words in his remaining ten years, although the document was in use, scrutinized by later leaders of the world oil industry. He was writing from memory, without documents or figures, but only trivial details have needed alteration. He gives, as he claims, 'a faithful picture'.

'In 1895–1910, German political and economic influence had become dominant in every direction in Turkey. The German Government supported all German enterprises most vigorously and opposed competition by every means. The grip which the German Government had on the Turkish Government was such that there was no chance for other nations to have any success. British enterprises were very much behind through lack of support.

'A great event happened in 1908–9. I refer to the Young Turk Revolution. which at once diminished the influence of the Sultan, and new sympathies and policies were in the air. The British Government thought that this was a first-class opportunity to resume energetic activity in the Near East.

'At the beginning particularly, the Young Turks' sympathies were pro-British.[1] It was thought that there should be in Constantinople a centre of purely British financial influence.

'The magnates of the City, such as Lord Revelstoke, of Baring Brothers, Lord Farringdon and Sir Ernest Cassel were consulted. Particularly, Lord Revelstoke then had the full confidence of the Foreign Office in all financial matters.

'It was decided that Sir Ernest Cassel should proceed to Constantinople, on behalf of the British Financial Consortium, to establish a bank on the lines of the National Bank of Egypt, which was then a purely British concern. In order to ensure the British character of this institution, the British Government decided to lend Sir Henry Babbington-Smith, a very distinguished Civil Servant, to become Governor of the projected Bank.

[1] The Young Turks enjoyed a brief spell of popularity in Britain in comparison with that of Sultan Abdul Hamid, who was deposed on 27th April, 1909. The new constitution which they brought in was ostensibly liberal. Confidence was first shaken in 1909 by the massacre at Adana. Brutal suppressions of the Albanian Rising in 1911 finally destroyed liberal Britain's sympathies with the Young Turks.

'Owing to my experience of the economic conditions in Turkey, I was nominated as financial and economic adviser to the Turkish Embassies in Paris and London. A year or two later, I was nominated by the Turkish Government as the Chief Financial Adviser of the Government, being at the same time Turkish financial agent in Paris and London.

'Owing to those functions, I was asked by Sir Ernest Cassel to accompany the British Mission to Turkey as technical adviser, which I accepted with pleasure, being very keen to see British influence get the upper hand in Turkey in 1910.

'I placed all my experience, knowledge and connections unreservedly at the disposal of the founders of the Bank.

'On the return of our Mission from Constantinople, the National Bank of Turkey was founded and all the capital was privately subscribed by Lord Revelstoke, Lord Farringdon and Sir Ernest Cassel, so that it was a purely British concern.

'I was also nominated to the Executive Committee of the Bank as a Director in London.

'It was decided by the founders of the Bank that its policy should be on sound British banking lines, and that it should gradually take an interest in, or support, British enterprises in Turkey.

'I emphasized all along that purely banking business in Turkey was not at all remunerative, owing to the fierce competition of the German, French and Italian banks, who accepted such risks as we could not entertain. Although, in practice, my opinion later proved to be correct, at the inception it was not shared by my colleagues, who were eminent bankers, nominated by the founders, but lacking any practical experience of the country. The Bank later took interest in Mesopotamian irrigation, the Baghdad Tramways, electricity, etc. . . . but it took some time before the Committee realized the poor prospects of pure banking in Turkey.

'At a meeting with Sir Ernest Cassel and his associates, I referred to a scheme of petroleum concessions and monopoly in Turkey, which, at the outset of the Young Turks' Revolution, I had submitted to the Turkish Government in conjunction with Mr Frederick Lane. I explained that we had had no success owing to the indirect opposition of the German interests.

'Sir Ernest Cassel proffered that he was a great friend of the German Emperor and had great influence in German high finance. He said that although he was reluctant that the Bank should indulge in oil speculations, if I personally took an important share with himself, he would arrange to bring Sir Henry Babbington-Smith into immediate

contact with Von Gwinner, the head of the Deutsche Bank, and also
introduce the former to the German Chancellor.

'This proposal was a most welcome and unexpected opening for
me, who had had in view the development of Mesopotamia for the
preceding twenty years.

'I had met Von Gwinner on several occasions on oil business—
in conjunction with the Royal Dutch-Shell interests—but had never
discussed anything about Mesopotamia with him, because I knew it
would lead to failure.

'Sir Ernest Cassel and his associates left it to me to mature with
Sir Henry Babbington-Smith the way to proceed, after Sir Henry
had got in touch with the German authorities.

'The first overtures were made by Sir Henry, and Von Gwinner
welcomed collaboration with the highest British finance.

'I at once realized that the quick response of the Deutsche Bank
was not a question of mere sympathy for Sir Ernest Cassel, but that the
German financiers thought a splendid opportunity presented itself of
getting British financial support—to begin with on the pretext of
petroleum explorations, but really for railways.

'As I was an oil man, the founders of the Bank—although they
had very great confidence in me—did not want me to mix any of my
oil friends (viz. the Royal Dutch-Shell group) in the negotiations until
matters were settled. It was decided that Sir Henry Babbington-Smith
should conduct the negotiations, myself acting as his technical adviser.

'The German financiers had endeavoured by different means to get
financial assistance in the City of London, but, for political reasons,
they had failed.

'There was some disappointment on the part of Von Gwinner
when he heard that I was behind Sir Henry Babbington-Smith as the
latter's technical adviser. He knew of my friendship with Lane, as
both of us had previously been antagonists to his interests in other
parts of the world.'

Here Gulbenkian cross-heads his next section 'Birth of the Turkish
Petroleum Company' and continues:

'Sir Henry was a very eminent but very cautious Civil Servant.
I soon gained his confidence to the extent that he continuously put
forward to the Germans my criticisms and remarks, which, naturally,
were all the time intended to safeguard the British group interests,
but were very often unpalatable to the Germans.

'The negotiations between the National Bank of Turkey, the
Deutsche Bank and their associates ended in the Deutsche Bank
bringing in Anatolia-Baghdad Railways to form a British limited

liability company. In consideration of the Railway's mining rights (20 kilometres both sides) and the *Lettre Vizirielle* (of 1888, promising Germany preferential treatment regarding mining rights), the limited liability company would defray certain expenses and pass 25 per cent of its share capital free of charge (to the Germans).

'As soon as the agreement between the British and the Germans was signed by Sir Henry Babbington-Smith and Von Gwinner, we started temporarily making use of the Articles of Association of an African mining company[1] (which belonged to Sir Ernest Cassel). Soon after, in 1912, the name was changed to the Turkish Petroleum Company.

'The Board of the Company was at once constituted with Sir Henry Babbington-Smith as Chairman, Hugo Baring (brother of Lord Revelstoke) and myself, as directors, on the British side. On the German side, as far as I remember, were Von Stauss (who was still alive two years before the outbreak of the Second World War), Von Helferrich (Chancellor of the Reich during the First World War) and another gentleman.

'To begin with, we had offices in Cornhill in the same building as the National Bank of Turkey. All the secretarial and administrative arrangements were carried out by Sir Henry Babbington-Smith.

'The Company, at its inception, issued 80,000 shares of £1 each, of which 20,000 (i.e. 25 per cent, according to the agreement) were allotted free of payment to the Deutsche Bank and Anatolia Railways; 32,000 shares were put at my disposal for myself and for the oil group, *the choice of which was left to me*. The balance was subscribed by Sir Ernest Cassel and the National Bank of Turkey. Apart from the shares allotted to the Deutsche Bank, all the other shares were subscribed in cash.'

Mr Five Per Cent's own factual account of the formation of the National Bank of Turkey and its transition into the Turkish Petroleum Company—given with no false modesty, no vain boasting and no slant—can hardly be improved. But I venture to emphasize several aspects.

Notable, first of all, is the alacrity with which he seized his opportunity, unwittingly presented by Sir Ernest Cassel, of reconciling British and German oil aspirations, which had so long bedevilled a decision by the Turks. While Britain and Germany were at loggerheads, the dying hand of the Ottoman Empire—weak, capricious and corrupt—could not be persuaded to embark on major industrial development.

Then there was the tact with which he weaned his associates from

---

[1] African and Eastern Concessions.

pure banking to the main, but ill-recognized, chance in Turkey, namely a petroleum concession; and his powers of persuasion, which must somehow have convinced the greatest financiers in the City that there was indeed oil in commercial quantities in Mesopotamia, although it had yet to be discovered. There was the instinct with which he detected that the Germans were primarily intent on using the British, and the ingenuity with which he then proceeded to make use of the Germans himself. When the Young Turks returned the Ottoman oil properties from the Privy Purse to the Ministry of Finance in May 1909, the Germans' Vizirial promise of 1888 might have been thought to be rendered valueless. But—when Gulbenkian threw it into the scales as a make-weight to his own understanding with the Privy Purse and the Ministry of Mines—it fortified his own standing. Of this the Germans were unaware.

Gulbenkian enjoyed the advantage of being a lone wolf—uncomplicated by executive office in the Royal Dutch-Shell—which enabled him to work freely for his own ends, to fix his own terms and to profit from the unique position he was carving for himself.

In bringing the Turkish Petroleum Company into existence, Gulbenkian cleared his first, very high, hurdle in the international race for the suspected Mesopotamian oil riches.

3. Second Fence: Dutch Treat

The next obstacle was Gulbenkian's new set of conflicting interests. He had to reconcile his key position in the Turkish Petroleum Company with his old ties to the Royal Dutch-Shell. Up to 1912 the Royal Dutch-Shell's efforts to obtain a Mesopotamian oil concession—with and without the aid of Gulbenkian—had proved as futile as the parallel activities of the Anglo-Persian Oil Company.

Suddenly he found himself in the big business jungle. The National Bank insisted that he, as the brain behind it, should always vote with it. The Royal Dutch-Shell, on the other hand, relied on him, as one of its three creators, to support its interests. The Germans, whose claims in Constantinople were the strongest, expected to dominate the whole thing. Sir Ernest Cassel and his fellow "pure" bankers, were none too happy about the oil venture and were continually on the point of backing out. The British Government, flushed with the sudden success of the all-British Anglo-Persian Oil Company, lost enthusiasm for the National Bank and its transformation into a rival oil company and lent itself to Anglo-Persian Oil Company intrigues. In addition, personal quarrels introduced vicious cross-currents.

It fell on Gulbenkian to subordinate the primeval competitive instincts of the Cornhill jungle denizens to the civilized procedure of live and let live.

His *Memoirs* recapture the clash and heat of this historic free for all.

'In view of my connection with the Royal Dutch-Shell group,' he writes, 'and the urgent necessity of having an oil organization capable of carrying out practical work, I felt that in order to serve the best interests of myself, the Turkish Petroleum Company itself and the British interests, it would be well to offer my friend Lane and the Royal Dutch combine part of the shares which had been placed at my disposal.

'I therefore offered them 20,000 shares, that is to say 25 per cent of the Company, to Lane and the Royal Dutch-Shell group, keeping for myself 12,000 shares, i.e. 15 per cent.

'It is a vital point to note how the Royal Dutch-Shell group came into the Turkish Petroleum Company, as this was exclusively due to my introduction.

'The Company was therefore constituted as follows:

		shares
Deutsche Bank and Anatolia Railway (25 per cent)	*Free*	20,000
Royal Dutch-Shell group (25 per cent)	*For cash*	20,000
C. S. Gulbenkian (15 per cent)	*For cash*	12,000
Sir Ernest Cassel and the National Bank of Turkey (35 per cent)	*For cash*	28,000
		80,000

'The founders of the Bank did not want to indulge in oil speculations, but their intention was to be connected with this new enterprise in order to have future banking advantages.

'As an oil man, I knew that 15 per cent was a big participation because I could very well gauge the enormous capital outlays necessary. However, I thought that I could keep the 15 per cent temporarily and watch events, as I felt sure that I could at any time dispose of the whole amount.

'Mr Deterding, head of the Royal Dutch-Shell combine, was exceedingly pleased and expressed his gratitude and appreciation to me for having succeeded in making this organization because his

technical advisers were most optimistic about the potentialities of
Mesopotamia.

'Mr Deterding prevented Mr Lane from having a private interest
because the latter gentleman was on the Executive Board of the
Royal Dutch-Shell combine, whilst I myself, although very intimately
connected with it, had not the some restrictions—not being on the
Executive.

'I again emphasize that, although I became a Director of many
subsidiary companies of the Royal Dutch-Shell combine in which I was
directly interested, I however avoided any Executive function that
might create impediments to my freedom of action. This, in later years,
as I have pointed out, has worked both ways—to my advantage and
disadvantage—by rousing great jealousies.

'It may be interesting at this juncture to refer to Mr Deterding,
who was head of the Royal Dutch-Shell combine when Mr Frederick
Lane made the initial arrangements to which I have referred. Mr Lane
had to give 60 per cent of all the arrangements to the Dutch interests.
The reason for this was that the Royal Dutch and its allied companies
had bigger assets than the British and Russian concerns.

'Owing to these facts, Mr Deterding became Chief (of the Royal
Dutch-Shell) and at the beginning we all worked very smoothly, but
year after year Mr Deterding endeavoured to reduce the power and
influence of Mr Frederick Lane, and ultimately the latter was practically obliged to retire, although the foundation and the initiative
were entirely due to him.

'When the participation of the Royal Dutch-Shell group (in the
Turkish Petroleum Company) was arranged as aforesaid, Mr Deterding
and Mr Frederick Lane also joined the Board.

'Although I was intimately connected with the Royal Dutch-Shell,
the Bank insisted, in virtue of my being the prime mover in the
arrangements, that I should always vote with it.

'On the other hand, I had undertaken with Mr Deterding—with
the knowledge of the Bank—that I should safeguard the interests of
the Royal Dutch-Shell and that the Bank should not be superseded
by the German interests.

'My position in the team was delicate and not in any way a pleasant
one.

'Von Gwinner, who was a very able and cunning personality,
endeavoured to get the upper hand, which I had to forestall. He
complained to Sir Henry Babbington-Smith that both I and Mr Lane
thought that the Germans were "up to Armenian and Maltese tricks"
—the Armenian being myself and, although Mr Lane was not

a Maltese, the latter part of the criticism referred to him all the same.

'I must emphasize that during 1911–12 the relations between the Deutsche Bank and the Royal Dutch-Shell were very far from friendly.

'Personally, both Mr Deterding and Von Gwinner were antagonistic and unfriendly. Luckily, with the help of Sir Henry Babbington-Smith and my backing from Sir Ernest Cassel and Lord Revelstoke, we succeeded in starting our work—at the cost of much patience and adaptability.

'We thought that the best way of making progress was to get the Anatolian Railway representatives in Constantinople to take steps to ask for further concessions and for consolidating the rights already obtained.

'With this object, I arranged with the Directors of the National Bank to instruct their agents in Constantinople, who started actively and efficiently on those lines. Sir Henry Babbington-Smith and I had several interviews with the representatives of the German interests of the Anatolian Railway.

'In view of the antagonism which existed between the Germans and the Royal Dutch, Mr Deterding and Mr Lane did not appear in any of the discussions or negotiations. In order to avoid friction, it was decided to hold as few board meetings as possible.

'I must confess that the Germans started to handle the whole matter in a most efficient way. The necessary applications were made in Constantinople for obtaining concessions, rights, etc., and I personally felt very gratified that at last, after so many years, I had succeeded in organizing a group to work in the right manner to attain my aims.'

4. Third Fence: Persian Slam

The third high hurdle Gulbenkian had to clear was the intrusion of the Anglo-Persian Oil Company. The background, according to his *Memoirs*, was this:

'In about 1900 the D'Arcy Syndicate (the future Anglo-Persian Oil Company) sent Mr H. E. Nichols (later one of their directors) to Constantinople to endeavour to get concessions. Mr Nichols spent considerable sums, but obtained nothing and returned absolutely empty-handed.

'At the same period, I was informed that the Royal Dutch-Shell interests subventioned an English Colonel (by name Piggott, if I remember right) to go on the same mission as Mr Nichols. The Colonel's mission was a complete failure.

'The two missions cost £80,000. This sum was absolutely wasted; nothing was obtained; but the two above-named corporations availed themselves of opportunities later and unfairly recouped this amount from the Iraq Petroleum Company and induced the other associated groups to bear their *pro rata* share of the wasted money.

'Yet I, in spite of having myself spent considerable sums with practical results, was never allowed to obtain reimbursement for any part of my expenses.'

Not only had D'Arcy got the better of him in Persia but he had also diddled him over expenses. Gulbenkian was bitter. The *Memoirs* continue:

'Unfortunately, my illusions (about a smooth-working organization for the Turkish Petroleum Company) did not last long. The greatest of storms about the scheme we had put on foot started very unexpectedly.

'About 1912–13 the Anglo-Persian Oil Company (now the Anglo-Iranian Oil Company) having been acquainted with the fact that an organization was set on foot for the development of Mesopotamia, in which they had no interests, at once got exceedingly upset and decided by hook or by crook to have the upper hand in our Company.

'German pressure had compelled Mr Nichols to come back ten years previously from Turkey empty-handed.

'The problem for the Anglo-Persian Oil Company was to exclude the interests of the National Bank of Turkey, the Royal Dutch-Shell and mine, thus appropriating 60,000 shares out of 80,000, the total capital of the Turkish Petroleum Company.

'It was quite plain that, had they succeeded, they would have had the privilege of a link (with the Germans) without which they could do nothing in Anatolia. By securing this link with the Germans, they were also to have the co-operation of the Turkish Government.'

That is to say, the Anglo-Persian Oil Company sought to oust the Bank, the Royal Dutch-Shell and Gulbenkian from the Turkish Petroleum Company and (having appropriated their shares) to use the Germans' influence in Constantinople to secure the Mesopotamian oil concession.

The *Memoirs* say the onslaught of the Anglo-Persian Oil Company developed thus: 'In about 1913, Sir Henry Babbington-Smith and Sir Ernest Cassel were told that it was the desire of the British Government that their interests should be transferred to the Anglo-Persian Oil Company.

'Soon after, Sir Ernest Cassel communicated to me that, in virtue of his personal relations with King Edward VII, and his intimate relations with the British Government, and as he was not an oil man and the oil business had been instigated by me, he had decided (along with his associates and the National Bank of Turkey) to place their 28,000 shares at the disposal of the British Government.

'At the same time he told me that I was expected to do likewise, but, as I was a private individual, who had worked so persistently without remuneration and had invested cash in the Turkish Petroleum Company, it was for me to decide with the Royal Dutch-Shell group what we should do.

'The difficult position in which I found myself can easily be imagined, the more so as during these *pourparlers* I received a telegram from Mr Alwyn Parker[1] (a Foreign Office official, then in charge of the Near East Department), by which I was informed that it had been decided that I should transfer my shares at once. The style was somewhat peremptory.

'The position became very much confused owing to the National Bank and Sir Ernest Cassel and their associates getting out and leaving us with the Germans, who were astonished at these most unexpected developments.

'Being greatly disillusioned and seeing the crushing of all my hopes and endeavours, I felt it was my duty—before ceding my rights and in view of my intimate connections with the Royal Dutch-Shell—to discuss the position with Mr Deterding.

'When I had acquainted him with the facts communicated to me by Sir Ernest Cassel and Sir Henry Babbington-Smith, and had told him what we were expected to do, Mr Deterding got into a state of frenzy. He became wild and stated that he would never agree to it. He threatened that if I should decide to part with my shares without his consent, it would mean a definite rupture between us.

'The rage into which he got was altogether non-academic—particularly in so far as he hated the Chairman of the Anglo-Persian, Sir Charles Greenway (later Lord Greenway). Mr Deterding had, in fact, a great contempt for the personality of this gentleman and whenever he happened to mention his name he invariably did so in the most ruthless way.

'Mr Deterding always emphasized that if this gentleman had not had the backing of the British Government, he would certainly not have been anywhere near the head of a corporation. In the same way, although his ability bore no comparison with that of Mr Deterding,

---

[1] Later a director of Lloyds Bank Ltd.

Sir Charles Greenway reciprocated the former's feelings and considered Deterding to be a man of no breeding.

'Mr Deterding made a point that I should sit tight and do nothing, and that he himself would take up the challenge against Sir Charles Greenway and his friends' machinations and intrigues.

'Mr Deterding, being a Dutchman, decided to take immediate steps with his Government on the lines that a Dutch corporation with legitimate participation in a British company was being unfairly subjected to pressure to renounce its rights. He was convinced that no British Government would allow such a risky policy because of possessing very considerable interests in the Dutch colonies—also for political reasons.

'In this strained situation between Mr Deterding and Sir Charles Greenway, the Anglo-Persian Company (strongly backed by the British Government) endeavoured to checkmate the progress of the Turkish Petroleum Company in the matter of getting further concessions.

'The Turkish Government, being at that time short of money, wanted to increase the Customs Duties, which could not however be effected owing to the Treaty known as "Capitulations".[1] This was still binding on Turkey and before the Turkish Government could take any steps towards the alterations of the Customs Duties, the consent of all the privileged Signatory Powers in the Capitulations Treaty was needed.

'As Senior Financial Adviser to the Turkish Government I was fully posted with what was taking place. I was informed that the British Government would not agree to any alteration of the Customs Duties if any oil concessions were granted to the Turkish Petroleum Company or the German groups.

'Although the Germans were politically very powerful, it was not possible for them to upset the international agreements embodied in the Capitulations.

'All the time the Deutsche Bank interests in the Turkish Petroleum Company were pressing us to come to terms with the Anglo-Persian Company or to find a *modus vivendi* to put an end to this troublesome situation, which continued during the latter part of 1912 and in 1913, causing great difficulties for the Turkish Government.

'The Turkish Ambassador in London, Tefyk Pasha, formerly a Grand Vizier, recommended the Sublime Porte to delegate a high Turkish official especially to discuss matters with the British Govern-

---

[1] In 1675 the commercial privileges granted under Capitulations to several foreign nations were extended to the English, and in 1809 these were confirmed by Treaty. Later the *ad valorem* Duty was increased from 8 per cent to 11 per cent.

ment—also with the interested parties—so as to come to an understanding and enable the Turkish Government to increase the Customs Duties.

'The recommendations of Tefyk Pasha were accepted. Hakki Pasha, a prominent lawyer and also a former Grand Vizier, was empowered to proceed to London to negotiate.'

We now see Mr Five Per Cent at his deftest.

'In 1913,' he continues, 'the official negotiations between the British Government, our Turkish Petroleum Company and the Royal Dutch-Shell group passed out of my hands to those of Mr Deterding, who relied on the support, if necessary, of the Dutch Government.

'I was in fact the pilot of his negotiations. I was in daily contact with Mr Deterding, although I did not appear.

'My advice to him was that it was our imperative duty to carry the good graces of the British Government and that, further, it was not wise to be antagonistic all the time to the Anglo-Persian Company, as this would only open the door to more trouble.

'*In order to show my genuine desire for peace and satisfaction, I placed at the disposal of Deterding two-thirds of my participation in the Turkish Petroleum Company: that is to say out of my 15 per cent I authorized him to dispose of 10 per cent, if a basis could be found for a general agreement.*

'Although no official or legal change took place between me and the other interested parties, Deterding knew that he had my authorization to deal with 10 per cent. *This is how my 15 per cent became 5 per cent.*

'This is an important point, which should be borne in mind, as regards my final participation of 5 per cent. I had paid cash for it and here I must again emphasize that *no remuneration or commission has ever been paid to me* (for the surrendered 10 per cent).'

When Hakki Pasha arrived in London towards the end of 1913, he and Gulbenkian, who then played in the dual role of founder-director of the Turkish Petroleum Company and Senior Financial Adviser to the Turkish Government, had many discussions together.

'He was pressed by British interests to arrange the grant of concessions to the Anglo-Persian group,' writes Gulbenkian, 'but this could not be done and I know as a fact that no promise was given, because it would have encountered, among other difficulties, the staunchest opposition from the German Government and the Deutsche Bank group.' This is debatable. The Anglo-Persian bid, backed by Britain, was not unwelcome to the Germans as it offered a broader basis for Anglo-German co-operation.

'Numerous negotiations and various machinations,' he continues, 'played their role, until (early in 1914), after strenuous *pourparlers,* it was decided to hold a conference at the Foreign Office between representatives of the Turkish Government, the British Government, the German Government, the Deutsche Bank and the Dutch oil group, in order to find a *modus vivendi*.

'The final conference took place at the Foreign Office on 24th March, 1914, in the presence of all the above representatives. The resulting agreement was signed by the German Ambassador, Sir Eyre Crowe for the British Government, and all the other representatives.'

Gulbenkian had reconciled the irreconcilable—all except the Americans' Rear-Admiral Chester, who gave up his draft concession indignantly, despite diplomatic intervention by the United States.

But at what a cost! Gulbenkian was carved up. He found to his astonishment that he had been left with no say at all in the enterprise which he had envisaged, pushed and at last created.

The agreement provided that 50 per cent of the shares in his Turkish Petroleum Company went to the pirate Anglo-Persian Oil Company who put up £160,000; 25 per cent to the Deutsche Bank; and 25 per cent to the Anglo-Saxon Petroleum Company (Royal Dutch-Shell). The National Bank of Turkey shareholding disappeared and a 5 per cent interest was provided in equal parts by the Anglo-Persian Oil Company and Anglo-Saxon for Gulbenkian for life. He was left voiceless in the future of the Turkish Petroleum Company, at the mercy of Sir Charles Greenway and Henri Deterding.

'My stupefaction was great,' he writes, 'when a copy of the Agreement was handed to me and I discovered that at the last moment and without consulting me or asking for my consent, this important 1914 document, bearing the signatures of most eminent personalities, usurped my rights—in spite of the fact that I had been throughout the conceiver, founder and artisan of the Turkish Petroleum combine.

'This was a preposterous usurpation of power, crushing a minority without even consultation or seeking advice. The entry of the Anglo-Persian group into the Turkish Petroleum Company was effected at the expense of the 35 per cent participation of the National Bank of Turkey and Sir Ernest Cassel's group and 15 per cent of my personal participation, making together 50 per cent. Neither the German interests nor the Royal Dutch-Shell group gave anything away. Only 2½ per cent from each of the two English groups was reserved for me for life. The Anglo-Persian would have had no participation had it not been for the influence of the British Government. Later, the Anglo-Persian claimed to have had a promise of concession from Hakki Pasha. This could not have been so. Owing to my post as Senior Financial Adviser to the Turkish Government, I was fully *au courant* with everything that was taking place and I never heard of such promises.

'It was a great and profitable lesson to me to follow from various corners the intrigues, the misleading influence brought to bear by the oil interests, the insincerities, etc.: a most valuable experience indeed. I was the only one who had a direct insight into what was taking place and I believe I did my utmost towards reaching an arrangement.'

5. Fourth Fence: Touching the Bar

Thus Gulbenkian no sooner became Mr Five Per Cent than he was abruptly confronted by the fourth hurdle on the Mesopotamian oil track: how to regain a voice in the transformed Turkish Petroleum Company.

'I immediately protested to Mr Deterding,' he writes in his *Memoirs*, 'whom I had myself brought into the Turkish Petroleum Company. The whole participation of his group was in fact due to me.

'Although Mr Deterding was then my friend, oil friendships are slippery. He assured me that he had done his level best, but that the Governments and the Anglo-Persian Company had compelled him to accept the arrangement.

'At the same time he stated that it was a preposterous arrangement as far as I was concerned, and that I certainly ought not to accept an illegality.

'My first step was to take the advice of the then foremost Counsel (Sir Wilfrid Greene, later Lord Greene; the late Sir Douglas Hogg, later Lord Hailsham; Sir John Simon, later Viscount Simon) and several other lawyers. They all assured me that this was an inconceivable decision and that I should not worry, because—not being a party to the Foreign Office Agreement—my rights could not in any way be affected. Sooner or later I could rely on the signatories of the Agreement making a satisfactory arrangement with me.'

War was in the offing and Gulbenkian was content to let his personal problem ride for the time being. There were more vital matters.

The *Memoirs'* parting shot at the double-crossing contains a homily: 'The iniquity of this Agreement is an example of what the oil groups can do through the ropes they control to influence Government circles. It is a great pity, because ultimately such policies will work against their very interests.'

6. Fifth Fence: Post Haste

By April 1914 the international situation was deteriorating fast.
The fifth hurdle—ratification of the Foreign Office Agreement by the
Ottoman régime—became urgent.

No shares had been transferred. No concession had been formally
signed. Operations could not yet begin. Procrastination at the Sublime
Porte could still hold up practical progress indefinitely. At any moment
war might undo Gulbenkian's work of a quarter of a century.

The atmosphere was not propitious. The brief flirtation between
Britain and the Young Turks evaporated, largely on account of
redoubled massacres under Enver Pasha, the small, dapper, boyish-
faced and debonair leader; Talaat Bey, who threatened he would 'deal
the Armenians such a blow as would stop them talking autonomy for
fifty years'; and Javid the Jew, who loved life, laughter, women and
power and could slit a throat without a qualm.

The Grey-Lichnowsky Agreement of January 1914, smoothing
Anglo-German issues, remained unratified and the spirit in which the
Foreign Office oil negotiations had started was dead. The renewed
animosity was reflected in the relations between the Deutsche Bank
and the Anglo-Dutch interests in the Turkish Petroleum Company.
The unmasked Young Turks veered back towards the pro-German
attitude of Sultan Abdul Hamid.

Such was the cold climate in which Gulbenkian's *Memoirs* resume:
'Owing to the agitated political atmosphere it was not possible for
me to make progress. Also there was no sincerity between the Royal
Dutch and the Anglo-Persian groups. And the tension with the
German Government gradually became very acute.

'I had several contacts with Sir Charles Greenway and Mr Nichols
of the Anglo-Persian so as to arrange a satisfactory *modus vivendi*
for the Company and its working. But these *pourparlers* did not lead
to any definite results because various technical matters had to be
settled, which took time.

'Before anything tangible was decided, war was declared on
4th August, 1914, and my activities came to a standstill at once.'

Here there is a vital omission. It can be explained by Gulbenkian's
obsession with the injustice he had received and with the Anglo-
Persian machinations; his preoccupation with the Foreign Office
Agreement in March, which was an historic advance in itself; and an
assumption that the neglected facts were public property.

Not until he comes to deal with the events of 1920 does he make a passing reference to 'the acquired rights promised to the Turkish Petroleum Company by the Ottoman Grand Vizier in his letter of 28th June, 1914, to the British and German Ambassadors at the Sublime Porte.'

That letter was the crux of the future Iraq Petroleum Company and his Mesopotamian oil fortune.

Longrigg's *Oil in the Middle East* explains: 'The letter from the Grand Vizier, Said Halim Pasha, stated that the Ministry of Finance agreed to lease the petroleum deposits "discovered or to be discovered" in the *vilayets* (provinces) of Baghdad and Mosul to the Turkish Petroleum Company and reserved to itself the right to decide later both its own share of the proceeds and the general terms of the concession. . . . This letter, less authoritative than a legally sanctioned concession, was yet a formal and solemn promise given by the highest of all Turkish authorities. The fulfilment was, no doubt, prevented only by the outbreak of war five weeks afterwards. Ten years later it was to form the basis of the Turkish Petroleum Company's approach to the Government of Iraq, as the successor state in the two *vilayets*.'

Mr Five Per Cent was in the nick of time. The European War broke out on 4th August, 1914, and Great Britain and Turkey were at war from 5th November, 1915, until the Treaty of Lausanne on 24th July, 1923.

Nubar Gulbenkian reveals the incisive skill with which his father cut through Turkish obstruction to obtain the vital letter: 'Said Halim was an Abdul Hamid man of the devious old school. He was persuaded to back Britain in writing because Turkey was broke as usual and urgently needed to raise the Customs Duties, which were fixed by Capitulations. Father traded an increase in tariffs (with the support of the British Government) for oil rights. He could rely on the British Government because of his association with Lord Revelstoke who had the full confidence of the Foreign Office in financial matters. He also had the confidence of the Turks as he was their Senior Financial Adviser. He was on the inside at both ends of the negotiations. It was as simple as that!'

Mr Five Per Cent had produced a *volte face*. A year earlier the British Government had been backing the Anglo-Persian Oil Company, which was working with the Germans against the Turkish Petroleum Company. Rather than risk the Germans swallowing the whole concession at the last moment, Britain somersaulted and backed Gulbenkian and the Turkish Petroleum Company.

*   *   *   *   *

One pre-1914 question remains incompletely answered.

Having suggested a Turkish oil *monopoly* to Frederick Lane in 1908, why did Gulbenkian successively reduce his interest from *40 per cent* (in African & Eastern Concessions Ltd.) in 1911, to *15 per cent* (in Turkish Petroleum Company) in 1912, and *5 per cent* (in the Turkish Petroleum Company) in 1913?

The explanation does not lie entirely in 'the enormous capital outlays', which he realized he would have to share proportionately with his associates when it came to development. Nor does it lie in his innate instinct for compromise, which was epitomized in the phrase, 'I have done my utmost for reaching an arrangement.'

Both are partial explanations. But there was more to his moderation than that. Nubar Gulbenkian adds: 'Father was not fundamentally greedy. He only wanted value for the money. Negotiating was his hobby. He enjoyed it, not primarily for the rewards, which he valued as a token of success, but for the thrill he got from the battle of wits with the biggest and best financial brains in the world and the satisfaction of forcing great conflicting interests to compromise.

'To take a later instance, when he was forced to scrap the restrictive "Red Line" Agreement in 1948 and let his American partners into Arabia without him, he did not harbour resentment, nor look at the outcome from the point of view of how much money he would be losing in Arabia. He made the best of circumstances—he never believed in crying for the moon.

'Although he disliked American monopolistic methods, which he believed were against the long-term interests of the oil industry, he did not, like his partners, oppose the entry of the Americans into the Turkish Petroleum Company in 1920 from the outset. He bowed to the inevitable and admonished: "Don't let's have a row with the Americans, let's have them in."

'Father never worried about what might have been. Oil diplomacy, like politics, he considered to be the art of the possible.'

Atvarte Essayan adds: 'If Calouste had had a powerful Western nation behind him he would never have parted with such a large proportion of his interest. After all, the concession was really 100 per cent his and there is a difference between 100 and 5 per cent! As one of the persecuted and unpopular Armenian race and an exile, he dared not hang on to more. Deep down he had a racial inferiority complex.'

Whatever the whole truth was, Mr Five Per Cent did not do too badly. His famous interest was bringing him £5,000,000 *a year* when he died, with an early annual prospect of £10,000,000 or more.

13

"LORD BAYSWATER"

B Y 1914 Mr Five Per Cent was forty-five. Half his working life had
gone and he was settling down into a middle-aged routine. He
was going prematurely bald and his beard looked so ridiculous
that he shaved it off. His distinguishing features were his fierce
twirling moustache and his piercing eyes.

Nevarte was in her fortieth year, getting plump, but still attractive,
though she was becoming slightly deaf. She was as bright and sociable
as ever, and ambitious.

Nubar had just gone up to Cambridge.

Since 1900 the family had been established at 38 Hyde Park
Gardens, Bayswater, where Nevarte (with the unwitting help of the
new Jewish aristocracy) had become a Society hostess.

Rita, the only daughter, was born at Bayswater in 1900, when
Calouste was thirty-two and Nevarte twenty-seven. She was not a
beautiful child, apart from the fact that she had inherited her mother's
great brown eyes; but she was bright and vigorous. After English
nurses and French governesses, in the Essayan tradition, by 1914 she
had started at a boarding-school in Sussex.

In 1902, Calouste had become a naturalized British subject. He
thus had a great Western Power's protection—at the same time keeping
a foot in the Oriental camp, as Financial Adviser to the Turks. But
he never became really integrated with his adopted country. Although
he had been headquartered in London for the best part of twenty
years by 1914, his English was guttural and he often made *faux pas*,
which made people snigger. He was essentially an internationalist.

Besides the Bayswater mansion, he kept a house at 27 Quai d'Orsay,
Paris—where he could conveniently entertain his contacts in the
neighbouring Ministries or pop round the corner to see them. He was
constantly crossing the Channel equally secretly on both business and
pleasure. The journey did not worry him as he travelled light and was
a good sailor.

He also kept permanent suites at the Ritz in London and Paris.
In the latter he installed his successive mistresses. Life was taking on
such a complicated pattern that he required a social secretary. For

this exacting role he engaged Rita's French schoolmistress, Elize Soulas, who tactfully performed the dual part of mistress of the mistresses' wardrobes and private secretary to Nevarte.

But he was not encumbered with office routine and rarely visited the Turkish Petroleum Company quarters in the City. He did his paper work in the comfort of an armchair at home in Bayswater or the Quai d'Orsay or one of his Ritz suites. His thinking was done on his daily walks. The world-wide ramifications of his business—in Russia, the Middle East, Europe, and America—were carried in his head. He was not littered with files or submerged with correspondence. His business secretary was no more than a short-hand typist—one of the earliest, as longhand was only just going out of ordinary office use. Much of his work was done by telegraph.

Calouste was what would now be called, opprobriously, "a dessicated calculating machine". Yet it was the foresight, energy and genius of Gulbenkian and his kind which made Britain the greatest power on earth and financed the victories in two World Wars.

By 1914, Calouste Gulbenkian had brought together and imposed his will upon a group of the toughest, shrewdest and most dynamic men who have ever shaped the destiny of a great country and a civilization.

Up-and-coming Winston Churchill, then First Lord of the Admiralty, and the terrifying Lord Fisher, First Sea Lord, were already convinced of Gulbenkian's twenty-five-year-old prophecy of the decisive important of oil at sea and were emerging from the thick of the hard-fought "oil *versus* steam" battle with the Admiralty, Treasury, the Cabinet, Parliament, and vested coal interests.

In tapping hitherto unfathomed forces, the new oil men necessarily waxed rich and they made a virtue out of it.

What were they like, these modern oil kings? Let us go on one of little Mr Five Per Cent's walks from Bayswater and have a look at their set.

Round the corner from Hyde Park Gardens was Herbert Louis Samuel in 32 Porchester Terrace—a year younger than Gulbenkian, a leading Liberal politician, a future High Commissioner in Palestine, elder statesman and philosopher—one of the brilliant Samuel family, who created Shell. As Viscount Samuel, aged eighty-seven, he is the last survivor of that thrusting set of financial Empire-builders and his address is still the same.

Up the Bayswater Road to Marble Arch and there, at 36 Great Cumberland Place, was Thomas Baring, the second Lord Northbrook, who had been Viceroy of India in 1872–6 and was the head of the famous "overbearing Baring" family—Baring Bros., the merchant bankers, who were established in 1763, registered in 1890, and have ever since been to the fore in finance, oil, and diplomacy.

At 90 Wimpole Street was the Earl of Cromer, formerly Sir Evelyn Baring, who had now finished his two historic spells in Egypt (1877–9 and 1884–1907). In 1914 he was seventy-three and in retirement, but still a link with the days of Nubar Pasha, the erratic Khedives, and Britain's absorption into Middle East affairs.

Down Park Lane was Sir Ernest Cassel, by then sixty-two, the amazing German Jew, who became the confidant of King Edward VII, and was founder of the National Bank of Turkey—the enterprise which launched Gulbenkian on the reconciliation of Ottoman oil interests.

At the Piccadilly end of Park Lane, at 2 Hamilton Place, was Marcus Samuel, by then aged sixty-one, already a baronet, Churchill's right-hand man in the "oil *versus* steam" controversy, and the future Viscount Bearsted—the founder of the Shell Transport and Trading Company.

On through Piccadilly to the Ritz and at 18 Arlington Street Lord Farringdon was to be found—one of the first magnates with whom Gulbenkian got in touch when he returned to London at the end of 1896. As Alexander Henderson, he had become Chairman of the Great Central Railway and Gulbenkian interested him in countering the Germans' Baghdad Railway plans for oil. *The Financial Times* describing him as 'a cautious and ultra-conservative Scot with a magic touch for converting people and especially Railway Stock into real hard money'.

Down St James's and Pall Mall to the majesty of Carlton House Terrace and at No. 3 we find that paragon of financial rectitude, Lord Revelstoke II. He was another Baring. He was fifty-one, six years older than Gulbenkian, on whom he looked down as his junior and as a foreign upstart.

Senior partner in Baring Bros. & Co., with a capital of £1,025,000, which was doubled in 1930; a director of the Bank of England; a Lieutenant of the City of London; President of the Territorial Association; owner of 10,000 acres; Revelstoke lived in splendid isolation —icy poles apart from the crafty, Oriental Armenian, who became his co-Director in the National Bank of Turkey.

Such rip-snorting activities as the oil trade in America, Trans-caucasia and the decaying Ottoman Empire hardly belonged to Revelstoke's world and one may assume that it was he—as much as Cassel and King Edward—who shunned Gulbenkian's petroleum plans and took the National Bank out of the Turkish Petroleum Company. It seems that only at the last moment, when Gulbenkian dreamed up the means of restraining German oil diplomacy in Mesopotamia, did Revelstoke awake to the real stake and throw his weight into the Foreign Office Agreement, behind Mr Five Per Cent.

But Revelstoke never approved of Gulbenkian's acquisitive instincts when it came to women. It was all right by Revelstoke's Victorian code to covet money, domestic comfort, power and position. Oriental erotics were no part of Baring's make-up.

And so we pass on, across Horse Guards' Parade to Whitehall and the Foreign Office, where Gulbenkian had his diplomatic contacts.

Not one of these magnates was English by origin. Farringdon was a Scot and the others were Jews by racial origin.

The routine Mr Five Per Cent worked out for himself by middle age is described by Nubar:

'He could play a waiting game as well as anybody, but he hated wasting time and made the most of it. He made a practice of starting to telephone his associates, his staff and members of the family from 8 a.m. onwards, so as to make sure of getting them—and perhaps catching them off their guard. He would then fix telephone appointments at intervals for the rest of the day, so as to keep them on the hop and under control. Often it was very irritating.

'Until 1925, when the lease of 38 Hyde Park Gardens ran out and he built 51 Avenue d'Iéna as his official residence, he slept increasingly less at home. After 1925, he gave up any pretence of sharing a bedroom with my mother. He always slept at the Carlton in London or the Ritz in Paris.

'He would breakfast at the hotel—do his "arms upward stretch" or "down on the knees, bend"—and have a massage. Then he would read his correspondence and reports, dictate letters and send off a sheaf of menacing telegrams.

'After business appointments and a snoop round the Ministries, he would arrive home to collect his mail and lunch—having taken a brisk morning walk in Hyde Park or the Bois, followed by his car, which would pick him up at a given signal.

'Luncheon got later and later yearly, much to the fury of his wife and family. He expected the food to be "just so": and we were kept kicking our heels. We put up with the delay so long as we could get the meal over between 2 p.m. and 3.30 p.m. But when, eventually, it came to serving lunch at 4 p.m., we plucked up our courage and let him eat by himself. He protested. But we got away with it. Pa was like that. He respected people who stood up to him. He didn't insist on the impossible.

'His business lunches were usually held at the old Carlton Restaurant, where he was affectionately known to the hotel staff as "Hell Fire Jack", because on his tantrums and insistence on split-second service.

'After lunch, he would go for another brisk walk in the Park—again followed by his chauffeur—and then keep another round of appointments, bury himself in art galleries or visit antique shops.

'If my mother was having a party or he steeled himself to attend some worth-while reception, he might look in for a moment. But he had almost no ordinary social life. He stuck to what he called the "essentials" and his "vision".

'By 7 p.m. he would usually be back home again to change for dinner at the Ritz in Paris or the Carlton in London, where he would dine with a friend at about nine o'clock.

'He was seldom in bed before midnight—incessantly on the telephone to his immediate circle and indeed all over the world—carrying in his head a mass of detail, running great risks and attending instantly to each problem as it cropped up. He was always on the ball. Day and night he kept a sheaf of small blank cards by him, either in his waistcoat pocket or on his bedside table. He forgot nothing, from a whisper of disloyalty to a dent in his top hat or a new recipe, or a new invention, to a rumour of a picture for sale or the hint of a profitable investment. Down went a note. It was always "action this day". It was inhuman, but one couldn't help admiring his keenness. He was a terrific worker.'

His suite at the Ritz, London, was No. 420 on the fourth floor, overlooking the Green Park, and is now occupied by Nubar and Marie Gulbenkian. On the drawing-room floor is the same exquisite Persian carpet, which the old man enjoyed. Its intricate purple, crimson, blue and black pattern would grace a museum showcase.

By 1914, Gulbenkian had also found time to develop his artistic taste to a very high degree over a wide field.

Sir Kenneth Clark, Director of the National Gallery from 1934 to 1945 and, since 1954, Chairman of the Independent Television Authority, who was his adviser and confidant for twenty years, says:

'Only a fraction of his art treasures were shown in London, at the National Gallery (1937–47) and in the British Museum. His supreme taste rested in his racial feeling for textiles (his Oriental carpets were magnificent) and in furniture. Among the pieces he bought from the Hermitage sale, after the Russian Revolution, were the wonderful bedroom suite of the actor, Talmar, and Marie Antoinette's table.

'He set about systematically getting educated in the Arts. He took daily lessons from Benedict of the Corps de Louvre, visiting Versailles, the Hotel de Ville, the Louvre and all the other great French art collections—studying sculpture, architecture and painting.

'He developed a reliable classical taste for painting, founded on the French classical taste of the 1890s. He was not open to the romantic or charming schools. He liked the grand, the perfect and the imposing. He also developed a reasonably good judgement of architecture. He knew the work of Louis XIV's great architect, Gabriel, by heart, also Mansart. He knew all the fine staircases in Paris and used to walk one round them, until one nearly dropped, pointing out their merits.

'His taste in painting was less sure. It was prejudiced by his love of pretty girls and agreeable occasions. He couldn't adapt himself to antiquity in a face. But he had good rich man's taste.'

He made his first major art purchase in 1907—"View of Mira on the Brenta", by Francesco Guardi (1712–93); a 'superlative work', as the National Gallery catalogue said in 1937. Guardi was to remain one of Gulbenkian's favourite artists, for whose works he watched the market like a cat.

In 1910, the year he became an international banker at the age of forty-one, when the National Bank of Turkey was formed, he bought Corot's "A Road at Ville-D'Avray", a restful woodland road scene. Whenever possible he celebrated a business deal by investing some of the winnings in a work of art.

The Foreign Office Agreement of March 1914 justified his acquisition of Romney's "Portrait of Miss Constable". The purchase was made in June, when the Agreement was underscored by the Grand Vizier's promissory letter.

What with millions, mansions, mistresses and art treasures, Mr Five Per Cent was already "The Mystery Millionaire" by the outbreak of the First World War. Unlike his friends, rivals, and associates. he did not covet the public trappings of power.

In the Parliament Act crisis in 1911, when the Prime Minister, Mr Herbert Asquith, threatened to pack the House of Lords with two to three hundred Liberal peers if the Lords threw out the budget, Calouste Gulbenkian was offered a barony for £100,000.

Rita, aged eleven and then living with her parents at 38 Hyde Park Gardens, exclaimed excitedly: 'Now Papa will be Lord Bayswater and Nubar and I will be Honourable Lancaster Gates!' Nubar says: 'Father often recounted that he was offered the barony third-hand. The government was touting people alleged to have money which they would contribute to Liberal funds. You could still buy honours in those days.'

But Gulbenkian refused the honour—he was to be Mr, not Lord, Five Per Cent. 'I'd rather have the cash,' he said.

14

LIFEBLOOD

THE sinews of the First World War were oil. During it Clemenceau telegraphed to President Wilson: 'Each drop of oil secured to us, saves a drop of human blood.' Afterwards, Lord Curzon declared: 'The Allies floated to victory on a sea of oil.'

That did not come about automatically. The oil had lain sealed in the ground since time immemorial, until the pioneers, Gulbenkian among them, came along to locate, tap, organize and deliver it. Not even then were ordinary Western minds adjusted to the new facts of economic life and the revolution in power which the dawn of the Oil Age connoted.

The lesson did not finally sink in until the Suez Crisis of 1956-7, when western Europe suddenly woke up to the fact that it would soon cease to function—even in time of peace—without regular deliveries of Middle East oil. Oil had become so much part of our lives that it was difficult in mid-twentieth century to realize our dependence upon it—and still more difficult to recapture the drama of the "oil *versus* steam" battle of nearly fifty years ago.

Nothing less than the survival of Britain as a Great Power, in war and peace, was the context of Gulbenkian's twenty-five years' pre-war struggle to prevent Germany from grabbing the oil resources of the sprawling Ottoman Empire. In a sense the First World War was a battle for oil.

Gulbenkian and Bismarck were twenty years ahead of Britain (her leaders, such as Cassel and Revelstoke; the Foreign Office and Admiralty; as well as public opinion) in seeing the light.

This blindness explains Britain's sudden appointment of a Royal Commission of the Supply of Oil in 1912, her sudden patronage of the Anglo-Persian Oil Company in 1913, and her *volte face* at Constantinople in June 1914.

Anybody reading Winston Churchill's *World Crisis 1911–14* today might think it was he who had suddenly discovered the potentialities of oil and safeguarded Britain's supplies. What he did was convince the Cabinet and Industry of facts which Gulbenkian and other oil men had been preaching for years. It was the oil men, not the politicians, who had the vision and took the risks to secure British oil supplies in Persia, where they delivered the goods in the nick of time in 1913. It was also the oil men, notably Gulbenkian, in the face of Cabinet and Whitehall obstruction, who deprived the Germans of corresponding supplies from Mesopotamia.

Churchill mentioned in a letter to Lord Fisher in February 1912: 'Hopwood and Sir Marcus Samuel are hard at it over oil.' It was about time. The two arguments set forth by him were:

PRO

'In equal ships oil gave a large excess of speed over coal. It enabled this speed to be attained with far greater rapidity. It gave 40 per cent greater radius of action for the same weight of coal. It enabled a fleet to refuel at sea with great facility. An oil-burning fleet can, if need be, in calm weather keep its station at sea, nourishing itself from tankers without having to send a quarter of its strength continuously into harbour to coal, wasting fuel on the homeward and outward journey. The ordeal of coaling exhausted the whole ship's company. In war time it robbed them of their brief period of rest; it subjugated everyone to extreme discomfort.

With oil, a few pipes were connected with the shore or with a tanker and the ship sucked in its fuel with hardly a man having to lift a finger. Less than half the number of stokers was needed to tend and clean the oil furnaces. Oil could be stowed in spare places in a ship from which it would be impossible to bring coal. As a coal ship used up her coal, increasingly large numbers of men had to be taken, if necessary from the guns, to shovel coal from remote and inconvenient bunkers to bunkers nearer the furnaces or to the furnaces themselves, thus weakening the fighting efficiency of the ships perhaps at the most critical moment in the battle. . . .

The use of oil made it possible in every type of vessel to have more gunpower and more speed for less size and cost. It alone made it possible to realize the high speeds in certain types which were vital to their tactical purpose.'

CON

'To build any large additional number of oil-burning ships meant basing our naval supremacy upon oil. But oil was not found in appreciable quantities in our islands. If we acquired it, we must carry it by sea in peace or war from distant countries. We had, on the other hand, the finest supply of the best seam coal in the world. . . .

First there must be accumulated in Britain an enormous oil reserve large enough to enable us to fight for many months if necessary, without bringing in a single cargo of oil. To contain this reserve enormous installations of tanks must be erected near the various ports. Would they not be very vulnerable? Could they be protected? Could they be concealed or disguised? The word "camouflage" was not then known. Fleets of tankers had to be built to convoy the oil from distant oilfields across the oceans to the British Isles and others of different pattern to take it from our naval harbours to the fleets at sea.

Owing to the system of finance by which we had bound our-selves, we were not allowed to borrow even for capital or "once for all" expenditure. Every penny must be won from Parliament year by year, and constituted a definite addition to the inevitably rising and already fiercely challenged Naval Estimates. And beyond these difficulties loomed up the more intangible problem of markets and monopolies. The oil supplies of the world were in the hands of vast oil trusts under foreign control. To commit the Navy irrevocably to oil was indeed "to take arms against a sea of troubles".'

Asking Lord Fisher to preside over the Royal Commission on 11th June, 1912, Churchill wrote:

'This liquid fuel problem has got to be solved, and the natural, inherent, unavoidable difficulties are such that they require the drive and enthusiasm of a big man. I want you for this. . . .'

Reading the CONS and Churchill's invitation to Fisher, one might imagine that oil tankers were novelties, whereas they had been plying the high seas, for the oil companies, since 1892; that the wicked oil monopolies were refusing to sell oil to the Admiralty, whereas it was manifestly their interest to do so and in fact the Royal Navy was already substantially, though not predominantly, oil-driven; that it was the oil companies which were fouling the British Government's efforts to secure Midde East oil supplies, whereas the Government itself was frustrating the plans of the Turkish Petroleum Company and giving the Germans their chance in Mesopotamia. Sir Marcus Samuel, himself one of the biggest "monopolists", was sorting out the Government's largely self-made difficulties and easing the penalty for the Admiralty's years of blindness. Gulbenkian was also at the height of his labours to provide Britain with an assured oil supply in peace and war, and very scurvily the Foreign Office was to reward him for his labours.

The truth is much nearer the British Government seeking an oil monopoly of its own—as it succeeded in doing in Persia—and, in the process, trying to do the magnates out of the fruits of their vision, labour and investment in the Mesopotamian oil enterprise.

As we have read in Gulbenkian's *Memoirs*, the Persian oil concession was 'a drag on the market' and its success was 'sheer luck, due to no industrial or economic foresight'. Churchill himself admits: 'Fortune rewarded the continuous and steadfast facing of these difficulties by the Board of Admiralty and brought us a prize from fairyland beyond our brightest hopes.'

Yet it was on Persia that Churchill pinned his hopes and the future of island Britain. 'The three programmes of 1912, 1913, and 1914 comprised the greatest addition in power and cost ever made to the Royal Navy. . . . For the first time the supreme ships of the Navy, on which our life depended, were fed by oil and could only be fired by oil. . . . A decision like this involved our national safety as much as a battle at sea. It was as anxious and harassing as any hazard of war. It *was* war in a certain sense raging under a surface of unbroken peace.'

Churchill's whole Naval oil policy and the survival of Britain in the First World War were in fact only made possible by the faith, risks and energy of the oil "monopolists"—by William Knox D'Arcy's persistence, to the point of bankruptcy, in drilling—by the miraculous last-minute strike at Masjid-i-Sulaiman on 26th May, 1908—even by the original Persian pipeline, which was started before the British Government produced the cash to see the Anglo-Persian Oil Company through and so gained control of the Company.

Churchill's *World Crisis* suggests that somehow the success of the Anglo-Persian Oil Company was due to the Government, whereas the credit should go to the pioneers of the Company. He records:

'Finally (1909) we found our way to the Anglo-Persian Oil Agreement and contract, which (for an initial investment of two millions) has not only secured the Navy a very substantial proportion of its oil supply, but has led to the acquisition by the Government of a controlling share in oil properties and interests which at present [1923] are valued at scores of millions of sterling. . . .

. . . The oil fuel reserves, when created, were clearly, whether for peace or war, as much an asset as the gold reserve in the Bank of England.'

Yet the *World Crisis* repeats the smear against the oil magnates:

'The Anglo-Persian Oil Convention encountered a confusing variety of oppositions—economists deprecating naval expenditure; members of mining constituencies who were specially sensible of the danger of departing from the sound basis of British coal; oil magnates who objected to a national inroad upon their monopolies; Conservatives who disapproved of State trading; partisans who denounced the project as an unwarrantable gamble with public money and did not hesitate to impute actual corruption.'

I should think the oil magnates *did* object to the British Government's attempt to grab the fruits of their spade work—and at the same time stupidly opening the way for a counter-grab by Germany.

We had to wait until 1951, when the Anglo-Persian was expropriated, to realize Gulbenkian's wisdom in merging the interests of the Western Powers and their oil companies in the Iraq Petroleum Company. It is not so easy to expropriate a multinational public-private enterprise. We shall see how Gulbenkian and Deterding developed this idea and how time and time again, down to the Suez Canal Users' Association, Governments must come back to it. In order to pay, the self-interest in the oil world must be enlightened.

By 1890 Gulbenkian, before he came of age, was already foretelling the replacement of coke by oil in industrial furnaces, as well as in ships. Yet in the middle of the First World War, Lord Fisher was still exploding:

'The duffers [in the British War Cabinet]! Would you believe it? They are not convinced yet that if I am to put to sea on coal, I must have two hundred stokers more on board every warship of any size than if we stoked with oil. If they insist on coal, where am I to bunker it? These officials talk as if they can so regulate the war that it will always be fine weather. Most important, to win a sea battle I must have speed, and I can only get the maximum on fuel oil. . . . The bill for our warships will run into millions. The guns, and everything else I have put into these ships, are the last word in efficiency. But what use will it be if speed is denied us? A slow battleship is about as much good as a slow racehorse. If the Government won't give way to me, I'll retire and grow roses in Norfolk.'

William Knox D'Arcy, who lived until 1917, gave Lord Fisher the oil required and the Persian production was distributed under the control of the Lane-Gulbenkian-Deterding Royal Dutch-Shell combine.

The case for the much-maligned and little-understood oil monopolists or cartel-mongers has gone largely by default and through their own disregard of public relations. That is, putting their case to the public.

The European oil pioneers, with the noted exception of Alexander Mantachoff and Henri Deterding, were introverts and had an extraordinary gift for anonymity. Bearsted, Revelstoke and Cassel left no memoirs. Gulbenkian carried his passion for privacy to the extreme of playing hide-and-seek in half a dozen addresses at the same time. Statesmen closely involved in the momentous oil story never even mention him, which is a tribute to his camouflage but not to their coverage. Cromer, Curzon, Fisher, Lloyd George and Churchill, for instance, might never have heard of him. Yet in the final analysis, his impact must have been as telling as any.

Statesmen seem to have taken the oil for granted, although its sudden appearance in vast quantities at the crucial moment was due to the Gulbenkians of the industry. The oil magnates seem, equally incomprehensibly, to have been shy of their own contribution to progress or victory and to have been mesmerized into silence about their own activities. They seem to experience a sense of shame; in an inverted way, even Deterding manifested it.

Perhaps the real reason for the oil tycoons' shyness, reticence, or anonymity was the fact that the essence of oil diplomacy is secrecy. Perhaps it was hardly surprising that they became furtive. It served their pockets richly, but it impoverished their subsequent reputations and incidentally ruined what little popularity millionaires ever had as a class.

In 1919, Sir Marcus Samuel was accorded a vote of thanks from the Lord Commissioner of the Admiralty 'for services of the utmost importance to the fighting Services' and in 1921 he was raised to the Peerage. Deterding got his knighthood.

Gulbenkian hankered after no such frills. He was ever the realist. The reality of power through oil and money was good enough for him. He needed no handle for self-justification.

The solitary occasion when Mr Five Per Cent was tempted into any highflown justification for his existence was at the end of his *Memoirs*:

'It has been a source of vivid satisfaction to me that as a result of the events and developments, which I have outlined in these notes, Iraq Oil was made available to the Allied Powers during the Second World War at a point of such vital strategic importance as the Eastern Mediterranean. When the full story can be told, it will be seen that this is by no means the only service which the Iraq Petroleum Company and its elaborate and efficient organization have rendered to the Allied war effort in the Middle East.' Normally Mr Five Per Cent was satisfied with a silent pride in his own achievement. There was no better judge, nor harsher critic.

PHASE II

1914-1955

15

HISTORY INTERVENES

1. Great Events

ON 28th June, 1914, the Turkish Petroleum Company was running on all four cylinders—Anglo-Dutch, Anglo-Persian, German and Gulbenkian. Five weeks later, on 4th August, it seized up. It was a pre-war model and came to a full stop. An almost unrecognizable post-war model came off the Gulbenkian drawing-board fourteen years later.

Great events merged into each other in that long interval of turmoil. All the while the map and minds were changed Gulbenkian kept track of the connecting threads. How he did so—and made something out of the mess—is one of the intellectual marvels of modern business diplomacy.

Anglo-Persian sabotage got to work again at once and soon the Turkish Petroleum Company was insolvent. . . . The Germans were enemies and in March their partnership ceased to be worth the Foreign Office paper it was written on. Who was to fill the gap? In November 1914 the Turks, too, became our enemies. The Sick Man of Europe finally died in November 1922 and the principal of the estate passed to new heirs. The nucleus of the Ottoman Empire was replaced by the New Turkey of Mustapha Kemal Attaturk. The Imperial Russian Empire also collapsed and in truncated form passed into the hands of Lenin and the Bolsheviks. There was civil war in Asia Minor and Caucasia. The Western Powers intervened to stabilize the residue of the Sultan's and Tsar's estates and fell out among themselves. In the process Gulbenkian's Russian, Old Turk and Armenian contacts evaporated and the Armenian race was pulverized outside the Trans-caucasian province of Erevan. The Americans began to join in, and Gulbenkian was presented with a new world in which he virtually had to start the work of half a lifetime afresh.

So it seemed. But the struggle was really the same—as it always was and always will be—for mastery of the communications, wealth and minds of the weak peoples at the crossroads of the world. Only the names change. For caravan routes we read sea lanes or air lines.

For spices it is now oil. For Islam we read Marxism. The prizes in 1914–18 were the same in all but name as those for which Alexander, Tamerlane and Napoleon (and lesser conquerors also) have waged their various wars.

The Suez Crisis of 1956–7 is about the same fundamentals. In the end one Great Power, Greek, Roman, Persian, Turkish or British—now Russian or American?—always emerges to impose its will and order on the big area of the Middle East. Those were the essentials to which Gulbenkian clung. In 1914 he backed the winners, the Entente Cordiale. But he was never so foolish as to imagine that Anglo-French domination was more permanent than any other Middle East settlement. He continued to woo the Americans and Russians in pursuit of general reconciliation and a permanent balance of the Great Powers without which there can be no lasting peace at the grand junction of Europe, Asia and Africa.

That is the perspective in which we now watch the early and transitory oil set-up in the Middle East emerge—through Gulbenkian's eyes. The only way to grasp the detail of this vast canvas is to inspect it bit by bit.

2. Sabotage

When Turkey, as well as Germany, became an enemy of the Allies on 5th, November 1915, and the Public Trustee seized the Deutsche Bank shares in the Turkish Petroleum Company, anybody might have been forgiven for thinking the Company was dead: anybody except Mr Five Per Cent. The Anglo-Persian partners certainly took that view, boycotted the Company and set about looking to their own interests in the new situation, which had arisen and would have to be worked out at some distant date when the war finished. The Company was soon insolvent and Gulbenkian and Deterding had to put their hands in their own pockets to pay running expenses and keep it alive.

Gulbenkian's *Memoirs* relate sourly: 'In 1915–16, the Turkish Petroleum Company having no funds to defray its routine expenses, it became necessary to put up money for it. Mr Deterding came forward willingly to cover the share of his group and, at his request, I called on Sir Charles Greenway to ask him to let me have for the account of the Company 50 per cent of the sums necessary to carry on. (The

Anglo-Persian Oil Company shareholding in the Turkish Petroleum Company was 50 per cent.)

'The first time I called on him, Sir Hugh Barnes was also present. We had a very friendly and cordial talk, but I could get no reply from Sir Charles Greenway to my request, on behalf of Mr Deterding, to contribute his share.

'All along he avoided answering me and then adroitly started asking me for information about Persian pottery. . . . Sir Hugh Barnes in his turn referred to Persian miniatures. . . . The whole conversation was very cute, but I felt helpless and ultimately I left with the feeling that they did not want to discuss the position at all.

'I reported the conversation to Mr Deterding and told him that it had been a very cordial one, but that I had come out of it empty-handed.

'Mr Deterding got angry, qualifying the attitude of the Anglo-Persian group as "not being cricket" (a favourite expression of his) and he asked me to make another call on Sir Charles Greenway, which I did.

'Sir Charles, seeing my insistence, told me that he did not see his way to discussing the matter.

'This I reported to Mr Deterding, who immediately jumped to the conclusion that the Anglo-Persian was again up to some "tricks" to see us all out. He thought they were labouring under the belief that, once the war was over, the whole of Mesopotamia would become British and then there would be no room for any foreign Companies. He became, as usual, very vehement and said he would see them damned first.

'In the circumstances, Mr Deterding and I advanced the expenses for running the Company. The amount was not big because the Company had practically no activities and, as far as I can remember, it concerned mainly solicitors' bills, salaries and other petty expenses.

'The position of the Turkish Petroleum Company remained stagnant. No Directors were nominated by the Anglo-Persian group and they did not interfere with the Company.'

Had he known his Mr Five Per Cent better, Sir Charles might not have been so negligent. He made the strategic error of under-estimating his opponent and not projecting himself into his mind. Gulbenkian and Deterding made no such mistake and ferreted out every move Sir Charles made behind their backs.

The *Memoirs* continue: 'Sir Henri Deterding was most sceptical about the pretexts put forward by Sir Charles Greenway to justify

keeping aloof. Sir Charles explained that he had acted at the request of
the Foreign Office not to abide by the March, 1914, Agreement, owing
to war conditions.

'According to his statements, it appears that on November 23rd,
1914, Sir Charles had written at length to the Foreign Office drawing
attention to the importance of the provisions of the Agreement being
"carried through without delay in order that the interests of the
D'Arcy group (i.e. the Anglo-Persian Oil Company) may be preserved
no matter how the present war may eventuate, and also for the purpose
of clearing up the present somewhat involved position as regards
liability for expenditure already incurred."

'On November 23rd, 1915 (exactly a year later), Sir Maurice de
Bunsen of the Foreign Office wrote in reply: "After due consideration
Sir Edward Grey is of the opinion—shared by the heads of the various
other Departments concerned—that the Agreement of March, 1914,
has in the circumstances no longer any legal validity and that they will
decline to take this Agreement into account when the moment comes
to arrange for the future of the oil areas (in Mesopotamia). His
Majesty's Government are therefore of the opinion that you should
take no steps to carry out the arrangements embodied in the Agreement.
But I am to add that the necessity of safeguarding so far as possible the
interests of the British parties to that Agreement will not be lost sight
of."

'Sir Henri Deterding was of the opinion that the above correspondence had been engineered by Sir Charles Greenway, who had a
great pull with the Foreign Office, so as to justify the stand he had taken
in not carrying out the March, 1914, Agreement.

'As explained previously, neither the Royal Dutch nor the Anglo-
Persian had any tangible rights in Mesopotamia. In 1913 and earlier
the Anglo-Persian had been working through the British Ambassador
in Turkey in order to get concessions, but had obtained nothing apart
from vague statements in correspondence. Their expectations of
concessions were put forward later on as rights, which had never
existed.

'Between 1913 and 1918 a general atmosphere of uncertainty,
confusion and intrigue prevailed among the different groups. Each
wanted to predominate and try and play out the other associates.
For practically five years, the Turkish Petroleum Company remained
in a state of confusion and suspended animation.

'On top of those conditions, I had added another claimant. At my
instigation, the British Government had promised to pass the German
share over to the French.'

3. Enter the French

Until thirty years ago, France was completely out of the oil race. Her historic role in the Eastern Mediterranean, going back to Charlemagne and the Crusades, had been interrupted by the Napoleonic débâcle in Egypt. She regained a foothold with the construction of the Suez Canal by Ferdinand De Lesseps, but the British position in Egypt and the Sudan (after the Fashoda incident) and in Persia (after the formation of the Anglo-Persian Oil Company) was predominant. The Paris Rothschilds had helped with oil distribution in France, but France had no share in any oil wells. She was dependent on foreign oil supplies and largely on American distribution. In that condition she could hardly remain a first-class power, capable of independent action. This dependence on foreign oil was one of the fundamental, though unpublicized, factors which bound France to the Entente Cordiale.

Thanks entirely to Gulbenkian, as we shall now see, France became an oil power in her own right and regained her independence. 'In 1915–16' he writes, 'I was nominated Foreign Delegate of the Royal Dutch combine, my mission being to place myself at the disposal of the French Government to facilitate their oil supplies.

'Although the prize attached to success was very handsome from a material viewpoint, what I had at heart was to render a great service to France by creating a sound oil policy and economy.

'The French oil groups' so-called *"Industrie Nationale de Raffinage"* was nothing else than a monopolistic association of grocers.

'I mean to say that they had no industry and as regards petroleum France was in a pitiful condition—in spite of the fact that French refiners had accumulated enormous fortunes by price rigging and dubious methods such as bribing the press.

'They had been working all along for their own advantage without worrying at all to establish a sound economic policy to meet the. requirements of their country in war-time or exceptional circumstances.

'The oil trusts—particularly the American companies—held the major part of the French oil interests under their thumb.

'This screen encouraged the so-called French refiners in their unhealthy methods.

'The foreign oil trusts, especially the American companies, sold oil products to the French oil interests at very high prices, but they undertook not to compete locally. Nominally there were French refineries and American refineries, but none of them worked or carried out their functions genuinely.

'The whole machinery was got up so as to avoid import duties under the pretext of a national refining industry. In fact, the petroleum arrived in France already refined, but before leaving the port of shipment some chemical dirt was added inside the tanks and it was easily removed at the destination by the local refineries.

'This process was qualified as "*Raffinage*" and the organization as "*Industrie de Raffinage*!" . . . To be frank, the Royal Dutch combine also participated in this trade (to a smaller extent), so as to secure a footing in France.

'Like the American groups, the Royal Dutch combine also had refineries which were either leased to the French or worked in the same fashion I have described.'

When war was declared, the supply of oil to the French Army had become most complicated owing to the lack of local organization, and Gulbenkian's *Memoirs* go on to describe his plans for coping with the situation:

'My working plans can be summarized thus:

1 My personal desire was to be of service to France by making use of my knowledge of the poor state of the country's oil organization. This aim was independent of material aims and was prompted by sympathy for a country where I had been residing for many years.

2 My activities in France were directed so that I could rely on the full approval of the British Government, by contributing to the war effort and at the same time promoting French interests. It was indispensable to gain the support and friendship of the French Government, which was a delicate job, because the American groups then had the upper hand.

3 To break the unwholesome, selfish and unpatriotic grip of the French refiners on their country's oil trade.

4 To increase the trade and influence of the Royal Dutch combine against the American hold and prestige in France and Italy, in accordance with Sir Henri Deterding's instructions.

'In peacetime the realization of those plans would have been almost impossible. The grip of the French refiners (political, press, Chamber of Deputies and beyond) was such that they could unscrupulously checkmate the activities of anyone honestly working in the interest of the country. The French oil refiners only feared the big oil trusts, such as the American groups and the Royal Dutch, with whom they were compromised.

'Fortunately for my plan, their organization was in such a pitiful state when war was declared that they dreaded the military authorities' expressing great dissatisfaction, which in fact occurred very soon afterwards.

'Disorder and confusion were such that the Government was obliged to take special steps to reorganize the petroleum and fuel administration.

'I advised the competent authorities, through influential channels, to create a special Commissariat.

'This was done at the beginning of 1916 and M Henri Berenger, Chairman of the Senate Foreign Relations Committee, was appointed High Commissioner for Petroleum.

'He[1] was an astute parliamentarian, fully acquainted with all the political intricacies and, to my great satisfaction, he immediately saw the advantages to be derived from my schemes—not only from his personal political standpoint, but also from the point of view of national interest.

'M Berenger was a very well known political figure and owing to his connection with all the Government departments, I soon got in touch with all the elements that would facilitate my task.

'At the outset I had great difficulties which I overcame only because I confined myself devotedly to the highest interests of the country, leaving aside all other considerations for the time being.

'I imparted all my knowledge to the new High Commissioner for the improvement of the French oil economy. His Department was thus able to gain great influence in Government circles and for me personally a genuine atmosphere of cordiality and confidence was created.

'I also had the support of the enterprising and clever Minister of Industrial Production, M Loucheur.

'On behalf of the Royal Dutch combine, I offered important financial facilities to the French Government. I negotiated credits, then amounting to many millions of pounds sterling. In doing so, I rendered practical services to the French State and at the same time pushed the interests of the Companies I was representing.

'Mr Bedford, Sr, then had the American interests in France in his hands. Instead of meeting the French Government's requirements, as I did, he adopted a virtually dictatorial attitude, basing his behaviour on the old traditions of the American oil groups. His main concern was to prevent the competing interests of the Royal Dutch from gaining

[1] A classical scholar of the old school, whose motto was, 'Whatever you do, do it well.'

ground. Fortunately, the way he acted was not wise in the prevailing circumstances.

'Personally, I felt in no way bound to restrain my enterprise, which was founded on a thoroughly healthy basis—and events favoured my going ahead.'

The *Memoirs* now enter the diplomatic stage of what Mr Five Per Cent calls the 'Preliminaries of the French Participation in the Iraq Petroleum Company'—then, of course, the Turkish Petroleum Company, since the State of Iraq did not yet exist:

'The Deutsch Bank share in the Company had been taken over, as explained, by the British Treasury and the Custodian of Enemy Property. But according to the Articles of Association, no participation could be sold (but for the war and wartime legislation) to outsiders without the consent of the other shareholders, who had prior rights of acquiring them.

'I therefore felt the opportunity was excellent for arranging that the German participation should be handed over to the French State after the war.

'Naturally, I would not and could not have done this without the prior approval of the British Foreign Office and at the same time, I felt it was my duty to carry Sir Henri Deterding and the Royal Dutch group with me.

'Before taking any steps in France, I went to London and submitted my plan to Sir William Tyrrell[1] at the Foreign Office and convinced him of the appreciation the French would be bound to hold for such a contribution to the Entente Cordiale. The matter was referred to Lord Long, then in charge of oil questions, and ultimately I secured the concurrence of the Foreign Office to go ahead with my scheme.

'I then communicated my scheme to the French Government. It was most enthusiastically welcomed and, after long deliberation, it was agreed that M Henri Berenger, representing the French Government, should proceed to London to meet Lord Long and the Foreign Office.

'Letters were exchanged to confirm the British Government's promise that, at the end of the war, the German interest in the Turkish Petroleum Company (then in the hands of the Custodian), should be ceded to France. Later on, the Treaty of San Remo (April 24th, 1920) officially recognized this cession.'

Until it was far too late, Sir Charles Greenway and the Anglo-Persian Oil Company knew nothing about it.

---

[1] Private Secretary to Sir Edward (later Lord) Grey, the Foreign Secretary, and later Permanent Under-Secretary and Ambassador to Paris.

Gulbenkian remarks with relish: 'During my negotiations with the French, the Foreign Office and the Royal Dutch group, I had not approached the Anglo-Persian Company, whose participation had been agreed in 1914, but who all the time remained aloof.'

Greenway's disloyalty to the Turkish Petroleum Company and Gulbenkian, his misjudgment and standoffishness, eventually cost the Anglo-Persian Oil Company half its 50 per cent share-holding in the Company and the predominant say in its affairs.

At this point it is convenient to dispose of the marketing arrangements which Gulbenkian instigated in France. Again it was a battle.

His *Memoirs* say: 'Sir Henri Deterding gave his consent to the transfer of the German shares to the French, subject to the formation of a French Company in which the Royal Dutch would be predominant.

'He had at first been reluctant to agree to French participation, but later accepted my argument that the inclusion of the French Government in our Company would be another trump to deter designs of the Anglo-Persian Company, who only joined us finally in 1921, after San Remo, when American interests gave inklings of waking up and seeking a share in Mesopotamia under cloak of the "open door" policy. The Anglo-Persian aim hitherto, as I have said, was to secure the whole Mesopotamian concession for themselves alone.

'With the approval of the French authorities of the time, we and the Union Parisienne formed the Société Française pour l'Exploitation du Pétrole, under the Presidency of M Villars of the Union Parisienne.'

Thus Deterding's objections were overcome. The French were in and the 23¾ per cent German shareholding was transferred to the new Société.

But this was the beginning of more trouble.

The Société combined the existing Shell interests in France with the existing French oil interests. The addition of the German interest gave Deterding a dominant voice in Gulbenkian's Turkish Petroleum Company and upset the delicate balance exercised by his Five Per Cent.

Gulbenkian regarded this arrangement as another of Deterding's manœuvres to usurp power and another ruse by one of the big oil groups to crush him.

So more fuel was added to the explosion which was to blast the two giants' friendship to pieces in 1925.

But, with the advent of Raymond Poincaré as Prime Minister, the French Government adopted a chauvinistic attitude towards the Deterding-controlled Société, regardless of any services which Gulbenkian or any other foreigner, such as Deterding, might have rendered.

The *Memoirs* continue: 'There were great political changes and M Poincaré came into office. He took an extreme nationalistic view of petroleum questions—setting aside all other considerations—and at his instigation an entirely French company, called Compagnie Française des Pétroles, was created (in 1923).

'This company was to represent French oil interests throughout the world—starting with the French rights recognized by the treaty of San Remo.'

The Compagnie Française des Pétroles was organized by Ernest Mercier, with the French Government holding 35 per cent interest (with 40 per cent voting power after 1931). The remaining 65 (60) per cent was split between private companies, individuals and banks. So Deterding's hopes of dominating the Turkish Petroleum Company with the assistance of French oil interests, collapsed.

Gulbenkian adds: 'I was severely criticized by Sir Henri Deterding, who thought my policy wrong, seeing that the French Government was very ungrateful in ignoring all the services rendered to them and brushing aside all their former feelings of friendship and appreciation.

'I must confess that what took place provided serious grounds for Sir Henri Deterding's criticisms.'

Poincaré had not of course blocked the Anglo-Dutch bid for control of the French oil industry out of gratitude to Gulbenkian, although in effect the formation of the Compagnie Française des Pétroles instead of the Société helped to preserve the Five Per Cent as the balancing factor in the Turkish Petroleum Company.

Poincaré acted as he did because he realized that a nation which depends on foreign oil masters is no longer free.

No sooner was the Compagnie Française des Pétroles in possession of the German interest than it sided with the other oil groups to squash Gulbenkian.

The *Memoirs* say: 'The French Foreign Office, knowing thoroughly all the work I had done, was at all times most friendly. But when M Raymond Poincaré came into power and the Compagnie Française des Pétroles was founded, the leaders took up quite a different attitude, which was thoroughly opportunist—always siding with the groups and forgetting that their participation in the Turkish Petroleum Company was exclusively due to my initiative and work. The San Remo Treaty only ratified it.

'Without trespassing on the limits of modesty, had I not directed M Berenger, the French Government would never have entered the Iraq Petroleum Company.

'With the exception of petty interests in Rumania, the French had no petroleum exploitations and no notion of petroleum enterprise elsewhere.

'Our French friends now pride themselves on their rights under the Treaty of San Remo, but (and this is probably due to the fear of feeling themselves under an obligation) they always avoid remembering that it was due to my conception.'

This French defection landed Gulbenkian in the situation in 1925–28 where he found himself getting crude oil, instead of hard cash, for his Five Per Cent.

Behind his back the groups arranged with the Compagnie Française des Pétroles to sell the Iraq Petroleum Company's *entire* crude oil at cost to the shareholders, for tax-dodging purposes, leaving each participant to market the appropriate share.

That was an arrangement for which Gulbenkian had no inclination or organization. As he pointed out: 'I had risked capital in this venture with a view to obtaining profits in cash.'

His indignation was beyond words. The *Memoirs* merely add: 'It came out later that this contract with the Compagnie Française des Pétroles was on behalf of *all* the oil groups and that it was kept secret from me. . . . No comment!'

But the French got cold feet. Fortified by the opinion of his eminent British Counsel, Gulbenkian again threatened to go to law.

The *Memoirs* continue: 'The French group was frightened that its rights would become prejudiced if the turmoil went on.

'This, in my opinion, explained the sudden *volte face* and they were, no doubt, acting in conjunction with the groups to save their faces and avoid serious litigation.

'To my great surprise, during these years of negotiations, M Cayrol, one of the leading members of the Compagnie Française des Pétroles approached me in a most friendly way, when discussions were taking a bad turn, and not only advocated my points of view but went even further.'

The Compagnie Française des Pétroles was indeed to become Gulbenkian's staunchest ally in the Iraq Petroleum Company.

As explained later, he reached a satisfactory arrangement with them, whereby they marketed his crude oil at the prevailing market prices on 1st January and 30th June each year. This was embodied in the Red Line Working Agreement of 1928. It was reaffirmed in 1931 and lasted until 1940.

This section on the French entry can be closed with the note that the Germans appealed to the Mixed Arbitral Tribunal in 1927-28 against the confiscation of the Deutsche Bank interest in the Turkish Petroleum Company and its transference to the Compagnie Française des Pétroles. Afterwards litigation was abandoned.

4. *Exeunt Sultan and Tsar—Obit Armenia*

Gulbenkian's plan for passing Germany's Mesopotamian oil rights to France after the war assumed that the Sick Man of Europe would die without a kick. So did the Long-Berenger Agreement, the Sykes-Picot Agreement (November 1916), promising Mosul to France without prejudice to British oil rights, and amendments in the corroboratory Lloyd George-Clemenceau Agreement (as late as December 1918). So did the Anglo-Persian plans. But History intervened.

The great illusion lasted until 1920, when the Allies' preconceived ideas exploded and an unpremeditated Middle East settlement was brought to pass at the sword-point of Mustapha Kemal Attaturk.

Consequently the Turkish Petroleum Company did not take final shape as the Iraq Petroleum Company until 1929, with Gulbenkian retaining his 5 per cent and Anglo-Dutch, Anglo-Persian, French and American interests sharing the rest equally.

The path to that result was 'very tedious' and 'impossible to amplify', say Gulbenkian's *Memoirs*. Indeed, there has been no more fateful and involved period in this century. No conception of the obstacles Gulbenkian overcame can be formed without touching on the highlights and the events nearest to him.

The two governing developments were the emergence of the New Turkey and the Soviet Union, both of which so surprised and confused the Western Powers that they became the slaves—and not, as they imagined, the masters—of events.

In February-December 1915, the Gallipoli-Dardanelles Campaign failed and in the process relieved Turkey of pressure from the West and forged a history-maker—Mustapha Kemal, who was to seize the reins from the Sultan's dying hand, defy the Allies and lead Turkey to a more cohesive future than the Western war-leaders ever contemplated.

In October 1917, the Russian Revolution and its sequel, the separate peace of Brest-Litovsk between the Soviet Union and the Central Powers, freed Turkey's Eastern flank just when the Grand

Duke Nicholas was due to mount a most hopeful offensive, thus giving the Sick Man a further respite.

The Turks were left with one Front, to the South, where 100,000 British troops were bogged down in "Mespot" (the Kut-el-Amara disaster) until the end of the war, and even Allenby, with his whirlwind Arabs under Lawrence, was slowed down.

The Red Revolution also produced its unexpected history-maker, Joseph Stalin, the Georgian from Transcaucasia, who was Lenin's Commisar for Minorities and had no sympathy either for "self-determination", the rights of small nations, or—least of all—the dismemberment of Russia's oil-rich underbelly.

Britain and France underestimated Kemal and Stalin, clung to an outdated appreciation of the Middle East and pursued policies which did not fit the facts. In the confusion Britain and France fell out, the Arabs and the Jews were alike betrayed, the Greeks and Armenians, the Kurds and Georgians were equally abandoned and, inadvertently by the Entente, left hopeless and helpless before the militant leaders, Stalin and Attaturk. An unstable British domination emerged, based on *temporary* Soviet weakness.

While Britain and France strove to impose an outdated and ill-fitting policy, Gulbenkian followed each twist but did not shift his ground. He held firmly to three cards: the Foreign Office Agreement of March 1914; the Grand Vizier's letter of June 1914; the Long-Berenger Agreement of May 1916. That was the wood. The rest was trees. Few would have rated it a strong hand . . . but three deuces to a skilled poker-player can sometimes scoop a pot against better cards.

One forgotten cause of the Allied failure to impose their planned partition of the Near East was the betrayal, and consequent extinction, of the Armenians of the Ottoman Empire. Their strongholds were the six eastern provinces of Anatolia, from Erzeroum to the Caucasian border (the former Kingdom of Greater Armenia) and Cilicia, centred on Adana, Tarsus and Alexandretta at the north-east corner of the Mediterranean (the former kingdom of Lesser Armenia, with its spiritual headquarters at Sis).

In 1914, Constantinople ordered the enlistment of all Armenians of military age for guerilla fighting against the Russians in the Caucasus. In return the Armenians, Tartars and Georgians across the Russian frontier were promised autonomy after the victory of the Central Powers. Van and Erzeroum were to be ceded to the proposed Armenian State.

But the Armenians knew their Turks and preferred to put their money on the Western Powers, who had been pleading their cause for years, and on the Russians, who had given sanctuary to thousands of Armenians, allowed them to prosper, and posed as their protectors. Moreover, the Allies were Christian.

Armenians refused to join the Turkish colours and early in 1915 broke into revolt at Van, Kharput, Sivas and elsewhere. The Government newspaper in Constantinople, *Tanine*, demanded the extermination or forcible conversion of all Armenian women as 'the only means of saving the Empire'. Active steps were taken at once to get rid of 'the accursed race'.

In June and July, men, women and children were rounded up and herded away, destitute and starving, to be butchered or beaten into submission by Turkish guards. Thousands more died of exhaustion and exposure in headlong flight. It was ascertained that of 18,000 Armenians rounded-up in Kharput and Sivas, only 350 escaped with their lives. In the Kernekh Gorge, 20,000 Armenian women and children were murdered. By 12th September, 1915, the end of the Armenian race in Turkey was in sight. Talaat issued a nation-wide order: 'Regardless of women, children and invalids, and however deplorable the methods of destruction may seem, an end is to be put to the Armenians' existence, without any heed to feeling or conscience.' Later he was able to inform the German Government (in French!): '*La question arménienne n'existe plus.*'

Armenians who had held out against the Turks at Zeytoon in the Taurus Mountains for 500 years and styled themselves 'the British of the Caucasus' were also obliterated. Two Turkish Divisions were detached from the Suez Front (before the well-known "Arab Revolt") to round up these sturdy Armenians, who refused to be mobilized against the Allies. This weakened the Turkish threat to Egypt, but it was the death blow of the Armenian race in Cilicia. The men were butchered and 20,000 women, children and old people were marched into the desert to perish.

In order to tie down Turkish forces in the interior, so as to weaken the Turks in the Dardanelles and Caucasus, as well as the Levant, the Allies encouraged Armenians, Kurds, Arabs and other Turkish minorities to rebel by promising post-war benefits. In England the slogan ran: 'To deny Armenians their rights is to transplant the Balkan question from Europe to Asia Minor'. In France a Free Armenian Committee and an Armenian Legion were formed under Government auspices. The (Tsarist) Russians actually *did* something for the Armenians. Supported by native and refugee Armenians, the Tsarist Army attacked the Turks in the East.

Enver Pasha, the Turkish Dictator, who had long nursed grandiose

Pan-Turkish ideas of sweeping through the Caucasus, wiping out the Armenians, and pressing on into Central Asia, attacked first. He set forth from Erzeroum in January 1915 with a large army, but only 12,000 of his 100,000 men survived the Russian counter-attacks and the blizzards.

The Russians swept back to capture Van, Bitlis, Mush and the great fortress of Erzeroum (all Armenian centres) and busied themselves with roads, railways and administration with a view to the next move. Half a million Armenians were thus saved from the Armenian provinces of Turkey.

Allied promises to the Armenians were renewed and enlarged—this time as much with a view to creating a post-war Armenian buffer state against Russia as to weakening the Turks.

At the same time conflicting promises were made secretly to the Arabs and to the Jews: Armenian, Arab or Jewish, any stick was good enough to beat Britain's enemies.

Had the Armenians known that their historic southern province, Cilicia, was secretly promised to Emir Faisal and the Arabs, as part of the proposed French sphere of influence in the Middle East, they would not have been so eager to resist the Turks. But the Armenians continued their resistance in Anatolia and the deluded Free Armenian Committee in Paris was led further up the garden path.

Mustapha Kemal was sent east to annihilate the remnants of the Armenians. Any captured Armenian was hanged or bastinadoed. He recaptured Van, Bitlis and Mush, despite gallant Armenian and Georgian guerilla action, and advanced on the Tsar's Black Sea oil port, Batum. But by the summer of 1917, the Turkish Army was out on a limb and in poor condition. Defeatism and desertion were spreading like wildfire. It was only saved from the imminent Tsarist counter-offensive by the October Revolution.

Kiazim, Kemal's second-in-command, ignored the Treaty of Brest-Litovsk, which was supposed to stop the fighting and redress the frontier in Turkey's favour. He pressed on, looting and massacring, to take Alexandropol (only recently renamed Leninkhan) and the fleeing Armenians took refuge in the rump of Russian Armenia.

The young Soviets were too feeble to wield authority as far south as the Caucasus, and the Allies took the opportunity to weaken Red Russia, grasp Baku oil and stiffen local resistance to the Turks by proclaiming free and independent states of Armenia and Georgia, with the backing of the ruling classes in each.

The Turkish capitulation to the Allies on 30th October, 1918, induced Kiazim's withdrawal from the Caucasus. But Kemal defied

the French occupation of Cilicia and Alexandretta, determined by the
Allies. Two hundred thousand Armenians who fled there immediately
after the Armistice, in anticipation of French protection, were massacred
and that was the end, once and for all time, of the last vestiges of the
Kingdom of Lesser Armenia. So much for Allied—and particularly
French—promises to the Armenians. As Fridtjof Nansen, the great
internationalist, sadly and sardonically observed: 'There was no oil
in Cilicia.'

In the oil-rich Caucasus the British were not so easily rebuffed.
A British Military Mission was sent, to co-operate with the "White"
Russian General Wrangel. In conjunction with other "White" inter-
ventions, under Denikin and Kolchak, it was hoped to unseat the
Communists by concentric attacks on the infant Soviet Union from
south, north and east. More specifically, Wrangel was to save the Baku
oilfields for their mainly Western owners. The bait, first held out by
the Turks in 1914, was again dangled before the long-suffering
Armenians—a free and independent Armenian State, including the
Russian province of Erevan and its spiritual capital, Etchmiadzin
Cathedral, together with the six Armenian provinces of eastern Turkey.

As a start in the dismemberment of Turkey, the Greeks moved in
force into Smyrna and the Aegean Coast in May 1919; the French took
over Syria from the British in December, having been assured (as
Gulbenkian's *Memoirs* note) of a share in his Turkish Petroleum
Company. The British remained in Mesopotamia, astride the oilfields.
Faisal, third son of ex-King Hussein of the Hedjaz, was proclaimed
King of an independent Syria in defiance of the Allies in March 1920,
and promptly fled. In compensation, the British made him King of
the new Mesopotamian State of Iraq in August 1921.

The Allies also occupied Constantinople in March 1920, and ruled
Turkey through the pro-British Sultan Vaheddin and weak Grand
Viziers. In April 1920, at San Remo, Turkey's oil was formally made
over to the Anglo-French-Dutch combination calling itself the
Turkish Petroleum Company—in which no Turk or Turkish corporation had a share! The question whether Turkey was to survive in any
shape or form began to arise. And Mustapha Kemal had little difficulty
in rousing national feeling against the satellite Sultan and his Anglo-
French-Greek backers.

The Bolsheviks, too, awoke to the danger of Turkey's disappearance from the map, the erection of a jig-saw of small Near East satellites
coming into existence on Russia's doorstep, mainly under British
influence, and the final removal of the Transcaucasion minorities
(with their oilwells) passing finally out of Soviet control. By the end

of 1917 they had established an Oriental Propaganda Department, divided into three bureaux (Islamic, Indian and Far Eastern). At the end of 1919, Lenin and Stalin issued a Manifesto:

'Mussulmans of the World, victims of the Capitalists, Awake! No Turkish territory will be given to Armenia, the Dardanelles Straits will be yours, and Constantinople will remain the capital of the Mussulman World. Long Live the Alliance of the Revolutionary Peoples of Europe and Asia!'

Early in 1920 they issued a more detailed Manifesto, preparing the way for the annexation of Armenia, Georgia and Azerbaijan, although each became an independent member of the League of Nations when it was formed in January.

There was thus a complete somersault. Russian and Turk—at loggerheads for centuries—made common cause. Kemal accepted Bolshevik arms and money to fight the Entente—but on his own terms. 'There are no oppressors and no oppressed,' he said. 'There are only those who allow themselves to be oppressed. The Turks are not among them. The Turks can look after themselves. Let others do the same.'

Oblivious of these historic changes, Woodrow Wilson, Lloyd George and Clemenceau committed their colossal blunder. They promulgated the Treaty of Sèvres. Having already recognized Armenia, Georgia and Azerbaijan as sovereign members of the League of Nations, the Allies now proposed: an extension of Armenia to Erzeroum, thus subtracting the eastern third of Anatolia from Turkey; independence for Kurdistan, across the southern third of Anatolia; the continuation of the Greek administration of Smyrna and the Aegean Coast of Anatolia; perpetuation of the Anglo-French sphere of influence to the south in Syria-Lebanon, Mesopotamia (Iraq), Palestine and Jordan.

What the frontiers of "Kurdistan" were to be, nobody has ever discovered. But the Kurds were worth some encouragement; they roamed the oil districts.

Clearly Turkey was to be virtually blotted off the map and a chain of hostile satellites was to be set up astride the South Russian borders, depriving the Soviet Union of oil supplies.

The effect was electrifying. Mustapha Kemal reasoned: 'The Ottoman Empire is dead. It is now a question of saving Turkey.' The Bolsheviks broke off inter-Armenian negotiations in Paris and definitely decided on the annexation of the infant Armenian, Georgian and Azerbaijani states. For Russia, too, it was a question of survival.

Kemal dispatched Kiazim eastwards to exterminate the last remnants of Armenians in Turkey. In the autumn the Bolsheviks smashed Wrangel. Armenia—independent for two years, for the first time since 1375[1]—was annexed. So were Georgia and Azerbaijan (with its oil). The three tiny states were incorporated in the Transcaucasian Soviet Republic in 1922 and re-separated into three separate republics in 1926.

Turkey rose to a man behind Mustapha Kemal, who was acclaimed Commander-in-Chief and Dictator in August 1921. He started hammering the Greeks in Smyrna and the mighty peacemakers at Versailles found to their dismay that they were quite incapable of imposing their terms on the ragamuffin Bolsheviks and Kemalists—even as the royal and imperial houses of Europe were dismayed by the victories won by ragged levies led by Dumourez and Bunapoulez.

The French, tired of their frustration in Syria and Cilicia, began to back out, and in January 1922 formally restored Cilicia to Turkey. The British, foiled in Caucasia and left with the obstreperous baby in Turkey, began to think it was time to "Bring the Boys Home".

In desperation the Allies turned to Venizelos, the quiet, pleasant, plausible Greek leader, who offered to move 100,000 crack troops into Smyrna and cut Mustapha Kemal down to his proper size. Within a fortnight the Greeks were crushed by Mustapha Kemal at the Battle of Sakaria on 14th August, 1921, and less than a month later the Turks reoccupied Smyrna.

Kemal pursued the fugitive Greeks by land in the direction of Adrianople, but was blocked by the British, on the Straits at Chanak, under General Sir Charles Harrington, who was bluffed into letting the Turks across the water.

The British had had enough and prepared to withdraw, and the Greeks found themselves deserted in Thrace.

In November 1922, Kemal abolished the Sultanate and thus set about shaping a modern state. At the Treaty of Lausanne a year later he obtained all he sought. Turkey kept East Thrace. The British evacuated Constantinople. The Turkish Straits were demilitarized and guaranteed by the Great Powers. Turkey ceded Syria, Mesopotamia, Palestine and Arabia and renounced nominal suzerainty over Egypt, Cyprus and the Sudan. But Turkey proper survived.

Not a thing was done for the Armenians and Kurds. Although they had served as the Allies' Fifth Column for four years and the Armenians had been British protégés for seventy years, they were abandoned to the mercies of the "Ghazi" ("The Destroyer of

---

[1] When Leo VI was deposed by the Mameluke Invasion. He died, a wanderer in exile, in Paris in 1393.

Christians") as Mustapha Kemal was proud to be called, until he took the title Ataturk.

He promptly set about their remnants—for revenge, and in order to remove two minorities, who were still objects of Russian propaganda. In 1925-9 the Armenians and Kurds buried their mutual hatred and made common cause against Kemal, who settled the rebellion by sending 15,000 picked troops against them. Censorship and Martial Law were introduced and there was no quarter on either side. Every Turk captured by the rebels was tried by summary Court Martial and then mutilated. The Turks replied with mass executions and the bastinado. After 3,000 years, the history of the Armenians in Asia Minor ended; also a pathetic chapter in British and French diplomacy.

Only about a million Armenians escaped from Turkish persecutions between 1890 and 1920. Most of these went to Russia, but 115,000 reached western Europe and 125,000 found refuge in Syria-Lebanon. In 1946-7 about 60,000 Armenians from the Middle East, Greece and France were enticed back to Soviet Armenia by elaborate propaganda. In Europe the main colonies are now: 17,500 in France, 6,000 in Greece, 2,000 in Britain and 500 in Belgium. In Russia there are 1,500,000 in the Armenian Republic and another 1,400,000 in the rest of the U.S.S.R. In the United States there are probably about 1,000,000. Allowing for the prodigious Armenian birth-rate, which seems to be some sort of natural compensation for persecution and helps to explain Armenian survival, there are possibly as many as 5,000,000 Armenians in the world today.

Now for the reckoning.

16

TURKISH DELIGHT

1. Profit and Loss

THE October Revolution meant the expropriation of foreign interests in Russian oil—Swedish (the Nobels), French (Rothschilds), Armenian (Mantachoff), and Germans—and an end to the "handsome material rewards", which Gulbenkian earned from the Russian business he brought into the Royal Dutch-Shell combine. Robert Nobel managed to dispose of his oil wells at Grosnyi for £20,000 to long-term speculators, gambling on a Tsarist Restoration. Leon Mantachoff managed to sell his late father's wells to Deterding for £635,000, but nevertheless died in poverty. Such pre-Revolution stocks are still dealt in and, at moments of East-West rapprochement, retain some market value. But to all intents, Gulbenkian, his relatives and associates, lost all their Russian millions.

Nor, with the expiration of the White Interventions in 1920, was there the slightest chance of getting back. The Bolsheviks were shy and self-sufficient. Baku passed under the control of a new type of man: Stalin, the Georgian cobbler's son, Beria, a mechanic and son of a peasant, Lazar Kaganovitch, a Jewish leather worker, and (sure enough) another Armenian, Anastas Mikoyan. There was no business to be done with these Marxist "workers and peasants". Gulbenkian's carefully cultivated group of Russian and foreign oil magnates was superfluous.

The most menacing fact of all was that Russian oil production, which was second only to that of the United States, was removed from the world orbit. The balance was therefore tipped heavily again in favour of Standard Oil. Price-cutting loomed up once more as a matter of life and death for the European companies. The search for fresh sources and the battle to enter all markets were intensified.

The Turkish Revolution removed Mesopotamian oil from the control of Constantinople, where Gulbenkian held his greatest advantage for reasons of family, languages, experience, contacts and services rendered. Mustapha Kemal Attaturk cut the last Byzantine links, including the removal of the capital to Ankara and the elimination of foreign influence. Those rich and informed Armenians who were smart enough to escape the holocaust, like the Essayans and Gulbenkians, were driven into exile, their wealth seized and their return made suicidal. Calouste Gulbenkian's chain of Middle East Armenian contacts also became superfluous.

Two of the three documents on which he pinned his Mesopotamian oil hopes, the Foreign Office Agreement and the *Lettre Vizirielle* of 1914, had been signed by officials of a defunct régime in a country now changed beyond recognition.

The actual oil passed from Turkish hands under the control of half a dozen new petty Arab Emirs, Kings and Presidents, whose authority was uncertain, since they were puppets of the Sultan's successors, namely Britian and France, the Mandatory powers under the League of Nations. This unique relationship had to be worked out. Frontiers had to be settled. Law and order had to be established. Anglo-French jealousies had to be smoothed. In addition there was the Palestine problem. The natural transit routes for the oil, from the deserts of the Mid-east interior to the Mediterranean sea lanes, became congested with artificial frontiers, racial hatred and danger. It had been complicated enough under the lethargic and corrupt Turk, but then it had had the advantage of homogeneity. Under the haphazard Anglo-French set-up it only made a modicum of sense—so long as British power imposed order, which took years and did not last. It was an artificial and piece-meal arrangement—with the Near East firmly divided at the Soviet frontier, the overlapping oilfields bisected, and the Americans outside the picture. Such a situation could only be temporary. Mr Five Per Cent had to make the best he could of it.

His world had changed out of all recognition, but not entirely for the worse. By 1922 there were 315,000 cars licensed on the English roads and petrol pumps were beginning to appear in numbers. There were still no civil airlines, but the Royal Flying Corps had indicated that there was a great peacetime future in aviation. The Royal Navy had triumphed on liquid fuel. A limitless expansion of the petroleum industry was imminent. And what he did not know about petroleum was not worth knowing. Oil business was booming. If only he could button up the Mesopotamian concession and get production going. . . .

Persia, next door, was already producing 1,000,000 tons a year by the end of the war, which augured well for Mosul. The British were in physical possession of Mesopotamia and the coveted oil wells. The British Army had fought a long campaign to hold "Mespot", thus staking a strong moral claim to keeping it as part of the spoils of war.

Moreover, the British Government—particularly Lloyd George

—felt strongly that British claims should be recognized by the Allies. And Gulbenkian had done much spadework on his own behalf at the British and French Foreign offices during the war.

Up his sleeve he also had his three precious documents, which, at the worst, were useful debating points. But it was a long step from ethics and old documents to an operative concession. This was how it worked out. . . .

2.   *Three Big Rows*

The events immediately following the 1918 Armistice are covered in bare outline by the *Memoirs,* as follows:—

'Immediately after the Armistice, circumstance began to change in that every claimant became very active.

'The French Government started to press its claims to the share of the Deutsche Bank's participation in the Turkish Petroleum Company, as promised to them by Lord Long and the Foreign Office.

'Great confusion ensued in the negotiations owing to the insincerity of the participants. Although the French had had the promise, both the Anglo-Persian and the Royal Dutch endeavoured to checkmate and reduce the extent of that promise.

'My personal position grew very difficult.

'On one hand, the 1914 Foreign Office Agreement was practically broken owing to the war. Further, it contained invalid stipulations regarding my own participation.

'On the other hand, the same Agreement defined participations of the Royal Dutch-Shell group and the Anglo-Persian Company.

'We also had to consider the French claims (as above).

'These complications caused great trouble to the British and French Governments.

'Notwithstanding my friendly relations and the services I had rendered to the different oil groups, they endeavoured to diminish my personal rights. A vicious atmosphere was created by these quibbles.

'Having personal interests to safeguard, I decided, in spite of my relations with the Royal Dutch combine, to act independently and follow a line which I deemed fair to all concerned.

'In view of all the difficulties put forward by the oil groups, I collaborated, independently of them, with M Phillippe Berthelot (Secretary-General of the French Foreign Office) and Sir William Tyrrell (of the British Foreign Office) to find a satisfactory solution.

'My activities in both Foreign Offices were slandered. This was probably due to intrigues and jealousies.

'M. Berthelot showed me a personal letter he had received from the then French Ambassador in London, M Fleuriau, advising M Berthelot to be careful of my activities because he knew me to be a confidential Foreign Office agent.

'M Berthelot also told me that M Raymond Poincaré, the Prime Minister, took umbrage at my intervention and that he had warned M Aristide Briand, Minister of Foreign Affairs, against my freedom of movement in the Ministry.

'M Berthelot replied that he was so convinced of my genuine collaboration that, although his own hand was writing and signing the documents, it was, in fact, my hand that guided his.

'It was a time of intense activity and political turmoil, and I was gratified when a satisfactory settlement was finally reached, which dispelled the difficulties between the French, the Anglo-Persian Company and the Royal Dutch-Shell—and the Treaty of San Remo and its annexes ratified the understandings.'

At this point the *Memoirs* assume the reader has a great deal of historical knowledge and proceed straight to American attempts to muscle in.

The gap is filled in by Nubar Gulbenkian, who was in the French Ministry of Supply from 1917 to 1919, working on oil problems and enjoying his father's confidence.

Nubar divides the 1914–28 period into "Six Big Rows".

First Big Row: 1914–15

Anglo-Persian, backed by the British Government, claimed the whole Mesopotamian oil concession and boycotted the Turkish Petroleum Company, in which it had a 50 per cent interest.

Gulbenkian was furious, but, unlike Deterding, sought a reasonable settlement with the Anglo-Persian Oil Company.

Second Big Row: 1915–16

Unknown to his disloyal Anglo-Persian Oil Company partners, Gulbenkian obtained Foreign Office approval to advise the French to create an Oil Commissariat and form a French petroleum company in order to take over the 25 per cent German interest in the Turkish Petroleum Company after the war.

Deterding opposed this scheme violently at first, but came round to it when he realized it would help to counteract the Anglo-Persian Oil Company's plot.

The Lord Long—Henri Berenger correspondence confirmed French post-war participation. This was reaffirmed by the Sykes-Picot Agreement promising Mosul to France after the war, without prejudice to British oil rights—a vital clause which was inserted as a result of Mr Five Per Cent's lobbying.

Anglo-Persian strongly objected, when it heard of this secret arrangement, and the British Government returned to its premise that the Turkish Petroleum Company 1914 concession had no validity. This was a flat contradiction of the promises already made both to Gulbenkian and the French.

Third Big Row: 1918–20

In December, 1918, Lloyd George and Clemenceau agreed that Mosul should form part of British-controlled Iraq and that France should be compensated with Syria-Lebanon and Cilicia.

France was also to get 25 per cent of Mosul oil—*but not from the debatable Turkish Petroleum Company concession.*

The oil was to come from an Anglo-Persian Oil Company concession in Iraq, through which Lloyd George still aimed at securing a controlling interest by the British Government.

Gulbenkian was thus left alone out in the cold.

At this point the Americans entered in a big way and threw the negotiations into the melting pot once more.

President Wilson protested strongly against the Lloyd George-Clemenceau carve-up. He demanded that the United States, as an 'Allied and Associated Power' should get a share in the Mesopotamian oil—that there should be 'equal opportunities for all in the Mandates' and that an 'Open Door' policy should be adopted.

The big moment in Mr Five Per Cent's life was drawing near.

The Lloyd George-Clemenceau arrangement cut both ways from his viewpoint. In the sense that the British were to remain in physical occupation of Iraq, there was an advantage. There was no longer any political dispute about that. But the French oil case was weakened by the elimination of their political claims to Mosul. Gulbenkian was too much of a realist to need telling that possession is nine points of the law.

In desperation he turned to his friend Henri Berenger, now French Minister of Finance.

He found Berenger shaken and dominated by his Prime Minister,

Clemenceau, who was hand-in-glove with Lloyd George. Gulbenkian steadied him by promising to continue to press French oil claims, in the likely event of their being further whittled away. He rested his appeal on his friendship with Berenger and the services he had rendered. And he held out the prospect of "suitable rewards" if Berenger stood up for the Gulbenkian Five Per Cent interest. It was the master-stroke.

The deadlock at the San Remo Conference in April 1920 was quadruple.

Lloyd George was set on seizing the whole Mesopotamian oil concession for the Anglo-Persian Oil Company, promising to see that the French should have a 25 per cent interest in an otherwise all-British concern. Woodrow Wilson would not entertain such a one-sided solution. His insistence on equal opportunities upset the Lloyd George-Clemenceau plan. Clemenceau insisted on a French share, in view of repeated Foreign Office promises and the assignment of Iraq to Britain.

Gulbenkian stood on the March 1914 Foreign Office Agreement, the *Lettre Vizirielle* of 1914, and the Long-Berenger Agreement: also on his secret understanding with Berenger.

The British Foreign Secretary, Lord Curzon, argued that 'American exclusiveness in the past was so marked that Britain might be allowed to benefit from the Turkish promise of 1914'—the promise declared in the very letter which Gulbenkian had been treasuring, although the British Government had maintained that it was "invalid".

To add to the confusion, the exiled Turkish Royal Family claimed the oil rights by virtue of the transferences to the Privy Purse in 1890 and 1899 and the disappearance of the Young Turk Government, which had later restored all oil properties to the Finance Ministry.

King Fuad of Egypt claimed he was *de facto* heir of the Sultans and suzerain of the Arab territories of the Ottoman Empire. As such, he pleaded, he was the rightful owner of the Mesopotamian oil.

Rival Turkish, Belgian-French and British concerns also entered the fray.

In the turmoil and deadlock, the Middle East situation went from bad to worse. No political settlement could be reached until the vital oil interests of the Great Powers had been arranged. Meanwhile the British case got no stronger.

Suddenly Lloyd George tired and yielded. Rather than let the Americans or new claimants into the Mosul oilfields, he abandoned his long struggle to win the concession for the British Government-controlled Anglo-Persian Oil Company.

Instead he settled on the original Long-Berenger solution of 1916, for which Berenger (primed by Mr Five Per Cent) had been working.

Far from being "invalid", the Turkish Petroleum Company had "acquired rights", which "took precedence over war-time arrangements". Anyway 'the oil did not belong to Britain but to the future State of Iraq, which had yet to be constituted.'

Whereupon everybody joined forces against the Americans and accepted Lloyd George's argument, although it flatly contradicted what he had been saying for the previous two years.

The Americans were out and—at last—after thirty years—Gulbenkian was in: for keeps.

The San Remo Oil Convention was signed on the spot, on 24th April, 1920, and the Turkish Petroleum Company was immediately reconstituted, as follows:

Anglo-Persian Oil Company	47½ per cent
Royal Dutch-Shell	22½ „ „
France	25 „ „
C. S. Gulbenkian	5 „ „

It is to be seen that Gulbenkian obtained his Five Per Cent at the expense of Anglo-Persian and the Royal Dutch-Shell *in his own right*—thus retrieving his disaster in the 1914 Foreign Office Agreement, which left him no direct voice in the affairs of the Company. He had not trusted in the legal opinion of two future Lord Chancellors and gone ahead in vain.

Nor did the faithful Berenger go empty-handed.

Shortly before San Remo, Gulbenkian had hastily acquired a mansion in the fashionable Rue de Grenelle in Paris, furnished it with antiques and fine pictures, and rented it to Berenger. After San Remo, Berenger no longer had to pay the rent. The house and its contents were his.

This had been called "bribery". Indeed Gulbenkian would hardly have been in the mood to pass this fine property to his friend if the French and he himself had been frozen out of Iraq.

On the other hand it is arguable that such a gift was nothing so vulgar as a direct bribe.

One can call it an "inducement", a "sweetener" or a "douceur". 'It is quite normal in the higher financial circles to mark the conclusion of a big deal with a gift.

In this case, Henri Berenger was doing nothing disloyal. On the contrary he obtained a great commercial asset for France. If he helped Mr Five Per Cent simultaneously, what of it? What was wrong with accepting a present?

Perhaps it's a matter of taste, which must vary from time to time and place to place, from individual to individual. To the conventional British businessman or politician, the Gulbenkian technique may seem unduly "oriental". On the other hand a little more realism of this sort might sometimes have served British interests.

Anyway—realism paid off.

In October-November 1920, an Iraq Government was established. And Rita, aged nineteen, married her second cousin, Kvork Essayan, aged twenty-three, according to the rites of the Armenian Church, at the Hyde Park Hotel, London. The reception was held at the Hyde Park Hotel and there were three hundred guests.

In the general jubilation, nobody noticed that the civil formalities were overlooked.

It was a great year for the Gulbenkians and Essayans, only clouded by the Armenian nadir in the Near East, which both families had so narrowly escaped.

What they lost in the swinging fortunes of Constantinople, they more than regained on the diplomatic roundabouts of San Remo.

17

ENTER THE AMERICANS

THREE more of what Nubar Gulbenkian calls the "Six Big Rows" still faced his father. The Americans had awakened too late to get their way at San Remo, but they were not to be fobbed off much longer.

1. Fourth Big Row: 1921–2 (Provisional Agreement)

They at once returned to their former arguments based on their position as an "Allied and Associated Power", regardless of "acquired rights".

Gulbenkian utterly discounted the American arguments. But he alone of the participants in the newly divided Turkish Petroleum Company supported the American entry bid.

The Company was not yet in the clear. The concession still had to be ratified by an elected Iraq Government. Iraq had also to be formally ceded by Turkey and recognized as a sovereign state by the League of Nations. The Mosul area was awaiting a League of Nations Frontier Commission to fix its location and boundaries. The Middle East was still in turmoil.

Besides, he calculated that the inclusion of an *independent* American oil group in the Turkish Petroleum Company would be a counter-weight to Standard Oil, whose monopolistic position had been strengthened by the elimination of Russian oil from the international set-up. Anyway, it would be better to have Americans in the Turkish Petroleum Company than disputing the Company's rights in Iraq and setting up business in competition.

His *Memoirs* take up the story again: 'We have seen that each time a new participant came into the Iraq Petroleum Company, it gave rise to a lot of strife, the old participants always resisting the newcomers. The entry of the Americans was no exception. The Anglo-Persian Company, the Royal Dutch-Shell group, and the French, endeavoured to impede the Americans. I must confess, too, that the

British Government, who had the matter in hand, was ill-advised from the start to follow the politics of the oil groups.

'The argument put forward by the old groups—that the concessions had been granted to the Turkish Petroleum Company as a private concern—was not correct. Owing to the war, the Turkish Petroleum Company's real assets were also in the melting pot. The negotiations between Washington and London grew increasingly unpleasant. The United States Government were not appeased by the arguments put forward, and tempers were getting frayed when Sir William Tyrrell, with whom I was in contact, asked for my advice.

'Personally, from the inception of the American crisis, I had held the opinion, taking the broader view, that it was sounder and higher policy to admit the Americans into the Turkish Petroleum Company, instead of letting them loose to compete in Iraq for concessions when in reality the Company had a very weak grip there.

'The oil groups are always tempted to seize what they see before them without looking ahead or following broader policies of collaboration. I suggested to Sir William Tyrrell that if he left the matter to the oil groups to come to an understanding, things would drag on and nothing would be achieved.

'I advised him that the best course was to call the leaders of the Royal Dutch-Shell and Anglo-Persian and impress them unequivocally that, by hook or crook, it was in the national interest that the Americans should be admitted as soon as possible—that, whatever the rights or wrongs of the matter, it was far more practical politics to make room for the Americans in the Mesopotamian oilfields.' The result was an ultimatum——

'My advice was promptly taken by Sir William Tyrrell and he gave the most emphatic directions. Very lengthy negotiations took place as to what the amount of the American participation in the Turkish Petroleum Company should be.

'The Americans claimed, as a matter of prestige, they could not accept less than anyone else—a view which was also pushed by the Royal Dutch-Shell, who did not desire that Anglo-Persian should obtain a controlling interest in the Company.

'Eventually it was agreed that about half the Anglo-Persian holdings should be surrendered to the Americans in exchange for an over-all royalty of 10 per cent of the oil produced.

'And so, after preserving my 5 per cent participation, the remaining shareholding was divided into four equal parts of 23¾ per cent each.'

It thus transpires that Gulbenkian, one of the original Big Three who struck at the Standard Oil monopoly and American price-cutting,

was the man who engineered the Americans' first entry into the Middle
East oilfields.

'A very elegant solution,' he remarked to his son.

He thus—above all others—set the present oil pattern of the
world outside the Soviet Union.

The strength of his native passion for compromise should at this
stage be evident.

2. Fifth Big Row: 1925 (Pre-Final Settlement)

The acrimonious entry of the Americans into the Turkish Petroleum
Company in 1922 was known as the Provisional Agreement.

Next year (1923) Turkey formally ceded Mesopotamia, which then
became officially known as Iraq. The Treaty of Lausanne made Iraq
a British Mandate and an Anglo-Iraq Treaty was signed. King Faisal I
ascended the throne. The way was cleared for a final settlement of the
oil rights.

This became urgent with the first discovery of oil in Iraq in commercial quantities—thirty-three years after Gulbenkian had first
reported on its possibilities to the Sultan.

Oddly, this historic discovery is omitted from the *Memoirs*—
probably, once more, because the facts were well known to
Gulbenkian's specialized readers.

The discovery was not made by the Turkish Petroleum Company
as such but by its restless constituent, the Anglo-Persian Oil Company.

The Anglo-Persian Oil Company 1901 concession covered the
so-called "transferred territories" of Iraq, covering 700 square miles,
which had been transferred from Persia to Turkey by an International
Frontier Commission in 1913–14.

Turkey had then undertaken to treat any territory that she might
gain through the Commission as being covered by the Anglo-Persian
Oil Company concession. The transfer was therefore one of lands
where the oil rights were already committed.

The 1923 strike occurred, after five years' drilling at Naftkhana,
in the border of the transferred territory; and by 1925 the time had
come to decide once for all to whom the disputed oil belonged—the
Anglo-Persian Oil Company or the Turkish Petroleum Company.

Sir Percy Cox, High Commissioner in the Middle East, approached
the Iraq Government, which proved open to reasonable terms.

In 1926 it was finally agreed that the Anglo-Persian should operate Naftkhana and, in return, build a refinery at Khanquin for Iraq's needs and pay a four-shilling (gold) royalty per ton to the Iraq Government. Henceforth, the Anglo-Persian Oil Company, on the Persian side of the border at Naft-i-Shah, and the Anglo-Persian Oil Company, on the Iraq side at Naftkhana, were to operate as twins, although politically completely separated.

By 1951, Naftkhana had yielded 5,000,000 tons of oil and paid almost £2,000,000 in royalties to Iraq. It continued to produce about 500,000 tons a year and the rights remained with the Anglo-Persian after 1951, when the Iraq Government bought the installations for £1,300,000.

The Naftkhana oil strike whetted the American group's appetite. Oil in Iraq was no longer theoretical, but a commercial fact; and the American instinct and tradition was to rush ahead, each for himself, in the spirit of rugged individualism.

Immediately west of the Tigris was the Mosul area, which was still awaiting assignment to Turkey or Iraq by a League of Nations Frontier Commission. It was already administered by Iraq, although it did not yet belong to her. The Turkish Petroleum Company regarded Mosul as a part of its concession, although this could not be finalized until the Frontier Commission had reached its decision. Mosul was therefore a tempting hunting-ground for the American group—and others.

The Americans hoped to grab Mosul for themselves, while acting under cover of a pretence that they were trying to secure the concession for their partners in the Turkish Petroleum Company.

But those tactics did not deceive Gulbenkian for a moment. He at once pointed out that all partners in the Turkish Petroleum Company were bound by a clause in the 1922 Provisional Agreement 'not to interest themselves in the production of oil in the Ottoman Empire in Europe or Asia except in association with their Turkish Petroleum colleagues'.

That agreement dated back to the formation of the Turkish Petroleum Company in 1912. It was repeated in successive changes in participation in 1913 (when the Royal Dutch-Shell entered), 1914 (when the Anglo-Persian joined) and in 1920 (when the French came in).

But the American group had accepted this self-denying clause in 1922 with the utmost reluctance and only then because they would not otherwise have been admitted. Gulbenkian himself had insisted on the clause, although he was the prime mover in introducing the

Americans. He had no intention (any more than his Anglo-Dutch-French colleagues) of allowing the Americans in merely to enable them to destroy the unity and strength of the Company by unilateral activity.

But now the Americans were in—and there was no getting them out. If it had been possible legally, which it wasn't, it would have been impossible politically. The Americans were therefore in a much stronger position than they had been three years previously.

Moreover the American group received full backing from President Coolidge. The American group insisted upon a revision of the 1922 Provisional Agreement. According to the Americans, the self-denying clause of 1912, 1913, 1914 and 1920 was out of date, contrary to the traditions of the oil industry and an affront to the principles of the Open Door and Equal Opportunities for All.

But those high-sounding phrases were in reality a bluff designed to elbow the other Turkish Petroleum Company partners out of future concessions in what had been the Turkish Empire. Mr Five Per Cent's *Memoirs* sum the American strategy up with sarcasm:

'The American group, presumably to carry their Government with them, had evolved a formula known as the Open Door. This they translated into an attempt to obtain a concession in Mosul and Baghdad for the Turkish Petroleum Company from the new Iraq Government—adding one obligation on the Turkish Petroleum Company to make use of only twenty-four plots of 8 square miles each—and another obligation to put similar plots up to world auction at regular intervals.

'This Open Door policy must have been given the limelight in order to convince governments that the oil groups were non-monopolistic and broad-minded.

'It was inherently eyewash that the whole world could participate in the exploitation of oil in Mesopotamia.'

So the argument went on across the Atlantic, the American group (backed by the State Department) demanding an end of the self-denying clause, and the other partners (backed by the British Government, which was in turned primed by Gulbenkian) demanding its retention.

Once more there was complete deadlock. The League of Nations decision on Mosul was getting nearer, and ratification of the 1922 Provisional Agreement could not be postponed much longer. The Company was on the point of collapse. If the oft-repeated self-denying clause was not valid, then the Company itself was not valid. Its very existence was based on the old agreements which Gulbenkian had piloted through the war and the San Remo Conference.

At this point he produced the master phrase: 'Then nobody has a concession.'

Nubar Gulbenkian comments pertinently: 'Then everybody saw the light.'

The Company was saved again. The American group consented to remain in it. But Gulbenkian and his Anglo-Dutch- French associates had to pay the American price . . . temporarily.

Gulbenkian had his own plan for sabotaging the Open Door and the Plot System which the Americans imagined they had imposed upon the Company.

When H. E. Nichols, Acting-Chairman of the Turkish Petroleum Company in 1925–6, went to Baghdad for the ratification of the San Remo Oil Convention by King Faisal I and his council of Ministers,[1] he had £40,000 in sterling from Gulbenkian's directors with him. It was a little present for the monarch: just to celebrate the occasion, but was never used because the British Government brought the necessary pressure to bear.

3. Sixth Big Row: 1928 (The Thick "Red Line")

The March 1925 Agreement, Nubar Gulbenkian calls the Pre-Final Settlement. The sixth "big row" (the last for twenty years) had now to be fought.

In December 1925 the League of Nations Frontier Commission formally awarded the Mosul area to Iraq[2] and this, the Government argued, was not covered by the existing concession for 'the whole of Iraq except Basra and the Transferred Territory'. The Government reckoned it had a new concession to sell and by 1925 there were several concession-hunters, besides the Turkish Petroleum Company and its egocentric American group.

There was Eastern and General (Major Frank Holmes of New Zealand, the oil-pioneer of Arabia); Lord Inverforth, who formed British Oil Development, Ltd., with Mosul as his objective; Lord Cowdray, with whom Gulbenkian had already done very considerable business in Mexico.

British Oil Development entered into direct negotiations with

---

[1] As yet there was no Parliament.
[2] Turkey was compensated with a 10 per cent royalty on Iraq's oil revenue from the Turkish Petroleum Company for ten years.

the Iraq Government at the same time as the Turkish Petroleum Company spokesman, E. H. Keeling, and carried on a flirtation with the ex-Sultan of Turkey's heirs, who pursue the argument that Mesopotamian oil rights belonged to the Privy Purse.

Then in June 1927 came the tremendous oil-strike at Baba Gurgur (the Burning Fiery Furnace, near Kirkuk) in the established Turkish Petroleum Company concession. This immediately added enormous importance to the disputed Mosul area on the west bank of the Tigris.

Next year British Oil Development proposed to build a Kirkuk-Mediterranean Railway, primarily to curry favour with the Government.

Meanwhile the Pre-Final Settlement, with its Open Door and Plot System, had come into operation. The American group pressed on, but Gulbenkian played for time. He persuaded his non-American partners not to pick the twenty-four plots for the Company's use and the twenty-four plots for auction. Through the good offices of the Government he got the date for a choice postponed until 1929, but then the Government (under pressure from British Oil Development) gave way and granted the concession to Lord Inverforth.

It looked as if Gulbenkian had been defeated but he played a waiting game with a poker face.

The British Oil Development grant still had to be ratified. The Americans had seen the futility of their unilateral tactics. Moreover Gulbenkian calculated that British Oil Development would not be able to raise enough extra capital to build the projected railway. He had whittled his own participation in the Turkish Petroleum Company down to 5 per cent because of the huge capital required for the development of an oil concession: he reckoned he could estimate capital requirements more accurately than Lord Inverforth. The chances were that the British Oil Development sales talk to the Government would boomerang.

Ratification of the British Oil Development concession did not pass the Iraq Parliament until May 1932. In December the British Oil Development was obliged to seek fresh capital abroad and to form Mosul Oilfields, under the chairmanship of Lord Goschen, but with Italian, German, Dutch, French-Swiss and Iraq interests holding 54 per cent control.

In 1935, British Oil Development was obliged to sign a formal undertaking to build the railway. But the Company was by then in such low water that it found difficulty in paying its £200,000-a-year (gold) royalty to the Iraq Government.

In 1936 the Italian Directors opened discussions with the Turkish Petroleum Company, through an American intermediary, and received cash to carry on. The Turkish Petroleum Company formed Mosul Holdings and then quietly bought up the German and Italian shares in Mosul Oil Fields. By 1937 the Turkish Petroleum Company was in effective control; the German and Italian drillers were withdrawn during the Munich Crisis of October 1938. And in 1941 Mosul Holdings (renamed Mosul Petroleum Company) received the British Oil Development concession. Thereupon the Mosul Petroleum Company merged with the Turkish Petroleum Company.

Thus another 46,000 square miles of Iraq passed under the control of the Gulbenkian Company. It was one of his smoothest and most nerve-wracking performances.

Only the Basra area in Southern Iraq remained unallotted. Up to 1938 nobody showed much interest in it. But in that year rich finds were made farther down the Persian Gulf in Kuwait, on the Al-Hasa coast of Arabia and in the island sheikhdom of Bahrain. These immediately gave Basra a value.

This time there was no free-for-all. Even the Iraq Government had learned the folly of encouraging oil rivalry in a country—the uncertainty, the waste of time and money, and the international embarassments. The Gulbenkian lesson, which he had been preaching for years, had sunk in. Basra passed to the Turkish Petroleum Company in July 1938 smoothly.

The annual terms were £200,000 (gold), 4 gold shillings a ton royalty, a rent of £200,000 (gold) pending exports, 20 per cent of the oil to Iraq, 12,000 feet of drilling guaranteed and rising to 20,000 feet after striking oil and an undertaking to ship 1,000,000 to 2,000,000 tons of oil within seven and a half years.

So, after forty-eight years, Gulbenkian got the whole of Iraq.

But the conclusion of the Sixth Big Row still has to be recorded.

By 1928 the American group in the Turkish Petroleum Company was begining to see that double-talk over the Open Door and Turkish Petroleum Company claims in the Mosul area was getting nobody anywhere.

Sir John Cadman, the new Turkish Petroleum Company Chairman, had been in Washington, exposing the nonsense behind the Open Door propaganda.

In October 1927 another great oil-strike in Kirkuk followed the finds at Baba Gurgur a few months earlier and it looked as if there would be plenty of oil for all Turkish Petroleum participants in Iraq.

Gulbenkian objected to being left out of potential new concessions within the borders of the former Ottoman Empire, in defiance of past agreements, and to limitations on his own area of activity, by the Plots System.

His *Memoirs* put his attitude this way: 'It was suggested that the other oil groups would endeavour to obtain concessions themselves, leaving me out, but this was stopped by the threat of legal proceedings to enforce the provisions against competition contained in the Foreign Office Agreement of 1914.'

Now that he had won his point about retaining a 5 per cent interest in the Turkish Petroleum Company in his own right, thus correcting the 1914 Agreement after the war, Gulbenkian's lone legal stand was not to be taken lightly.

An Anglo-American diplomatic conference was held with Gulbenkian and the Anglo-French-Dutch-American groups in July 1928. Three years of bitter legal and international argument ended with Gulbenkian winning his point. The 1912 self-denying clause was still binding. The Americans had to give way—not with a very good grace.

That was not quite the end of the row. What exactly were the boundaries of the former Ottoman Empire in which the Turkish Petroleum Company participants were restricted?

This question could involve untold millions in view of the recent triumphs at Naftkhana, Baba Gurgur and Kirkuk; nearly 5,000,000 tons production in adjoining Persia in 1927; and sudden new expectations in Arabia.

Besides, the Gulf Corporation of Pennsylvania (one of the American Companies in the American group of the Turkish Petroleum Company) was already interested in Kuwait and Bahrain, although there had as yet been no oil-strike in either sheikhdom.

The British Government, too, had special interests in the Arabian Peninsular, for example treaties with a number of sheikhs, who had never admitted Ottoman claims to sovereignty over them.

The Americans could not make head or tail of all this research into remote and bygone history, which seemed to them dead and meaningless. If they couldn't have an Open Door, they could at least go ahead. There was oil in the ground and the business of an oil corporation was to get it out of the ground and sell it. Talk of ancient treaties and boundaries between microscopic tribes seemed to the sometimes brash and naïve Americans to be some Limey trick or Armenian swindle. They were exasperated.

But there was the self-denying clause, which they so reluctantly accepted. And Gulbenkian was not to be shaken.

Nebuchandezzar's 'Burning
Fiery Furnace', at Baba
Gurgur, near Kirkuk, Iraq

Left: Calouste Gulbenkian as a child with his mother, Dirouhi. *Right:* The first
successful mechanical drilling for oil: by a former railroad guard, Col. Edwin Drake
(in stovepipe hat): at 69 feet, in Titusville, Pennsylvania, on 27th August, 1859. The
start of the modern oil industry

Where he mastered the mysteries of backsheesh

Where the Sultan wove his plots. Throne to right. Divans for concubines
background

THE ESSAYANS ABOUT 1890

Back: Nevarte, the future bride of Mr Five Per Cent; her brother, Yervante, her cousin. Vahan, and sister, Anna (Madame Frenkian). *Front:* Meguerditch (left) and Ohannes (right), one-time scrap metal pedlars and founders of the Essayan fortune, with their mother, Anna (left centre) and Ohannes' wife, Virginie (right centre)

THE GULBENKIANS

Calouste (bottom, centre) with his brothers, Karnig (left) and Vahan (right). His parents, Sarkis, one-time rug pedlar and founder of the Gulbenkian fortune (above), and wife, Dirouhi.

The guest house and garden where Calouste courted Nevarte. *Left:* The house where Nevarte 'kept' Calouste when he was on the verge of bankruptcy

OHANNES ESSAYAN'S MANSION BUYUK-DERE BESIDE THE BOSPORUS

SULTAN ABDUL HAMID
'THE DAMNED'

The Ohannes Essayans on the eve of Nevarte's marriage in 1892. *Left to right:* Virginie, Hrand, Nevarte, Anna, Ohannes and Yervante

Calouste, aged twenty-three, Nevarte, aged seventeen, Rita, their volatile daughter, and Nubar, the 'problem child'

Top left: Nevarte, the woman who 'made' Mr Five Per Cent, on her presentation at Court in 1911. *Top right:* Nubar, the Beardless Wonder Boy, at the wedding of his sister, Rita, to their cousin, Kvork Essayan, 1920. *Bottom left:* Nubar's second wife, Doré Plowden, in her £80 white egret hat in Charlot's 1915 revue *5064 Gerrard*. *Bottom right:* Nevarte (left) and her sister, Anna, in Nice, 1897

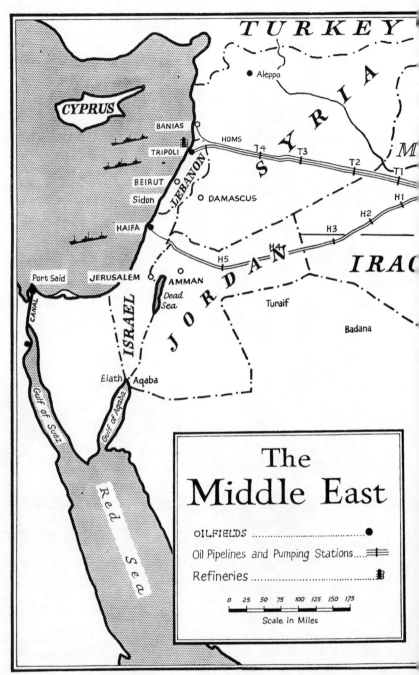

Iraq Petroleum Company Oil Concessions, including t
original I.P.C. Concession (1920), the Busra Petroleu
Company (1938) and the Mosul Petroleum Compa

AIN ZALAH
BUTMAH
MOSUL
I.P.C. 1920
BAI HASSAN
aiyarah
KIRKUK
K2
K1 JAMBUR
Pulkhana
*Transfered
Territory*
Injana
Samarra
Khanaqin
Naft Khana
Naft-ı-Shah
Fallujah
*Lake
Habbaniyah*
BAGHDAD

Karbala

Amara

Shabicha
B.P.C.
1938
Ratawi
ZUBAIR
Takhadid
RUMAILA
afha

*Neutral
Zone*
Qaisuma
*Neutral
Zone*

Nariya

Fadhill

RIYADH
o

Caspian   Sea

TEHRAN

P E R S I A

Isfahan

Tigris

Euphrates
Qurna
BASRA
Abadan
Fao

P e r s i a n   G u l f

KUWAIT
Burgan
KUWAIT

Ras Safaniyah

Abu
Hadriya

Ras Tanura

Qatif
Dammam
Abqaiq
Ain Dar
Shedgum
Uthmaniyan
Huiya
Haradh

Bahrein

DUKHAN
GHAWAR

QATAR

941). (It was confirmed that oil rights in the "Trans-
red Territory" belonged to the Anglo-Persian Oil Com-
ny in 1926 but they were nationalized in 1951 by Iran.)

MR FIVE PER CENT IN HIS PRIME

THE LAST PHOTOGRAPH
(1953)

MR FIVE PER CENT ON THE
CONTINENT BETWEEN THE
WARS, HIDING HIS BALDNESS

Above: Taking his daily 'constitutional'

Left: All dressed up for one of his rare
appearances at one of his wife's parties

1

2

SPARRING PARTNER

1—4 Sir Henr
Deterding of the Roy
Dutch; Sir Marcu
Samuel (Lord Bearstec
of Shell; Lord Greenwa
of Anglo-Persian; th
first Lord Cowdray c
the Mexican Eagle O
Company, etc.

3

4

THE CO-FOUNDERS, WIT
GULBENKIAN, OF TH
IRAQ PETROLEUM COM
PANY (AFRICAN AN
EASTERN CONCESSION
LTD) 1911

5—7 Sir Ernest Casse
Sir Henry Babington
Smith; the second Lo
Revelstoke

5

6

7

8

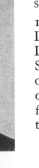

9

FAITHFUL FRIENDS

8—9 Senator Hen
Berenger and 'Willi
(Lord) Tyrrell

© *Harris's, Lond*

Left: Unused Gulbenkian burial plot in the British Cemetery, Lisbon, with the British Chaplain, Canon Hugh Farrie, in the background. *Right:* St Sarkis, Iverna Gardens, London, w8, built and endowed by Mr Five Per Cent and his (present) resting-place

The Supreme Catholicos of the Armenian Church, Vazgen I, with the Archbishop of Canterbury, Dr Geoffrey Fisher, at St Sarkis in 1956

TWO OF MR FIVE PER CENT'S 'CHILDREN'

Above: Bronze cast of Houdon's 'Diana', commissioned by Catherine the Great but rejected as 'indecent'. The marble original was bought by Gulbenkian from the Russians 'under the counter', thus outwitting Duveen in the grandest art coup of modern times. *Left:* Gulbenkian's obsidian 'Macgregor head' of Amenhotep III, 'The King of Kings'—the 'finest sculpture which ever came out of Ancient Egypt' and presented for exhibition at the British Museum in an old newspaper

Geraldine Guinness at her St Margaret's, Westminster wedding in 1956 to Mikael Essayan: wearing the Georgian diamond tiara presented by Nubar to Marie and lent for this occasion. It is definitely *not* paste as some of Nevarte's jewellery was supposed to be

Mikael's father and mother, Kvork and Rita Essayan (front background) stepping out of St Margaret's. Four days later, having been married thirty-six years earlier at the Hyde Park Hotel according to the rites of the Armenian Church, they went through a second form of marriage at Caxton Hall

Kirkuk 1955

Drilling a submerged
'Continental Shelf'
from a £900,000 Shell
'oil island'

When the conference looked like foundering, he again produced one of his brainwaves. He called for a large map of the Middle East, took a thick red pencil and slowly drew a red line round the central area.

'That was the Ottoman Empire which I knew in 1914,' he said. 'And I ought to know. I was born in it, lived in it and served it. If anybody knows better, carry on. . . .'

The British looked and found Kuwait was outside the red line, but not Bahrain, Qatar, Saudi Arabia nor the Sheikhdoms. The Americans looked and saw they were free to operate in Kuwait. The others looked and raised no objection. The Definitive Group or Working Agreement was through. Ever since it has been known as the "Red Line" Agreement.[1]

Gulbenkian had built a framework for Middle East oil development which lasted until 1948: another fantastic one-man feat, unsurpassed in international big business.

4. Buddies

Nubar Gulbenkian says: 'Pa was not interested in the subsequent formalities. He had imposed his will on insuperable opponents— achieved an impossible compromise—and produced a perfect solution, where none seemed possible. It was enough.'

The *Memoirs* merely say: 'The redundant Open Door was hermetically closed and no one talked about it any more. There could not have been a more closed Open Door policy than the one followed by all the oil groups trying to secure every possible concession from the Iraq Government in order to prevent other competitors applying for them.'

Mr Five Per Cent then chartered a yacht and took his daughter, Rita, for a Mediterranean cruise.

Leaning over the rails off Morocco, he pointed to a passing vessel and asked: 'What's that strange-looking boat with a funnel at the stern?' Rita told him.

At the age of fifty-nine, the oil king had seen an oil tanker for the first time.

In all his life he never saw the land of his oil dreams, either as Mesopotamia or Iraq.

[1] 'Father had the foresight to include territorial waters' (Nubar Gulbenkian).

For what he calls Fiscal Policy—otherwise tax-dodging—a non-profit-making Working Agreement was arranged for the Company, with the connivance of the British Government. Gulbenkian set up his own private subsidiary Company in Canada to receive his 5 per cent profits and the Groups made corresponding arrangements.

The *Memoirs* say briefly: 'The Americans were reluctant to pay British income tax, as they might have been obliged to do on this venture—a reluctance which was shared by the French.

'The British Government, being desirous that the headquarters of the Company should be in England and its Chairman a British subject, did not raise difficulties.

'The Americans, in co-operation with the French, evolved what was known as the Working Agreement, whereby the Company was in effect debarred from making profits.

'To give effect to this decision, Participations and Investments of Toronto (a Canadian Company) was formed and became the owner of 5 per cent of the Company. Since its formation I have been the President and Managing-Director.'

This arrangement was embodied in the Red Line Agreement. Mr Five Per Cent could not be bothered to sign it. Instead he sent his son, Nubar, as a Director of Participations and Investments (Pandi). For "fiscal" reasons the signature had to be attached outside British territory and off Nubar went to Ostend.

This is his account: 'I chartered a private Handley-Page aeroplane and set off for Dover with Mr Duncan Smith (the Gulbenkian solicitor) and Miss Everest (the faithful typist). On arrival we found it seated only two passengers. Somebody had to be left out and we had an argument. I settled it by suggesting that Captain Olley, the pilot (later the founder of Olley Airways) should be appointed a Director of Pandi on the spot and fly to sign the Agreement instead of me. He was thrilled—little realizing that he could be removed from the Board as quickly as he was installed. But they wouldn't hear of abandoning me. So we *all* piled in—defying the Regulations—and somehow reached our destination safely. After signing, we celebrated on excellent champagne and turbot straight out of the North Sea, which I had ordered in advance.' So somebody had some fun out of the Six Big Rows.

Mr Five Per Cent was offered the grade of the Legion of Honour which is usually reserved for Royalty, but he refused. Say the *Memoirs*: 'The French Government was highly gratified by the inclusion of the Americans and high orders were bestowed on several participants in the negotiations. I was personally offered the highest French decoration.

But I declined this honour on the plea that, whatever I had done, I had been prompted by a feeling of friendship. For this particular reason, I could not and would not accept any reward. M Briand, the French Prime Minister, remarked jocularly: "Gulbenkian is just like myself; the only virgin thing he has left is his button-hole. . . ." '

Nubar adds: 'Papa also told the French, "If you want to show your gratitude to me, do something for my son. He has been working in your Ministry of Supply for three years." That is how I became a Commander of the Legion of Honour—at the fantastic age of only thirty-two. I always wear it in France. It's polite. It also helps with the Customs and traffic police.'

Mr Five Per Cent also received praise from Britain for his part in the Six Big Rows. On 10th October, 1924, Lord Tyrrell wrote from the Foreign Office: 'The Secretary of State desires me to express his earnest hope that you, who were from the outset so instrumental in bringing in American Participation, will be similarly prepared to make every endeavour to meet the Turkish Petroleum Company in the same spirit, and thereby avoid an impasse which could only have regrettable results for all the interests concerned.'

Mr Five Per Cent "endeavoured" and on 7th December, 1925, Lord Tyrrell wrote again: 'I am very much in debt for the very full information you sent me with regard to your differences with the Turkish Petroleum Company. I can't tell you how relieved I was to hear that resort is to be made to arbitration, and I am convinced that your share in contributing to so satisfactory a solution cannot be exaggerated.

'It is further proof of your public spirit and disinterestedness. I hope now that we may be able to maintain American participation in the Company, and present a united front to the attacks upon it, from whatever quarter they may come. I am sure you will think this is good news.

'Moreover, a statement will be made this week in the House of Commons, in reply to a question, exactly defining the attitude of the British Government towards the Turkish Petroleum Company, as being in their opinion the only valid title to oil in Mosul.

'I hope you are keeping well and will not fail to let me know when you are in London.'

Even the Americans had a good word to spare for Mr Five Per Cent. Mr Montagu Piesse, the London lawyer of the American groups, wrote to Colonel F. Mercier, head of the Compagnie Française des Pétroles, on 9th April, 1926:

'I am glad to see that the French Group will agree to the arrangements with Mr Gulbenkian upon the basis of the memorandum, which Mr Teagle[1] has communicated to you.

'I wish to thank you for your kind reference to myself in bringing so far, to a successful conclusion, the negotiations with Mr Gulbenkian, but I do not wish to take entire credit for this, for great credit is due to Mr Gulbenkian himself.

'As you know he has all along put forward certain claims to which he considered he was justly entitled, but the Groups have not been prepared to admit some of these claims, which has been the cause of the long delay in bringing this matter to a position where the American Group could take up its participation in the Turkish Petroleum Company Limited.

'I have in no way convinced Mr Gulbenkian that his claims were not justified, but, in order to facilitate the great desire of all parties interested and of the three Governments concerned to bring about co-operation of international oil groups in Mesopotamia, he has most generously agreed to modify his claims in a way indicated in the memorandum, which will now make it possible for the American Group to become a partner in the Turkish Petroleum Company Limited, and thus complete the much desired international association.

'I think great credit is due to him for the broad-minded way in which he has faced the situation and for making, what he considers, a considerable sacrifice to meet the above-mentioned desire.

'My negotiations with Mr Gulbenkian have been on the most friendly basis and we have both worked hard to bring about a settlement of all outstanding points which existed between him and the Groups, and this, I think, we have now done.

'I am writing you this letter as I wish to put these facts on record with the French Group.'

Eighteen years later, after more "Big Rows", Montagu Piesse wrote in the same strain on 5th April, 1944: 'I had forgotten the letter (of April 1926) but not the sentiments, which, I might say, have been reaffirmed by further experience gathered over a period of eighteen years since the letter was written.'

The *Memoirs* add: 'During the whole negotiations I believe I did not put forward an iota more than anything I was legitimately entitled to.

'It may not be superfluous to state here that in 1940, when I met

[1] Walter C. Teagle, one of J. D. Rockefeller, Senior's, bright young men from about 1900 and a Director of Standard Oil of New Jersey, one of the American Companies participating in the Turkish Petroleum Company. Gulbenkian and Deterding had been battling with him since 1907.

Mr Sellers (of the Socony-Vacuum participants) in London, he told me as a compliment that the American lawyers of his Company had remarked to him: "Although we are told Gulbenkian is a difficult man, we have never come across demands from him to which he is not fully entitled." '

For the time being the tycoons were buddies.

*   *   *   *   *

In 1929 the name of the Turkish Petroleum Company was changed to the Iraq Petroleum Company, by which it will be known for the rest of this book.

18

SIDELINES

THE story now shifts abruptly to Latin America.

From Mr Five Per Cent's *Memoirs* one might imagine this area was off his track. There is only one passing reference to it. Dealing with the Pre-Final Settlement of 1925, he wrote: 'At the time I had already had great divergences of view with the Anglo-Saxon (Royal Dutch-Shell) regarding mutual interests in the management of the Venezuelan Oil Concessions.'

But this was the turning point in his friendship with Henri Deterding, which had repercussions throughout the oil industry. We must see how Latin America fits into the picture.

In the early 1900s the oil industry was not greatly developed outside the United States and Russia. Alarmist talk about wasteful production methods, diminishing reserves and conservation had hardly started. Only a few progressive exploiters like Nobel and some Americans yet shared Gulbenkian's youthful views about efficient production.

But the importance of an oil company (with pretensions to worldwide operations) obtaining access to new fields as they opened up and penetrating all markets, was beginning to be understood. Universality was an essential safeguard against undercutting. That was the reason for the Royal Dutch-Shell merger of 1902-7.

Any new oilfield was, therefore, a matter of concern to a major oil company in the very early days; and as world consumption soared (and oil became the decisive raw material of power politics), the acquisition of fresh reserves became vital.

The withdrawal of Russian oil from the world market in 1917 suddenly put the European companies at a great disadvantage *vis-à-vis* the Americans in the price war. Coming at a time of enormous increase in the demand for oil, for peaceful as well as belligerent purposes, the Soviet oil exodus also produced a shortage, which had to be rectified by supplies from elsewhere.

That is the background to the Gulbenkian connection with Latin America.

1. A Basinful

About 1905 a husky young Englishman was nosing round the wild subtropical coast of the Republic of Venezuela in search of adventure—lost civilizations, deep-sea monsters and treasure.

This was F. A. Mitchell-Hedges, who was later to become a millionaire, famed archaeologist, record-holding big-game fisherman, Old English Silver connoisseur and best-selling author.

He picked up the chicle concession in Spanish Honduras and sold it to the Americans for chewing-gum. Likewise he bought and sold gold, timber and beef concessions in Central American Republics. He had his eyes wide open.

When he edged his boat from the Venezuelan coast up sweaty creeks into Lake Maraciabo, he immediately noticed oil was seeping through the ground all over the place and that the natives were caulking their canoes with asphalt. Naturally, he bought an oil concession.

'I paid "nothing" for it in terms of modern money,' he says, 'and when I returned to England I got rid of it for what you'd call a song today—maybe £20,000. I can't even remember. The buyer was a City financier, Duncan Elliot Alves, of Copthorne Avenue, Tunbridge Wells, who subsequently became a Lord-Lieutenant in Wales. He hawked my concession round London. That is how Venezuelan oil became known in this country.'

Deterding heard of it and, after studying reports, bought the Vigas Concession (covering much of the southern part of the Maraciabo Basin in Western Venezuela) in 1907. This was a failure.

Gulbenkian also got his private intelligence system working in Venezuela, but for several years reports were not encouraging.

Then in 1915, when he had come over to London from Paris (at the initiation of his intrigues with the French Government and British Foreign Office against the Anglo-Persian Oil Company), a swash-buckling Venezuelan General named Aranguren arrived to see him at the Ritz Hotel.

Mr Five Per Cent was never too busy to see anybody worthwhile. Although Aranguren was a flamboyant, in-and-out politician, as well as a General, Gulbenkian listened to him carefully about the oil prospects and (cross-checking with his own private information) bought the concession.

He then cut the Royal Dutch-Shell in on the deal, following his practice of running parallel activities with them and taking his share of the profit or loss of the ensuing business.

Deterding's version of the deal is given in his autobiography: 'I made the most speculative venture of my life. . . . Around five million dollars had been spent on working this concession fruitlessly and it had been hawked round the United States for some time. . . . It was that sixth sense again, that blind instinct which I believe every successful oil-operator must have, that drove me on. Somehow I felt in my bones that this big bid in Venezuela—sheer gamble though it seemed—would be justified. And so it ultimately was.'

That, according to Nubar Gulbenkian, who worked with Deterding on Latin American business, is 'a complete misrepresentation'.

What really happened, says Nubar, was this: 'Deterding had got fed up with the whole Venezuelan enterprise. So had the Royal Dutch-Shell—to such an extent that when Papa saw General Aranguren in London in 1915 and took an option on his concession (in the districts of Bolivar[1] and Maracaibo), he was laughed to scorn at the office.

'Sir Marcus Samuel said: "Why do you bring that muck here? This is a respectable office." And Deterding shared Samuel's contempt for Father's offer of a share in the concession. It was Pa's "nose for oil", not Deterding's "sixth sense" nor "blind instinct", which led to the Royal Dutch-Shell development in Venezuela. Pa "knew" there was oil in the Aranguren concession. He also had his principle: "Never abandon an oil concession".

'He argued Deterding into going ahead in Venezuela, instead of giving up in despair. What finally persuaded Father's doubting associates was his own readiness to put up 35 per cent of the capital out of his own pocket. Pa allowed them to buy the other 65 per cent because he never wanted to be bothered with the production and marketing side of the oil business. But for him, Royal Dutch-Shell probably wouldn't have stayed in Venezuela and would not be there today.'

It was from Mene Grande, in the Aranguren Concession, that the first commercial oil production and exports came two years later (1917), thus proving the sensitivity of Mr Five Per Cent's nose and encouraging the Royal Dutch-Shell to persevere.

And it was the Anglo-Dutch interest in Venezuelan oil which substantially helped Britain and Europe through the Suez oil crisis of 1956–7, when Middle East supplies were interrupted.

In 1955 Venezuela was the second greatest oil-producing country in the world, ranking only after the United States: 2,157,216 barrels a day in 1955.

---

[1] It was not until December 1922 that the fourth well drilled at La Rosa in the Bolivar District blew sensationally into uncontrolled production of 100,000 barrels a day at only 1,500 feet.

The Anglo-Dutch debt to Gulbenkian's courage and enterprise in Venezuela has yet to be publicly recognized. But he did not go unrewarded. He realized his Venezuelan interest in 1947, when (according to his son) he sold his 330,000 13s. 4d. shares for £6 10s. each, thus at one stroke adding £2,145,000 ($8,644,000) to his fortune.

His original stake in 1915 was less than £20,000. Nice "muck"!

2. Eagles Flutter

No direct reference to Mexico occurs in Gulbenkian's *Memoirs*, although the famous Mexican Eagles share-holding was one of the numerous interests which he introduced into the world-wide Royal Dutch-Shell combine in pursuit of global production and sales solidarity against the Americans.

Maybe the omission was because Gulbenkian was mainly concerned, as he stated, in tracing the development of the Iraq Petroleum Company. But still the omission is strange. The *Memoirs* are so frank and self-critical. He was widely blamed when Mexican Eagles nose-dived. Mexico was also one of the main causes of his breach with Deterding in 1925, to which the *Memoirs* repeatedly refer.

If ever Deterding had real cause to regret an oil deal with Gulbenkian, this was it.

Yet in *An International Oil Man*, which he wrote sixteen years later, the big Dutchman ignored the chance of getting some of his own back. He hogged both the credit for taking the initiative in Mexico and the blame for subsequent disappointments. The little Armenian might never have existed.

Deterding merely remarked ruefully: 'The years 1911–12 were momentous. . . . We also got busy, purchasing large properties in Mexico. . . . 1918–19 marked the negotiations resulting in our (Royal Dutch-Shell) Mexican-Eagle purchase, the gap in the years being explained by the war period. . . . Against the spectacular successes of petroleum production, you must offset the costly failures. In Mexico, it is estimated that of the wells bored fifty per cent proved dry holes. Imagine the wasted expenditure! Some of the bores cost £50,000 each! Wells have been successfully capped and subsequently produced nothing but salt water.'

That is a travesty of the facts, according to Nubar Gulbenkian. Deterding implies that he was the leading man in the development of the Mexican oilfields and that these were one of his few failures, in striking contrast to his many triumphs. He even makes a virtue of failure, maintaining: 'If I hadn't had a crop of failures in my harvest, I would indeed be a fool. Only a fool never makes a failure. Every man fails sometimes, unless he wraps himself in cotton-wool and evades all responsibility.'

Says Nubar: 'The truth was very different. Mexico was not a complete failure. Nor was Deterding the prime mover in the Mexican Eagle purchase. The fact of the matter is that Deterding took what seemed to him an unfortunate gamble in Mexico *before* the First World War and lost interest in the Mexican properties in the two years before 1914—indeed, until 1918, when my father intervened.'

What really happened was this. In mid-1918 Gulbenkian met the first Lord Cowdray in the Ritz, Paris, and heard how the latter had just struck oil while building a railway in Mexico.

Cowdray had sunk a shallow well amid natural seepages near the line and suddenly a huge gusher had broken forth, scattering rocks hundreds of yards and inundating the site with black petroleum. He had immediately obtained a concession, formed the Mexican Eagle Oil Company and started to erect a refinery.

But Cowdray was not an oil man and was preoccupied with his other interests. So he consulted Mr Five Per Cent.

Gulbenkian heard him out, excused himself and made post haste for London to consult Deterding, who agreed spontaneously: 'We must get Pearson (Lord Cowdray) to sell at any price. This will put us on top of the Americans.'

Soon Gulbenkian was back in Paris, before Cowdray had time to change his mind and anybody else could grab him and by 1919 the deal was completed.

This set the seal on the fortune behind the polo-ground at Cowdray Park, Sussex, where British polo has been kept alive since the Second World War and the Duke of Edinburgh plays with the present one-armed holder of the Cowdray Viscounty.

'The basis of the deal which father negotiated with Cowdray and Deterding was as follows,' says Nubar. 'Blocks of 98s shares were to be successively sold on the Stock Exchange, the Royal Dutch-Shell and Cowdray each taking 40 per cent of any profits over the 98s and Father the remaining 20 per cent. As a reward for his efforts Father also received 50,000 free shares at par from Cowdray.

'The Royal Dutch-Shell's geological reports were good. The so-called "golden lane" of wells, each producing at least 100,000 barrels a day, came into operation. Oilfield conservation was not then developed and production went ahead full tilt. Profits mounted rapidly and the shares rocketed.

'Soon the shares almost trebled in value, rising to £13, and at one moment father made a million on paper. Cowdray and Deterding of course profited proportionately.

'Then on Armistice Night, 1918, when I was nursing a sprained arm at home in Hyde Park Gardens, father and I learned the first ominous news from Mexico.

'A little salt water—not more than one per cent—had appeared in the most famous Mexican well at Potero Del Llano.

'Not so much importance was attached in those days to a small occurrence of salt water as it is today, when we know it is the beginning of the end. But still it cast a shadow over the prospects.

'Then another of the big wells caught fire and millions of barrels of oil went up in smoke.

'Notwithstanding the Royal Dutch-Shell and Cowdray continued to sell at well over 98s and cleared out in time.

'But father did *not* clear out. He held on to a last block of 500,000 shares—in spite of the untoward inside information from Mexico.

'He did *not*, as his secretary David Young has suggested, sell out *all* his Mexican stock immediately the first bad news arrived and continue to tell acquaintances to "buy, buy, buy".

'He was very conscious, as always, of his own interest and protected himself. But he was also conscious of having been primarily responsible for starting the boom in Mexican Eagles and that thousands of small shareholders would be ruined if the word went round that "Gulbenkian is selling" and the bottom consequently dropped out of the market. He was already a name in the City, despite his self-effacement.

'He therefore hung on far longer than necessary, against his own judgement, hoping against hope for better news from Mexico. In those days it was thought that if one well blew salt water it didn't necessarily mean that adjoining wells were bound to do the same.

'But eventually the true situation in Mexico leaked out. Mexican Eagles crashed and the public blamed father although he finally sold his remaining 500,000 98s shares for 15s each, thus losing half a million. In the end he probably didn't make £500,000 on the whole venture.

'In a few years Mexican production slumped from 200 million barrels a year to a tenth of that and Mexico has never since been one of the great producers. One year the Company paid 30 per cent dividend, then nothing for the next 20 years.'

Shortly before the Second World War, Mexico took a leaf out of the Soviet book and nationalized the oil industry, putting up a monstrous memorial in the capital to mark the occasion—a bad example which was to be imitated again in the Middle East, at Abadan and Suez.

Although Deterding (like Cowdray) took an enormous quick profit from Mexico, the enterprise was in the long run, as he wrote, a "costly failure". He burned his fingers badly. Hence, doubtless, his prejudiced account of the venture and his disdain for Gulbenkian.

This was another cause of the breach between the two men. But it went deeper than money. A question of principle was involved. Until the Mexican bubble burst about 1924 and expectations of production big enough to offset American competition evaporated, Deterding sought to dominate the Company.

Nubar explains: 'The Management Contract gave Deterding control of the Mexican Eagle Oil Company, and he wanted to run it in the interests of the Royal Dutch-Shell as a whole and not, as my father insisted, in the interests of the Company.

'Again the rights of minority shareholders became a burning issue between the two men. Father thought the Mexican Eagle shareholders, including himself, were being swindled.

'This is where I came in. Deterding was very intelligent and put me in charge of the Mexican department, calculating that Father would be loath to criticize his own son's work too harshly at the same time leaving me to yelp on behalf of Gulbenkian interests, if necessary. By 1922 this arrangement patched up the quarrel and peace was restored for the next two or three years.'

Anyway so far as Mexican Eagles were concerned, David Young's description of Calouste Gulbenkian as "The Meanest Man in the World" is not justified. Unlike Nubar Gulbenkian, he was not fully on the inside of Mr Five Per Cent's Stock Exchange dealings.

By his own account, Young was engaged at 30s a-week straight from school before the First World War as a shorthand writer who spoke French and during his twenty-six years' service was never paid much more than £8-a-week. He confesses that he was "devoted to him —yes, even to his incredibly mean ways and his insistence on attention to detail'. But he thinks his treatment was "pretty shabby" for a confidential secretary who was expected to work the clock round seven days a week.

Nubar Gulbenkian comments: 'Young was engaged as a shorthand typist with a knowledge of French and no more. He was paid what he was worth. When Young was called up in the First World War, Father continued to pay his wages and helped the family. But he was never under any obligation to him.'

This "devotion" of Young's is echoed by another member of Mr Five Per Cent's staff, who reckons he got a raw deal, namely Cyril Nisbet, a solicitor who is now a director of the Selection Trust. He informs me:

'I acted for him in pre-war days in connection with purely business matters. After the war I worked at the London office of his organization for two years.

'He was exceedingly difficult to please until he got exactly what he wanted, but he was equally generous and charming on occasions. Your inquiries have probably brought home to you that while many people with whom he had business relations considered him an unmitigated nuisance, they nearly all had very friendly feelings for him.

'It was the same with me. I left his service feeling anything but fairly treated but curiously enough continued to consider him as my friend. Whether I should have done so if I had not fallen into a better job I can't say, but I believe I would. You have a most intriguing subject. . . .'

Looking back on the Venezuelan and Mexican oil deals of 1915 and 1918 a philosopher might argue that Gulbenkian had already begun winning the next war by seeking fresh oil sinews to wage it.

19

THE BIG BUST-UP

THE wonder is not that Calouste Gulbenkian and Deterding quarrelled in 1925, but that they had worked together for a quarter of a century. The two men could hardly have been more different by nature—the little, secretive, patient Armenian—and the big, showy and impulsive Dutchman.

From the moment Gulbenkian introduced Deterding into the Turkish Petroleum Company in 1912, the latter was a cuckoo in the nest. 'Year after year Mr Deterding endeavoured to reduce the power and influence of Mr Frederick Lane. . . .' At first Deterding opposed Gulbenkian's efforts to reach a compromise with the Anglo-Persian, instead of waging mutually destructive policies *vis-à-vis* Mesopotamia. Deterding let down Gulbenkian at the Foreign Office Conference in March 1914, so that Gulbenkian was almost frozen out of his own company. Deterding also started off by opposing Gulbenkian's plans for compromise with the French in 1915–16 and the Americans in 1921–2.

Certain characteristics enabled them to overcome those differences.

Both men agreed from the start of the great Royal Dutch-Shell merger in 1902–3 that: (*a*) co-operation was the only means of fighting the ruinous price-cutting by Standard Oil; (*b*) world-wide participation in oil production and distribution was an essential insurance against the resumption of price-cutting; (*c*) compromise must be their keynote. Gulbenkian went all the way with Deterding in believing that 'an amalgamation should leave no party with the idea he has made a bad bargain and that the true test of an amalgamation is value for money.' If one man held this belief more persistently than the other, it was Gulbenkian. Contrary to Deterding and the oil groups, Gulbenkian was *always* prepared to cut his own demands in the interest of a smooth, long-term settlement, if his associates did likewise. He was the personification of the broad view and the long view.

Each man respected the other's brains and industry: 'Deterding was a brilliant commercial man.' And they hated idleness with equal intensity. Deterding wrote: 'A common delusion, existing in the minds of too many people today, is that because a job is big, it is bound to be complicated. Hard work, plus a little vision, provides better ignition fuel than wizardry for carrying a man to the top.'

Gulbenkian worked ten hours a day until he was over eighty and was constantly exclaiming: 'I can't stand people who don't work.' Deterding was once overheard to say: 'If I were dictator, I would shoot every idle man!'

Stronger than their common strategy and mutual respect was the bond of common interest. For many years each needed the other and made use of him. Gulbenkian, the Oriental exile, needed the framework of the great Anglo-Dutch combine. Deterding, the Hollander, needed the Armenian's Middle East subtlety and knowledge. Together they were a match for the colossus of Standard Oil and even for Governments. Gulbenkian's infinite patience, Deterding's quick vigour and Frederick Lane's statesmanship formed a tremendous combination. Together they created a unified oil industry for Europe, which could meet Standard Oil on equal terms and, incidentally, brought the Iraq Petroleum Company to life.

But the attraction of opposites could not last in the long run. In the end there was bound to be an explosion.

Deterding was the fourth of five children of a simple Dutch sea-faring family. His father was a Master Mariner, who died at the age of forty-two, when Henri was six, and left inadequate funds for the boy's education. But Henri, like Gulbenkian, was a child prodigy. On leaving school at sixteen, he was proficient in English, French and German and was two years ahead of his contemporaries. But it was a hard struggle for him and his mother.

He was apprenticed as a bank clerk at five shillings a week in Amsterdam and later recalled, sententiously: 'Mighty good tasted the couple of salted herrings and glass of beer on which, for a few cents, we used to be regaled in the office from a small night café, after working nearly round the clock. There is nothing like hard work for making a young man enjoy his food.'

His setting could hardly have been further removed from the oriental, international luxury—and the peril of massacre—of the wealthy Gulbenkian household in Constantinople.

Deterding loved hunting, shooting, skating on the frozen canals of Holland and skiing at St Moritz, with all the accompanying social gaiety. In England he spent three-quarters of an hour every morning astride a horse before going to work. After the age of sixty, he was still plunging vigorously into his swimming-pool, winter and summer, before breakfast—often breaking the ice. He was contemptuous of Gulbenkian, who risked nothing more violent than a constitutional in the park, Swedish drill or a gentle cruise in the Mediterranean. Gulbenkian thought Deterding was wasting his time and energy, instead of concentrating on essentials. For him the competition of the sale-room was the substitute for Deterding's enjoyment of the thrust and parry of sport.

Both men had violent tempers. Gulbenkian's *Memoirs* are punctuated with instances of the Dutchman's fury. He was liable to burst out with such pronouncements as: 'God damn gold! Let's have bimetallism!' When a Standard Oil executive patronized him with the remark, 'Aren't you the man from a company called the Royal Dutch?' Deterding was quick to retort, 'Yes, I am. And I sometimes think my parents showed great presumption in not asking permission from the Standard Oil Company for me to be born.' The London Ritz still remembers Gulbenkian fuming round the hall about the lawsuit he faced with Nubar: 'I'll ruin him. Yes, I'll ruin him!' The blistering telegrams he sent off daily are still recalled with terror by his staff. Two years after his death they speak of him with awe.

Both men were also sticklers for detail. 'Nothing escapes my attention, absolutely nothing,' and 'Check, check, check' were two of Gulbenkian's pet phrases. Deterding proudly recalled how, when he (and Gulbenkian) were negotiating the purchase of Mexican Eagles, Lord Cowdray afterwards asked the Chartered Accountant: 'Is Deterding also a Chartered Accountant? Within twenty minutes of looking through the figures, he discussed them as thoroughly as if he had been looking through them solidly for a month.' The moral he drew was: 'You will go a long way in business if you train yourself to appraise a balance sheet as rapidly and as shrewdly as a good judge of character can sum up his fellow-man.'

For their first twenty-five years together, Gulbenkian and Deterding were ideal sparring partners, brushing up their technique, sharpening their wits and trying out their strength against each other—for a common purpose. Then the sparring turned to a duel.

The human flaws in the partnership were Gulbenkian's spite and Deterding's conceit. Mr Five Per Cent's *Memoirs* are continually harping on the alleged sins of the Anglo-Persian Oil Company, its disloyalty, greed and ingratitude, which were really indistinguishable from the ordinary thrust and parry of oil rivalry and his own methods. What he could never forgive was the fact that the Anglo-Persian "got away with it".

Deterding, as we have seen, carried conceit to the extraordinary extreme of omitting a single mention of Gulbenkian in his autobiography, published nine years after their quarrel, and anybody reading *An International Oil Man* might imagine Deterding had built the Royal Dutch-Shell single-handed, apart from some transitory help from Kessler, Frederick Lane and Lord Bearsted: that Deterding alone had secured a footing for the Company in Latin America. Nobody would know that the Iraq Petroleum Company existed and that the Royal Dutch-Shell shared in it. Thirty words, in 30,000, is all he spares for his twenty-two years' association with this country: 'The new pipeline laid in Iraq at a cost of around ten million pounds sterling to convey oil to the Mediterranean, is the world's longest pipeline. It is over a thousand miles long.' Towards the end of his life Deterding could not bear to think he was indebted to anybody—let alone that any oil man might have got the better of him.

Instead of dealing with the Iraq Petroleum Company epic he pontificates: 'There are few worse forms of vanity and self-glory than to strive to appear too self-effacing,' or 'What has always proved an unfailing aid to hard thinking is a strenuous bout of physical exercise'— both obvious (if covert) sneers at his erstwhile friend and colleague, the coddled "Mystery Millionaire", Gulbenkian.

Cynics may well gloat over the fact that the inevitable explosion came in 1925, when the Pre-Final Settlement was reached for Iraq and the architecture of the Company was completed by the entry of the Americans—the very year of the two magnates' joint triumph, when they no longer needed each other to the same extent.

True, there were two unpleasantnesses outstanding from the Iraq negotiations—what Gulbenkian calls 'My objections to the Group Agreement' and 'Sale of Oil Agreement and the Compagnie Française des Pétroles'—both of which contributed to the breach. These must now be recorded. But, as the *Memoirs* say, the last straw was the rights of minority shareholders (including Gulbenkian) in Venezuela.

Mr Five Per Cent could never swallow Deterding's dictation, summed up in the latter's two phrases: 'I never put money in a business without a deciding voice in the management,' and My conditions for investing capital in the Venezuelan Oil Company provide that the Company is managed by us.'

A battle for power was on, in which riches were the token. The opposing weapons were the sledge-hammer and the rapier.

2

Since forming the Turkish Petroleum Company with Sir Henry Babington-Smith, Sir Ernest Cassel and Lord Revelstoke in 1911, Gulbenkian had not earned a penny in Iraq. Indeed, commercial production did not begin until 1927. So, when the Definitive "Red Line" Agreement was signed in 1928, he wanted cash—real money as the token of his success after long efforts, and of his power, as represented by his balancing 5 per cent interest in the newly named Iraq Petroleum Company.

What he got was . . . crude oil. And this did not interest him. He had no marketing organization of his own and anyway he could not be bothered with the technical details. For the disposal of his crude oil he was at the mercy of the groups.

This, he felt, was inconvenient, precarious and unjust, after all the trouble he had taken to introduce the Anglo-Dutch-French-American interests in turn.

The argument went back to 1925 and beyond, and his friend Deterding sided with the other groups against him. In fact, there was a conspiracy to squash his 5 per cent interest and eventually squeeze him out. A struggle between one David and four Goliaths was on.

The *Memoirs* expose the nakedness of this battle of the billions. 'The plan was most unfair and objectionable from my personal point of view. I had never had any compensation or reward for all the trouble I had taken or the expenses I had incurred. I had risked capital in this venture with a view to obtaining profits in cash and not barrels of crude oil.

'The groups took no account of my objection. Their eminent lawyer, Mr Harold Brown, told me they had said: "Gulbenkian can do his damnedest, but we are forging ahead, whatever he does". Eventually, acting on the advice of the Bank of England solicitors (Freshfield's) and fortified by the opinion of two future Lord Chancellors (Simon and Hailsham), to my great reluctance, I threatened legal proceedings unless some way was found of satisfying my elementary rights.

'The Anglo-Saxon (Deterding and the Royal Dutch-Shell) endeavoured to make political capital out of my attitude and tried to present me to the British Foreign Office as blocking the arrangements in connection with the American groups. However, the matter being explained to the British authorities, the justice of my position and contentions was made apparent. The oil groups were told to settle the matter on a fair basis amongst themselves or to accept the arbitration of Sir Warren Fisher (Head of the Treasury).

'The threat of an outside arbitrator, connected with the British Government, was quite sufficient to secure an agreement in principle by the groups. It was proposed that I should be assured of a regular outlet for my 5 per cent share of the oil produced.

'The difficulties were overcome after long and tedious deliberations by a contract between (Gulbenkian's) Participations and Investments and the Compagnie Française des Pétroles. The former obtained an option to sell its 5 per cent quota of oil to the French group at the mean market price ruling on 1st January and 1st July of each year—this price to apply to deliveries during the ensuing year.

'This contract has worked satisfactorily for all parties and if one looks at figures and actual current values, the results are practically the same.'

The dispute was not quite as simple as that. It was not merely a matter of a Foreign Office ultimatum. Mr Five Per Cent's *Memoirs* take a sweep back, as a matter of interest, to show just how low the oil groups could sink in their attempts to smash him.

'The American group became champions of the other major groups in finding means of eliminating my minority rights. The Americans wanted to buy oil from the Iraq Petroleum Company at cost, although legally such a course was altogether incompatible with my rights. Sir William Tyrrell and other Foreign Office officials were surprised and failed to understand how I could be subjected to such an onslaught, after I had worked so hard to bring the Americans in.

'At first I negotiated with Mr Teagle and Mr von Riedeman, who, if my memory is right, began by proposing a 1*d.* royalty per ton in place of any benefits due to my Company (Pandi).

'Before they came in, Sir Henri Deterding had proposed a basis of 12*d.* per ton, which I had declined, insisting on a gold shilling. Since then Mr von Riedeman always remembers me as "the gold shilling gentleman".

'He and Mr Teagle declared they could not entertain Sir Henri Deterding's proposal. . . .

'Technical arguments were advanced by Mr Teagle to convince me that my rights ought to be amply satisfied by their proposal (1*d.* a ton). As oil technology is my weak side, I asked for the help of my son, who was the assistant of Sir Henri Deterding and sufficiently acquainted with oil technology.

'My son's knowledge was not welcome to Mr Teagle and Mr von Riedeman, and they asked Sir Henri to tell him it was incorrect to take part in the discussions as he was an official of the Royal Dutch-Shell. My son had to retire. But this not very courteous incident stiffened my attitude. I refused to enter into technicalities. I maintained that I wanted a gold shilling per ton, or 2 per cent royalty. But I wanted a firm outlet for my 5 per cent oil.

'I was advised by foremost Counsel that the Americans were

bluffing and that I should not hesitate to call the bluff by instructing that an injunction should be issued against the Directors and Company. Luckily, it did not come to that.' The Foreign Office ultimatum was sufficient.

Mr Five Per Cent goes on to soliloquize: 'I am not writing this off-handedly, but after half a century of intimate connection with the oil combines, which entitles me to hold an opinion and express it straightforwardly.

'Apart from historical interest, all these details show what a vicious atmosphere can at times be created by the oil groups, misleading governments, twisting laws, etc.

'The oil groups, headed by the Americans, had only one aim—to wipe out the rights of the minority by hook or by crook, i.e. my 5 per cent participation.

'Several other unfair exigences, such as forcing the Company not to sell its oil freely to outsiders, forbidding trading and refining, etc. All these exigences were simply in the interest of the major groups and designed to prevent anyone disturbing the monopolistic rings in their markets.

'In an endeavour to bring pressure to bear on me, it was suggested that the groups should try to obtain fresh concessions on their own—leaving me out—but this was stopped by the threat of legal proceedings by the Compagnie Française des Pétroles in order to enforce the provisions against internal competition contained in the 1914 Foreign Office Agreement.

'To a philosopher, interested in oil, what reflections there would be for him today (1945) concerning the fact that the same oil groups, forgetting all their former traditions, are offering to carry out the Atlantic Charter—that Washington Oil Conferences are boldly declaring themselves the apostles of World Welfare and have the interests of oil economy at heart.

'It may be a miracle. But my personal opinion, as a Scotsman would say, is: "I ha'e ma doots about it. . . ." '

3

So Deterding deserted Gulbenkian in his hour of need, when it came to a showdown over the spoils of the Iraq Petroleum Company. And this coincided with the row over control of the Venezuelan

venture. Gulbenkian wanted the Venezuelan oil company to be run
in the interest of its shareholders, including himself. Deterding
(backed in 1925 with a 52 per cent Royal Dutch-Shell holding in total
Venezuelan oil properties) wanted to run the company to suit the
combine. What Nubar Gulbenkian called "The Big Bust-up" followed.

Nubar is the only survivor today who knows both sides. He was
not only the apple of his father's eye, his confidant and a director of
Participations and Investments. He was also Deterding's right-hand
man in the Royal Dutch-Shell, with specialized first-hand knowledge
of the Latin American business. This is his story:

'For years the pernickety interference of my father and the overbearing grandeur of Deterding had clashed. Their relations became
increasingly strained. Deterding did not like being constantly reminded
of the great obligations he was under to my father. And Papa was
offended at the way Deterding took past services for granted.

'To give Deterding his due, he was clever enough to foresee the
dangers of an eventual bust-up and to take precautions. That is where
I came in.

'When I left the French Ministry of Supply in 1919, Deterding
made me the liaison between himself and my father—in particular the
guardian of Gulbenkian interests in Venezuela and Mexico. Deterding
reckoned that Father would not criticize his son's work too much.
And I could yelp, on Father's behalf, if necessary.

'Papa agreed to this arrangement and it worked fairly well for a
time. I became "Deterding's Dauphin" and accompanied him to the
United States and South America and for two years had charge of the
South American business. I managed to keep the peace.

'Then Deterding wanted me to go and look after Venezuela:
partly because there was important work to be done: partly to keep me
out of trouble with Pa and so preserve my use as a buffer. When I was
in Rome on holiday, Deterding ordered me to Venezuela "at once".
But Papa had me off the train in Paris and hauled me back. I never
got to Venezuela. Father thought Deterding was banishing me so
that he would be free to interfere with Gulbenkian interests.

'Papa, with his 35 per cent interest in Venezuela, did all the work
and wanted no limelight. But—having brought Deterding into
Venezuela—insisted on the rights of minority shareholders. He stuck
rigidly to his principles and in adopting this line, he frankly made
himself a damned nuisance to the Royal Dutch-Shell.

'The fact is, both men got too big for their boots as they grew
older.

'Deterding, later in life, developed a *folie de grandeur*. He expected to get the kudos for everything. He loved to cut a public figure, making speeches at banquets and sitting on Commissions. Unlike Papa, he accepted a title. This megalomania led him to forsake the "consortium" principle, of which he had been one of the early originators, and to ride roughshod over the rights of minorities.

'I must say Papa's quarrel was not entirely selfish. Of course he was looking after his own interests and had his eye on the main chance. But he was also genuinely concerned about small investors. By 1925 people were following him on the Stock Exchange, thinking "If Gulbenkian is buying, it must be a good thing". In later life, Deterding paid little more than lip-service to such considerations.

'Who was the more to blame, I still can't say, although I was on the inside. As father wrote in his *Memoirs* "oil friendships are slippery". Perhaps it's best to leave it at that.

'For my part, I had become an irritant, instead of a lubricant—the obstacle over whom the two men stumbled. One day I was summoned to Deterding's office and told peremptorily to "get out". The long Gulbenkian-Deterding era of co-operation was over.

'I didn't only lose an income of £5,000 a year and the chance of stepping into Deterding's shoes in the Royal Dutch-Shell. It also meant "back to father". Hence the showdown I was obliged to have with him over my own finances and the beginning of the clash of our two personalities, which eventually deprived me of a trusteeship under his will.'

It furthermore meant Mr Five Per Cent had lost an old ally in future struggles with the oil groups, during and after the Second World War—and a weakening of his own position as the world's only "One Man Oil Power".

4

The popular theory was that Deterding fell out with Gulbenkian over the beautiful Russian-born Lydia Bagratumi.

When they met her she was married to the "White" Armenian General Bagratumi, who was related to the famous Georgian General Bagration. (These surnames are the localized forms of the same name.)

Bagratumi and Bagration had both been fighting against the Reds in the Transcaucasian Civil War, after the Russian Revolution, and Lydia's husband had been unofficially proclaimed head of the new independent Armenian State.

Nubar Gulbenkian told me: 'Deterding met Lydia in London in the early 1920s, when he was introduced by the ex-Duma member, Adjemoff. My father, being interested in the fate of Armenia, met Lydia about the same time. On subsequent social occasions Deterding jumped to the conclusion that Father was trying to cut him out in Lydia's estimation.

'She was certainly an attractive woman and as she and father spoke the same language, they undoubtedly talked a lot together: and Deterding became jealous.

'Father was not really interested in Lydia, but Deterding's dismay amused him: especially when Deterding started heaping literally hundreds of thousands of pounds' worth of jewellery on her—in the mistaken belief that his imaginary rival was up to the same game.

'The great joke, according to Father, was when he learned that Deterding had ordered £300,000 of emeralds from Cartier for Lydia and couldn't pay for them because his annual director's fees had not yet come in.

'I am sure, as Father is concerned anyway, that no woman ever came between him and Deterding. When Deterding and Lydia were free to marry, Father said (and meant) good luck to them.

'When the heir to the Romanoffs, the Grand Duke Cyril, made Lydia "Princesse de Donskaya", father was not impressed. He just laughed. He certainly didn't regret having missed something. Anyway, Lydia dropped this artificial title a few years later.'

In Paris I asked Lady Deterding about the persistent rumour over the breach between her husband and Gulbenkian. She replied: 'In 1924-5, when my husband and Gulbenkian were parting company, I was expecting a baby and knew little about their business.

'I only met Gulbenkian three or four times, when I was married to the Armenian General Bagratumi, who was the last Commander-in-Chief of the Free Armenian Army and was recognized as ruler of the country by Woodrow Wilson, after the First World War.

'There is no truth in the society gossip that my future husband, Henri Deterding, fell out with Gulbenkian over me.

'So far as I know, they never competed to win me with jewels. It's nonsense. Gulbenkian could be charming, if he liked, but I didn't see much of him, as I've said. He was not the type of man to give away something for nothing and I certainly received nothing from him.'

If some woman did come between the two tycoons, it was a detail. The origin of their differences was very much deeper.

20

FAMILY FEUDS

PERHAPS a row between father and son was inevitable in 1925. Calouste Gulbenkian, now fifty-six, had been under tremendous pressure for twelve years, battling single-handed for his rights with the Great Powers and big oil combines. He was no longer so resilient. He was just established as the "One Man Oil Power" and wielded immense influence, which began to go to his head. He became more and more suspicious, as he grew to have more and more to lose. Never having suffered fools gladly, he became a dictator. Everybody —his family, as well as Governments and oil associates—must obey him. Deterding was the first to rebel.

Nubar was next. He was now in his thirtieth year, having made a brilliant start in life: French Prizes at Harrow; two Honours Degrees at Trinity College, Cambridge; the Legion of Honour for his work in the French Ministry of Supply; and five years at Deterding's right hand, where he had established himself as "The Dutchman's Dauphin". Nubar, out of Royal Dutch-Shell, had reached the stage where he wanted paternal recognition, his own money and independence— none of which Mr Five Per Cent was prepared to concede.

Nubar was not the sort of son expected of such a father. He was not cowed into submission and never became another faithful "Yes-man". Nor was he a prodigal son, a playboy, although he had already developed the philosophy that "the object of life is to enjoy it"—and that required appropriate spending money. Nor yet did Nubar cut adrift from Father, in disgust or horror, out of sheer bravado or cowardice, and make a totally different career on his own. On the contrary he reckoned he had as good a brain as his father, if not better, and he knew that some of their oil associates shared this view. So did Mr Five Per Cent. Up to a point Father was proud of Nubar. 'I was the apple of his eye,' says the latter.

But Father was not prepared to yield his patriarchal and paternal authority nor to meet Nubar on equal intellectual terms. 'He consulted me about everything, but he expected me to obey him,' Nubar adds. Up to a point, too, Nubar "respected and admired father", but at the same time he was "absolutely terrified of him" and "resented being treated like a small boy".

In 1925 the "Big Bust-up" with Deterding placed Nubar com-

pletely in his father's power and *eliminated his immediate usefulness.*
Mr Five Per Cent decided it was time his son toed the line. Nubar
realized that now or never was the time for a showdown if he was
ever going to be able to call his soul his own.

Today Nubar looks back on the second phase of "The Big Bust-up"
like this: 'My mother and I were in the same financial predicament.
We were kept on a golden chain, always without a regular allowance
or any money which we could call our own. By the time I was nearing
thirty, I'd still never had a fixed allowance.

'Nor had I ever received a salary from father, although he had been
discussing all his business problems with me for years and sometimes
taking my advice. I worked very hard for him. I bore a good deal of
responsibility and relieved him of much worry. I therefore resented
always having to go to him cap-in-hand for cash.

'I could always have money for a new Rolls or a hunting-box or
another hunter or foreign travel. He wouldn't even refuse me money for
parties or buying jewels for my girl-friends. In his way, he was generous
and understanding. As I have often told you, I was the apple of his eye.

'But we were too much alike. If you insist, we were both men of
character and temperament. I wanted my independence. He wanted
to keep me under his thumb, as if I'd never grown up.

'This ordinary latent father-son antagonism was bound to come to
a head. Although I was terrified of him, I insisted I should be paid a
proper share in the proceeds of "our" business, as of right, and should
cease to be merely the recipient of arbitrary sums, doled out as a favour.
Father protested fiercely that I was always over-spending and didn't
know how to look after money. In reality, he just wanted to keep me
under control. But I knew that he respected people who stood up to
him and took a chance.'

There was another difficulty. Nubar passionately wanted to get
married: for the second time. He couldn't do so without an assured
income. Moreover the girl was anathema to Mr Five Per Cent and
Nubar knew he ran the risk of being cut off unless his income was
assured.

2. *Hermina and Doré*

Nubar's first marriage had caused enough trouble.

When Mr Five Per Cent, Deterding and Cowdray were deep in
the Mexican Eagles deal during the 1918 Armistice and England was

going gay in expectation of "a world fit for heroes to live in", the twenty-two-year-old Nubar's mind was not on business.

Beardless, slim and well-groomed, a gay, witty and attractive man-about-town, Nubar naturally gravitated into the set of post-war "Bright Young Things", the new social world of emancipated women, knee-high skirts and jazz.

He preferred the ball-room to the board-room and, of course, he was to be found at the Victory Ball at the Albert Hall. There his large, brown and already monocled eye caught a glimpse of a dark, lissom young girl, sparkling and vivacious, dancing the fox-trot.

Nubar fell in love at first sight. He relates: 'I was infatuated. She turned out to be Hermina Rodriguez-Feijo, daughter of a middle-class business man from Corunna, who owned slaves in Cuba. She was dazzling—a real Spanish beauty. We had lots of fun.

'Her father amused me by telling of one of his slaves, named Pedro, who always carried his Panama hat under his arm when it rained. Asked why, Pedro replied: "My head belongs to Mr Rodriguez, but my hat belongs to me."

'But Mr Five Per Cent was not amused. He thought Hermina wasn't good enough for his only son. Besides, she and her parents were staunch Roman Catholics, who would give their consent to our marriage only on condition that our children should be brought up in that faith. Father did not object to my sowing wild oats, but he violently opposed what he considered was an unsuitable marriage. In spite of his own many affaires, he deeply respected marriage as an institution, and he had little sympathy with what he thought was my more light-hearted and less business-like approach to it. He hadn't much time for sentiment. Moreover he cut a figure as a patron of the Armenian Church and took a poor view of his son marrying outside it.

'So—he refused to meet my beautiful Spaniard: and four years passed—father all the time trusting that my infatuation would blow over.

'Eventually, in 1922, we plucked up courage and got married in my rooms on the fifth floor of the London Ritz, directly above the suite then occupied by my father. Neither of the families was represented.

'We deliberately had no wedding picture taken, in case it should leak out and cause the sort of personal publicity which Father hated and despised. We chose the Ritz for the same reason. We had influence there and could trust the management to keep the ceremony as secret as possible. There was no point in gratuitously antagonizing Father any more than necessary. Three years later, Hermina and I woke up to reality and we parted.'

Mr Five Per Cent had the dubious pleasure of saying to his son 'I told you so'. Next time, he hoped, Nubar would think more seriously and choose a more suitable girl—a girl from Society, whom he would marry according to the rites of the Armenian Church.

But there was more matrimonial trouble immediately ahead. By 1925 Nubar already had his twinkling eye on the former music hall star, Doré Plowden, two years his senior.

By then she had been married twice—to Henry O'Hara, an Irish-Australian, who lived in the United States, and Tim Freeland, a wealthy Englishman and had retired from the stage.

In 1914 she was starring in *Keep Smiling* at the Alhambra, where she made a grand entrance down a long flight of steps half-way through the show to sing "I do kind of feel I'm in love". Subalterns in the Guards used to arrive late, just in time for this appearance, and give her a terrific ovation as she sang to them from the footlights.

In 1915 she was starring in the Charlot Revue *5064 Gerrard*, also at the Alhambra, wearing a black and a white egret hat, each costing £80.

Her next war-time show was a C. B. Cochran Revue at the Ambassadors Theatre. Co-starring with her was Alice Delysia. Afterward she succeeded the late Gertrude Lawrence in *Buzz-Buzz*. Between 1916 and 1919, she did some filming in Hollywood. Then she retired.

When Nubar met her, he was already beginning to be noticed in the gossip columns. He had taken up fox-hunting—much to his cautious father's annoyance. Nubar had also started his since unbroken fashion of wearing an orchid in his buttonhole—even when riding to hounds— a foible which once goaded an M.F.H. to remark: 'Don't you think it's rather strange to wear an orchid in the hunting field?' To which Nubar replied: 'No stranger than seeing a bearded and monocled Oriental on horseback.'

Soon Nubar and the glittering dark Doré were noticed about together in international society and the West End, and the omniscient Mr Five Per Cent got to hear of it. He did not approve—of the girl, the orchid, or the publicity.

The breach with Hermina was bad enough. All the difficulties of divorce proceedings with a Roman Catholic were looming up. And now it looked as if Nubar was heading straight for another scandal with a twice-married woman. To Mr Five Per Cent this seemed irresponsible, indecent and impossible.

That was the set-up, coinciding with the Deterding "bust-up", in which Nubar sought recognition from Father and money in his own right. His requests were inevitably refused.

3. First Showdown

Father and son were hardly on speaking terms. But Nubar stuck to his arguments. He had protected Gulbenkian interests in the Royal Dutch-Shell, particularly in Venezuela, for five years—without receiving any pay from his father. He had served as a buffer between his father and Deterding—relieving the former of much worry and unpleasantness—and had received no pay from Mr Five Per Cent for this either. Now he had lost a £5,000-a-year job, entirely through his father's intervention, and he was receiving no compensation. Finally, he had lost his position as Deterding's "Dauphin" and all expectations of a directorship in the Royal Dutch, for which he also demanded compensation.

Mr Five Per Cent replied with counter-charges: that the "bust-up" had occurred because of Nubar's "inefficiency", "impetuosity" and "short-sightedness"; that Nubar's loyalty was not above suspicion. In addition there were the criticisms of Nubar's private life—his "irresponsibility", "extravagance" and "inability to handle money".

In the middle of this battle of wills, Mr Five Per Cent moved out of 38 Hyde Park Gardens, which he had been so proud to occupy a quarter of a century earlier, and started to build a palace in Paris. Rita was left in No. 38 to live out the remainder of the lease there, and so the English Channel was put between father and son. Nubar categorically refused to go and share the house at 27 Quai D'Orsay with his parents. He was courting Doré in England.

Emboldened by Nubar, Rita's husband, too, started a battle for recognition and independence. Kvork Essayan had also been working for Mr Five Per Cent for years, without a regular, fixed salary. Most of the Essayan millions had either been lost in Attaturk's Revolution, devoted to Armenian charities or frittered away by the second generation. Kvork was just as dependent on the tyrannical whim of Gulbenkian as was Nubar.

It was a miserable time for Nevarte. She was fast getting very plump but could still dance two or three young men off their feet in an evening. Calouste had virtually walked out of the house and was fobbing her off with the new art palace at 51 Avenue D'Iéna, a stone's throw from the Eiffel Tower and Arc de Triomphe. He himself was well known in his own small circle to keep a retinue of mistresses, including the current favourite at the Paris Ritz. But Nevarte was still the matriarch, to whom Calouste paid formal respects daily, and as such she retained an influence. All she wanted was peace—and fun. Her sympathies were therefore with Nubar and Rita's husband.

Mr Five Per Cent thus found that his family ranged against him. True to character he calculated that the opposing forces were too strong for him alone—that he had better compromise—and tacitly admitted that his case was none too strong.

He gave way. Nubar relates: 'He formally provided me with 5 per cent in his own 5 per cent in the Iraq Petroleum Company, plus £5,000 on account and £500 a year for three years. Kvork, who had been in much the same invidious position, was also provided with a 2½ per cent interest in the famous Iraq Petroleum Company 5 per Cent and some ready money.

The face-saving clause was, of course, the "three years". The family had got away with it for a time. They were still on the golden thread—only it was just a little longer.

Father-and-son relations were still strained, but Mr Five Per Cent did not give way to malice for long, either in private or petroleum business.

Nubar harboured no resentment: 'Having stood up to Father for the first time and won, I felt better and I think I earned his respect. Of course he continued to try and dominate me and the rest of the family and to keep tabs on everything we said or did. He was incredibly suspicious. And he loved to feel he had us in his power. That was his nature.

'But one couldn't help admiring his incredible energy and attention to detail, which were some of the secrets of his success. And, in his way, he was generous. It was not a question of how much one spent, but how one spent it. He could not bear waste. Where we disagreed was on what one could define as extravagance. He chose to invest in pictures. I preferred to invest in life. I have only one.'

4. Doré and Diana

Nubar was now in a position to think constructively about divorce and re-marriage. With difficulty, a decree was obtained in France, dissolving his marriage with Hermina, who thereupon faded from the picture until eleven years later.

As soon as he was free, in 1928, Nubar and Doré got married quietly at Prince's Row Registrar's Office, London. Thirty years later, she is still a shapely, vivacious and smart woman. Allowing for the dated fashions and photography of the time, she must have been dazzling.

She told me: 'Although our marriage ended twenty years ago and I had two previous husbands, Nubar was—and is—the great love of my life. I still keep the photograph of him as a baby, given to me by his mother, in the most prominent position on my piano. I never travel without it.

'Now we are both more than sixty. I suppose we should both have steadied down. But we haven't. The small boy in Nubar has never died. He still likes to dress up and show off. And I am off to New York, California and Las Vegas for six months to see an old boy-friend and have a good time. But I shall never find another Nubar.

'We had a lot of fun—"baby parties" and all the absurd things we "Bright Young Things" used to get up to in the 'twenties. I learned to drive Nubar's fast cars and we won more than one Concours d'elegance on the Riviera. Then there was our craze for golf.

'Our great disappointment was never having a baby. It wasn't for want of trying. If we had had a son, perhaps Calouste would eventually have become reconciled to our marriage. But he never was convinced that I, twice-married previously and an ex-actress, was the right wife for his only son.

'Nubar only dared introduce me to him once before our wedding. Calouste was charming and polite—as one expects from a man who is interested in women. But our first conversation was superficial and Nubar and I agreed it was best not to tell him we had already arranged to get married.

'But a fortnight afterwards, on our golfing honeymoon in Paris, we broke the news to him. We expected an explosion. But he seemed to accept the *fait accompli*. Soon we became quite friends and he accepted me as a true daughter-in-law. He was quite sweet in many ways. In fact we got on so well that I was able to patch up the smouldering row he'd had with Nubar about money three years earlier. As a reward, Calouste gave me a jewelled bird in a nest of pearls.

'It was quite valueless—intrinsically. When I was burgled in 1956 it was left behind. The thieves must have been experts. They took my crocodile jewel-case, gold watches, pens and pencils, a gold frame and trinkets, which had real as well as sentimental value. But not the bird's nest. I still treasure it as a gesture of friendship from Nubar's father. Perhaps he was wise, as it happened, not to give me an expensive present. Otherwise I should have no token of his friendship today.

'For some years Nubar and I got along splendidly. We were very

happy and had fun. But I was too green and innocent—in spite of
having been on the stage and knocked about the world with two
previous husbands. I suspected nothing when Nubar and our friend,
Lady Diana Gibb (daughter of Lord Lovelace) were reported (wrongly
as it turned out) to have had an air crash together on the way down
to the Coronation Naval Review in 1937, only Nubar was in it. His
arms were badly burned and two passengers were killed. Diana used
to stay with us, in London and Paris, and I couldn't believe it when
a "kind friend" told me he was in love with her. But this was apparently
so. He started divorce proceedings to please her.

'It was all very complicated. I was still deeply in love with him and
sincerely wanted our marriage to go on. I didn't in the least want a
divorce. Nor was I mercenary. I just wanted to remain married to
Nubar.

'But, like his father, he is a perfectionist. He was not content with
a judicial separation. In the end he obtained a decree of nullity on the
grounds that at the time of his second marriage, to me, he was still
technically married to Hermina! And then Diana would have nothing
more to do with him!

'Poor Nubar. I was sorry for him. I am still devoted to him. He
and his new wife are good friends of mine. We often meet and lunch
together. Marie is a sweet and charming person. I am also friends with
Nubar's sister, Rita. We are joining each other in Las Vegas and Reno
for a spree.'

So Mr Five Per Cent's fears worked out again. Nubar *had* made a
mistake over his second marriage.

5. Marie: The Car Queen

No sooner was Nubar out of the divorce and nullity tangle which
seemed to Mr Five Per Cent's tidy mind a thoroughly slipshod business,
than a third ravishing brunette entered their lives.

Diana, the mousy companion of Nubar and Doré at "Baby
Parties", faded out and into her place rode Mrs Marie Samuelson.

She was married to Horace Samuelson, one of Nubar's Harrow
contemporaries who had survived the holocaust of the First World
War.

He was a wealthy member of Dreyfus & Co., the City merchants,
and they had two schoolboy sons; Tony, who was later to join the

Iraq Petroleum Co., and Peter, who was to serve in the Royal Navy in the approaching war and provide Marie with her first grandchild.

Oddly, the stylish Mrs Samuelson and Nubar Gulbenkian never met until 1934, although she was well known in the Shires and born a de Ayala, of the French champagne aristocracy; an heiress in her own right and a member of the international moneyed set which Nubar frequented. But it was in the hunting field they eventually found one another.

In wit, argument and vigour Nubar and Marie were well matched. She belonged to the cosmopolitan upper crust to which Mr Five Per Cent always hoped his son would aspire. She was wealthy, intelligent and experienced enough to make Nubar the sort of wife his father wanted for him. She shared the French background, which Mr Five Per Cent had adopted, and could even lip-read in French and English.

But by 1939 Nubar was hard up. Father had stopped his money.

A second big father-and-son row was stoking up and had yet to be settled. The war intervened and anyway Marie's divorce did not go through until April 1948.

It was in June 1948, in Lisbon, that Nubar and Marie got married, he for the third time, she for the second.

*   *   *   *   *

Pinpricks, mostly concerned with motor-cars, contributed to the second great family "bust-up".

Nubar and his future wife, Marie, loved fine cars as they loved thoroughbred hunters.

But Mr Five Per Cent—with his concentration on "essentials" and belief that 'privacy is the most precious thing money can buy'— was content with unobtrusive dark runabouts. Nubar did once succeed talking his father into a black Rolls, but they never really saw eye to eye with each other on cars.

For the last few years, two of the finest limousines Rolls-Royce and Hoopers, the coachbuilders, ever produced, have been regularly drawn up outside the London Ritz—numbered NSG 2 and NSG 3.

Marie says the numbers are 2 and 3 because Nubar Sarkis Gulbenkian has been married three times and his wife twice.

The truth is that Nubar, the perfectionist, traced NSG to Edinburgh as soon as three-letter number-plates came out before the war. Hoopers watched for NSG 1 to come up. But an Edinburgh City Councillor appropriated it.

NSG 2 is the magnificent Rolls with the purple bodywork, set off in dignified black, in which Nubar is driven—with the windows wide open for the fresh air and scenery—by his Portuguese chauffeur.

NSG 3 is the even more magnificent Rolls, belonging to Marie Gulbenkian—an eye-catching woman in her Persian lamb fur coat, Court shoes and diamonds.

This is her "Silver Cloud" model, the first of its kind Rolls-Royce produced, and she drives it herself. Over the back seat a perch is specially fitted for her miniature peach-coloured poodle to see out.

But neither vehicle is a match for Mr and Mrs Gulbenkian's unique Rolls-Royce, which they call the "Goldfish Bowl". This was built to their own specification and is kept on the Continent for touring.

The entire top is transparent plastic. "So that I can see out and my wife won't get blown about," says Nubar. "It's the perfect answer to how to remain happily married though motoring with one's wife. I have been married three times and I don't want to lose my third wife.'

This wonderful £6,000 (export) job in fawn and dark blue, with upholstery to match, is air-conditioned. It has an automatic pilot, which works out the speed for keeping the next appointment. But there is no radio, television nor cocktail cabinet because Nubar thinks they would be "out of place".

Now that Norah Docker has been dethroned and lost her Daimlers, Marie Gulbenkian is the undisputed "Car Queen". The "Goldfish Bowl" puts the Gold Car, the Zebra Car and "Stardust" in the shade. 'The only drawback about NSG 2 and 3 and the "Goldfish Bowl" is that everybody knows them and stops and stares,' says Marie. 'And you know how the Gulbenkians hate publicity.'

Nubar's pre-war cars were just as eye-catching and Mr Five Per Cent hated them.

There was the brown and beige open touring Rolls-Royce, which Nubar called 'the chocolate and sick'. This was the largest and most spectacular car of its kind in its day, before Hitler's giant Mercedes-Benz tourers appeared.

In 1935 a surprise call reached Nubar from an Air Marshal speaking on behalf of Buckingham Palace, and wanting to hire the "chocolate and sick" for King George V to use at the Silver Jubilee Royal Air Force Display.

Nubar was 'not in the car hire business', as he observed and all he asked was £2 for his chauffeur.

Next year King Edward VIII borrowed the car for the Naval Review in 1937, which explains how Nubar came to have his air crash.

In 1956, Queen Elizabeth II used Nubar's other Rolls-Royce—the

big green old-fashioned open tourer, which he kept on the Continent
and has now been replaced with the "Goldfish Bowl". It was ideal
as a vehicle for the Queen, coursing slowly through the African
crowds on the Nigerian Royal Tour, as well as for enabling Nubar to
see the view.

So he has the unique distinction of having lent his motor-car to
three reigning monarchs, which may seem harmless enough and indeed
gratifying. But that sort of thing did not appeal to furtive Mr Five Per
Cent. To him it seemed unnecessary ostentation, superfluous flaunting
of wealth and gratuitous propaganda for Communists and Socialists—
just the type of thing to bring more unwanted publicity to the
Gulbenkian family. Again there was a shindy. It just shows how father
and son were again getting on each other's nerves towards 1940.

6. Problem Child

It must be admitted, Nubar is rather special. 'A bundle of nerves.
He'll go out like a light one day,' they nod their heads at the Ritz.
'He eats too much, and upsets his tummy,' warns Doré. 'A fuss-pot,'
say the domestic staff. No wonder he irritated his equally fastidious
father.

I have listened spellbound to his altercation with the head chefs of
the Ritz and Savoy over the proper ingredients of Poulet Vendome
and Poulet Rose de Mai—whether one or the other is stuffed with
foie gras or something not quite so rich. He expects everything to be
just so.

There is a wonderful punctilio when you go to see him. 'Come and
see me at seventeen minutes past two,' he may say. 'I have to see
somebody else at three, but I can give you until three minutes to three.'

A snack is wheeled into his permanent £20-a-day suite at the
Ritz and he peels a peach with his own silver knife, like a surgeon
performing an eye operation, downs it with half a bottle of champagne
and luncheon is over.

'Black or white?' he says, offering the coffee. Then 'Milk or
cream?' Whereupon he takes the silver jug and, fixing his monocle on
the little Crown Derby cups, remarks: 'The object of the exercise is to
get the milk into the cup.'

'A glass of brandy? . . . Cognac, Spanish or Armenian?' You've
never tried Armenian. And he observes: 'There are some advantages

in being an Armenian Churchman and keeping in with the Armenian authorities.'

Or you may prefer sherry. 'Tio Pepe, Manzanilla or Brown?' He produces three bottles, wrapped in gold leaf, from what looks like an enormous cigar box, and says: 'I have just received these samples from the Directors at Xeres. And here's a summary of the history.' He opens another box. . . .

'And a cigar? . . . Havana or Jamaican? . . . Large, medium or short? . . . Right, let me pierce it for you.' And he produces a small gold cigar-cutter to perform another delicate operation.

'Now make yourself comfortable.' While you are doing so, you notice the detail of the astonishing figure opposite, as it settles into the arm-chair with the back to the light, thus exposing your own features to the full glare. . . .

The rigid monocle; the glistening, long, blue-rinsed beard; the pearl tie-pin fastening the cravat in the pin-stripe City suiting; the manicured hands, fondling the carefully warmed tulip brandy-glass; the fresh orchid in the buttonhole; even the eyebrows seem to have been tweezered into place; surely the most immaculate man in the world, and, strangely, not in the least ridiculous, although he resembles a Soviet cartoonist's version of a "Capitalist Bloodsucker".

'A few minutes, Miss Wallace,' he says over your head, as a dumpy woman in black disappears into the bedroom. Then he whispers: 'She's done my hands for forty years.'

And now, what do you want? You explain and he answers in quickfire staccato, which would seize-up a dictaphone and reduce a champion stenographer to helplessness.

'Have you got that?' You haven't. He repeats it. 'All right, you can quote me on that. But are you sure you've got it right? Would you like me to go through it again? We must be accurate. Check, check, check . . . that was my father's motto . . . and it's mine too.'

When he was sixty, he developed a mysterious fever. Specialists in half a dozen countries couldn't diagnose it. But he managed to get a laugh out of the repeated blood-tests and injections. 'I call myself a human pin-cushion,' he said, adding: 'You can quote me on that.'

But when we were discussing his three marriages and their effect on his relationship with Mr Five Per Cent, he remarked: 'All my wives have been good ones. But you'd better go steady on that. Don't go calling me "The Blue Beard of the Ritz".'

He gets more fun out of two cheap toys than his three Rolls-Royces: a little bone hunting-horn, picked up for a few marks in Germany, and a baby set of bagpipes, bought for a few shillings off the pavement in

Oxford Street. It's a remarkable sight to see "Blue Beard" prancing round the Ritz blowing them.

As Doré says, Nubar has never quite grown up. When his sister, Rita, moved from the art-filled Gulbenkian palace at 51 Avenue d'Iéna, to a smaller house at 30 Rue Emile Menier, he delighted in calling the new address 'Emily Manure Street'.

He likes his little joke. When Rita unexpectedly found an expert from the French Ministry of Fine Arts under her bed, ear-marking the contents of No. 51 for Probate and Scheduling, Nubar could not resist remarking: 'At her time of life she ought to have felt very gratified. . . . I understand she was *not* included among the antiques!'

Nubar and Rita have always sparred. 'We have been good friends,' he says, 'since she got over putting her hair up when I was still at Harrow and stopped giving herself airs. She no longer imagines she is more advanced than I am, although she is four years younger.'

She is sensitive about her age. When we first met, she said outright: 'I want to talk to you. Aren't you the man who wrote I was four years *older*? I suppose that's Nubar. He's always talking to the Press.'

These Gulbenkians, they're sticklers for detail. When Nubar gets himself up for the aristocratic Portuguese sport of hunting hares on horseback, he wears fabulous dark-grey drain-pipes, an Eton-type red-lined jacket, black sash, boots with fur chaps and a large grey sombrero. (No orchids.) And Marie accompanies him in a similar costume.

He likes to boast of a "little deal" concerning his braces. He chose a decorative new Austrian pair. Price: 31 Austrian schillings (under 10s.). Then he showed the shop-assistant the pair he was wearing and said: 'I bought these here twenty years ago.' Asked the shop assistant: 'Would you care to sell them, Sir?' Nubar asked: 'How much?'

'Twenty schillings.'

'It's a deal.'

Nubar's later comment: 'Not the biggest deal of my life, but most successful.'

He had plenty of chuckles over the society "Wedding of the Year" in 1956, when his nephew, Mikael Essayan, married Geraldine Guinness at St Margaret's, Westminster.

"Dina" is daughter of the late Sir Kenelm Lee Guinness of K.L.G. Sparking Plugs. 'We supply the oil. She supplies the ignition,' he wisecracked. Alternatively—although she is not in the brewing branch of Guinnesses—'Now the family is properly lubricated.'

He was also amused by his stud-groom's comment down in Buckinghamshire: 'Good. So now money's coming into the family.'

He is the only really jolly millionaire I know: "Mr Hundred Per Cent". He ought to be appointed public relations officer for the diminishing and unpopular millionaire class. But, as his father's friend, Lord Radcliffe, has said to me: 'I am very fond of Nubar, although he can be very trying at times.' The wonder is that Mr Five Per Cent ever produced such a son. It's no wonder they quarrelled.

And now it's time to go. Nubar looks at his gold wrist-watch. It's three minutes to three. You hurriedly get your overcoat half on and, as you pass through the door, put out a hand for a farewell shake. 'Not across the threshold. It's very unlucky,' says Nubar, dragging you back.

Deep down, you learn, he is still a suspicious, Armenian oriental: like father, like son. His birthday massacre of 1896 has left its mark.

'Nubar is so clever that he makes mistakes which a stupid man could never have committed,' says his Uncle Atvarte, who is only four years older and a friend. 'The great weakness of the Armenian race is that we can't co-operate.'

So we come to the second great showdown between father and son, in 1940.

7. Second Showdown

The clock went back fifteen years. Again Nubar wanted paternal recognition, his own money and the independence it would give him to marry once more. And his case was stronger than in 1925. He had his father's formal agreement to let him have 5 per cent of the proceeds of the famous Five Per Cent interest in the Iraq Petroleum Company. The Iraq Petroleum Company, producing more than 3,500,000 tons for five years, so Nubar was entitled to more considerable sums than the £5,000 a year he had been receiving. He had helped to see his father through the "Red Line" crisis of 1928, the British Oil Development intervention in the 1930s and various marketing difficulties. He was a Director of Mr Five Per Cent's subsidiaries, Participations & Investments ("Pandi") of Toronto. Nubar was also forty-four.

But seventy-one-year-old Mr Five Per Cent was more difficult than ever.

The old arguments were revived—Nubar's alleged "irresponsibility", his "extravagance", "inability to look after money" and "frivolity". But what was really at stake was the huge fortune now pouring out of the deserts of Iraq annually. When it came to big money like this, Mr Five Per Cent formed second thoughts about giving Nubar and Kvork the freedom which such great wealth commands. He visualized his son and son-in-law getting out of all control. Besides, the war was on—the demand for oil would increase—the annual proceeds from Iraq might increase too—the family might get split up—and there was no knowing what Nubar might get away with. This nightmare was more than Mr Five Per Cent's power complex and innate suspicion could tolerate.

Nubar could get no satisfaction. Contact between father and son ceased. Life became wretched for Nevarte, who was the only link. This upset Nubar, who adored his mother, and he realized he had to act firmly once more.

He summed up his father's weaknesses thus—pride in his solitary victory against the world and a refusal to admit that anybody could get the better of him; pride in being the power behind the scenes and in the avoidance of publicity; pride in the power which unlimited wealth gives over people and represents as a token of success.

At those prides Nubar struck with a frontal attack. He brought a legal action against his father in the High Court for his legitimate share in his father's profits in "Pandi".

It was the "Phoney War" period and there was every prospect of a long, complicated and sensational case, revealing not only differences between father and son but much more of the Gulbenkian interests than Mr Five Per Cent cared to have known.

At the very start, the newspapers began referring to the eminent, but not widely known, C. S. Gulbenkian as "The Mystery Millionaire" and "The Richest Man in the World". The old man writhed.

'I'll ruin him . . . I'll ruin him!' he screamed round the vestibules of the London Ritz, to the astonishment of the suave staff.

Nubar says: 'The row was touched off by my bringing an 18s. 6d. roast chicken into the office for lunch. Father thought this was an ostentatious piece of extravagance and a breach of office discipline, which could not be tolerated. I took the view that I was a responsible man, nearing middle age, as well as a director, and that it was up to me when and where I chose to lunch and what I ate .

'The resulting lawsuit became a test whether father owned me lock-stock-and-barrel, mind-body-and-soul, whether I was simply his slave, with my freedom of action and personality under his control.

'My claims required an investigation of Father's business affairs for at least the previous ten years, in order that the amount of my 5 per cent of his Five Per Cent could be established.

'My lawyers accordingly compelled him to produce no less than

987,000 documents, weighing a ton, in the High Court. This attracted much publicity. So did reference to $1\frac{1}{2}$ tons of solid gold (then worth £450,000) which Father was stated to keep in his safes. One consignment was so heavy that it smashed its way through the steel shelf of a London safe deposit into somebody else's compartment.

'Father called the production of nearly a million documents "the hell of a nuisance", as it was. This, coupled with the unwonted publicity, was more than the old man could stand. I learned of this from a passing remark which Father made in private to his counsel: "Isn't it clever of my son to think of making me unearth all those papers?" The counsel replied: "I thought you were here to fight your son and now you are praising him!" To which Mr Five Per Cent answered: "He's getting tough. He's a chip of the old block."

'After three days washing Gulbenkian dirty linen in public, I withdrew my action unconditionally. Subsequently father paid me £7,500 over and above the £5,000 a year I was supposed to be getting and costs amounting to £30,000.

'That must have been the most expensive chicken that was ever cooked!'

Mr Five Per Cent agreed to "forget it". As usual, he reckoned it was no use having regrets. Diplomatic relations were resumed between father and son. Nubar thinks that the case actually won him more respect from his domineering father. For a few years they got along better.

But Mr Five Per Cent harboured a grudge deep down. Sir Kenneth Clark, then Director of the National Gallery and one of the old man's new cronies, told me: 'He was terribly upset by the lawsuit. He even suspected me—and other innocent people—of putting Nubar up to the action and helping to get him down. I have never known anybody so suspicious. He checked up on us to fantastic extremes—cross-checking every scrap of information—and even threatened us. I don't believe he ever quite got over the case.'

The wounds festered again three years later, in 1952–53, when the third great family row occurred over Nevarte's will and dowry recorded in Chapter 5. That in turn led to the removal of Nubar's name from the list of trustees of the future multi-million Gulbenkian Foundation in 1951 and a sea of trouble after his death.

*   *   *   *   *

Anyway, Nubar Gulbenkian was in a position to marry Marie Samuelson in 1948, when she came out of the Red Cross. The ceremony took place in Lisbon, where Mr Five Per Cent was then living. This time he was forewarned and gave his blessing.

'About time you got it right!' and 'Left it a bit late, haven't you?' were some of his comments. But he thoroughly approved. After all she had liquid assets—not oil, true, but Mr Five Per Cent could settle for champagne.

To everybody's astonishment, including Marie's, he left her an annuity of £2,000 a year.

His regret was that Nubar did not have a son and heir.

*　　　*　　　*　　　*　　　*

After Nubar, it was Rita's turn for a wigging.

Some ten years after her marriage (in 1920), she was robbed of her jewellery and this provoked another family row.

A relative recalls: 'Her father never distributed too much jewellery round the women of the family. But a rich man's daughter is bound to collect some odds and ends in time, such as Rita's twenty-first birthday emeralds. And she lost the lot. Father got to hear of this and there was another terrible scene. The result was that poor Rita's allowance was cut for a time and Kvork's own position was not exactly improved by the incident. It was some years before things were patched up.'

But in the end Kvork and Rita came out of their differences with Mr Five Per Cent better than Nubar.

21

CASANOVA

IN 1945, ten years before Mr Five Per Cent died, aged eighty-six, the
time came for a very direct question. A member of the family asked:
'Have you ever slipped up? If so, we feel we ought to know. We
don't want to find some strange little Gulbenkians clamouring for
support after you're gone. Please tell us if we've got a little relation
we don't know anything about.'

This question was not so impertinent as it may seem because little,
wizened five-feet-eight Mr Five Per Cent was a spare-time Casanova.
He went about the business of the boudoir and boardroom with equal
application. As he said, he regarded women as 'part of the rhythm of a
man's life'—an aid to equilibrium and efficiency.

His attitude towards sex was strictly Oriental.

He maintained a carefully selected and changing harem. Only the
best satisfied his collector's instinct. He was not a hoarder. One
exquisite acquisition was frequently being replaced by something better.
The discards were "disposed of" as if they were comparatively inferior
objets d'art.

Gulbenkian was also a pioneer. He sought untapped sources of
beauty as watchfully as fresh oilfields or unrecognized masterpieces.
He was a keen prospector who did not compete in well-worn fields or
in the open market; he preferred to develop his own discoveries. He
nurtured the flowers he gathered by the wayside as tenderly as the
gardener he claimed to be in his *Who's Who* recreations. They were,
so to speak, bedded out in luxurious private apartments in Paris and
elsewhere—wherever he happened to be living.

But the lease was never taken in the name of Gulbenkian. He was
no exhibitionist. His passion for a privacy, amounting to anonymity, applied not only to his business life and his official domestic
circle.

He was miserly over his mistresses. He gloated over them in the velvet and brocade magnificence of the regal quarters provided for them.

Occasionally, however, the girls insisted on getting an airing and displaying the gowns, gems and furs lavished upon them—but they were not exhibited until they were thoroughly groomed for stardom; then they appeared at his side in the opulent resorts he frequented.

He was tactful. There was no point in giving ammunition or offence to such straight-laced associates as Lord Revelstoke. His behaviour towards the girls in public was positively courtly, with appropriate Olde Worlde, Continental hand-kissing, dignified bows to right and left and an ever-ready arm to squire the ladies in. Not for Mr Five Per Cent from Old Stambul the more casual behaviour of Nubar's Bright Young Things.

He must have been one of the most earnest exponents of the now threadbare (and shallow) philosophy that he was 'not being *mentally* unfaithful to his wife', as he used to explain.

He and Nevarte remained workably married for sixty years. She also was Armenian and understood her husband's need for "rhythm". She even found her own amusements. She was often escorted by a handsome Swedish Count when her husband was otherwise engaged. Late in life, when she was buxom, she still maintained her quota of brave young men she whirled round the ballroom.

Sometimes Calouste and Nevarte even consulted each other about their extra-curriculum activities. She appreciated people and her ungregarious husband valued her advice. There was never much risk of either of them creating a public scandal or getting involved in divorce. Mr and Mrs Gulbenkian reached a practical understanding, which was in keeping with their background and their time. Nevarte's miseries were caused by his perpetual spying and restraint, his temper and constant interference—not by his other women. She remained the matriarch and she knew it. Besides, she was good tempered by nature.

Calouste's wealth enabled them to evolve their double system of double life. Their paths seldom crossed, except at the customary noon and evening appearances of Mr Five Per Cent at home.

Nevarte's habitat, after 1925, was the finest private house in Paris, 51 Avenue d'Iéna, off the Champs Elysées, where was housed the most valuable private art collection in Europe. The staff was run by a distant Armenian relative, Virginie Keurhadjian, herself a professional photographer. This arrangement baulked prying eyes and gossip. The setting was superbly adapted for the parties Nevarte adored.

Her brother Atvarte says: 'The house was flanked by a thirty-foot barricade and festooned with every imaginable burglar alarm—it cost thousands of pounds—and everybody spied on everybody else. The fabulous contents were constantly being checked and cross-checked to see that nobody stole anything. Nevertheless, Nevarte managed to have fun there.'

Calouste preferred the intimacy of his permanent suite at the Ritz in the Place Vendôme, near the theatres and smart restaurants. With entrances fore and aft, a maze of corridors, several staircases and lifts, he could come and go unnoticed. At the same time he could keep an eye on visiting magnates. He could infiltrate or extricate his little "distractions" unobtrusively. He might even spot a new diversion.

His money, and his old connection with César Ritz commanded the loyalty of the hotel staff; there was no gossip about him in the bars which, anyway, he never frequented. Occasionally Nevarte even accompanied him to the Ritz, when he had done his stint at home. The suite was no secret.

His "rhythm" was conducted with precision and depended on the orchestration of a remarkable woman, Elize Soulas. She was the French teacher from Rita's English school during the First World War. One day Mr Gulbenkian paid a surprise visit to his lively young daughter and asked her 'Who's your favourite member of the staff?'

Rita answered: 'Mlle Soulas.'

She was engaged almost immediately (at a greatly increased salary) as Rita's resident private governess.

Elize fitted perfectly into the complicated Gulbenkian household and developed a genius for dealing with the delicate matrimonial situation she found there. She was French and sophisticated enough to take in her stride the comings and goings of her employers; moreover, she could efface herself like a chameleon.

She became indispensable to Mr and Mrs Gulbenkian in arranging their varying rendezvous, buying suitable presents, paying bills, taking or delivering messages, and generally smoothing out difficulties. Every member of the family was temperamental, but Elize coped with them all.

There was the day when her employers' respective escorts each had a car smash. First Mrs Gulbenkian's Swedish Count was taken to hospital and the grief-stricken mistress of the house had to be soothed. The best doctors and a private ward had to be arranged for the Swede. Flowers had to be sent. Repeated inquiries had to be made.

In the midst of this panic, another S O S reached Elize by telephone. The Canadian lovely, of whom Mr Gulbenkian was then enamoured, had also crashed and been taken to hospital. And he was frantic. Was she disfigured? Was a plastic surgeon needed? Was she comfortable? A torrent of questions had to be answered convincingly and the protocol issue of flowers, fruit and candies delivered. Nothing but the best would do. And, of course, the Gulbenkian name had to be kept out of the newspapers in both cases.

A great diplomat was lost to the Embassies when Mlle Elize Soulas took private service.

One of her duties was to attend to the beautification of Gulbenkian's raw material. Sometimes he spotted a simple girl in a café, or even on the street, and decided there and then she had the makings of a master-piece. Elize then had to locate her, talk her into taking up residence in the luxurious flat kept for this purpose. Next, the girl had to be set up in fitting style. Elize escorted her to the leading *couturières* and jewellers, selected her new hair style, decided on an appropriate perfume. Elocution and lessons in etiquette sometimes had to be arranged, too. The product had to be perfect. Gulbenkian was satisfied with nothing short of perfection.

Occasionally there was a hitch: parents had to be pacified; a girl, taken out of her natural surroundings and her own circle would get lonely and break into tears or hysterics.

There was the awful occasion when Nicole—just out of the slums of Paris—disgraced herself and Calouste in public. It was her first outing with Gulbenkian. He and Elize having judged she was ready for presentation to cosmopolitan society. They had taken more pains with her than, perhaps, any of his other fancies. She was gowned and jewelled like a queen, and looked like one. He told her so, and confided in Elize that he had never taken more pride in introducing any woman to his own world. He almost purred as the *maître d'hôtel* bowed them to their table. He had, of course, ordered a superb dinner.

Course after course followed, with appropriate wines, and Nicole became more and more silent. At last her favourite sweet arrived. One spoonful, and she was tragically, pitifully and violently sick.

Many a man would have turned tail. Instead, Mr Five Per Cent calmly took her on his arm to the powder room and sent his car for Elize. Nicole was rushed home, sponged, given smelling salts and a sedative. Inside the hour, Elize had her back at the Ritz, in another lovely gown, and the evening continued.

Little was beyond Elize. She was even equal to the unenviable task of getting rid of the discards. Some of the girls began to take their miraculous luxury for granted and wouldn't give it up. Some hinted at legal proceedings. More than one pretended she was having a baby. There were scenes—rage, tears and hysteria. Elize had to be a psychologist, sympathetic and patient, but shrewd and firm. It was seldom easy. Gulbenkian had no time for such complications and would take no part in the unpleasantnesses. That was Elize's department.

Sometimes the situation had to be dealt with quickly. One occupant of the flat was seldom on her way out before her successor was on the way in.

The one ace in Elize's hand—which triumphed over all queens!—was Gulbenkian's generosity. He expected her to make a fair settlement, to see that the outgoing woman was comfortably set up for the future—not too extravagantly, but well. He never asked for the jewellery or furs to be returned.

I am told that several girls received £10,000 and one old faithful as much as £100,000.

'No,' was the family verdict, 'the "rhythm" never slipped up. In this department, too, Mr Five Per cent was a perfectionist.'

Elize Soulas died in 1952, a few weeks after Nevarte.

22

CONNOISSEUR

1. Inventory

MILLIONS of people who never heard of Mr Five Per Cent Gulbenkian, the oil king, knew of Gulbenkian the collector. More than thirty of his magnificent pictures were on loan to the National Gallery, London, from 1935 to 1949; for the last eight years they have been on view at the National Gallery, Washington, D.C.

The London catalogue (printed at his own expense) said:

'The collection formed by Mr C. S. Gulbenkian in his house in Paris is known to lovers of art as one of the finest and most varied on the Continent, but the masterpieces it contains have been comparatively little seen by the public. We are therefore fortunate in being able to show at the National Gallery a selection of Mr Gulbenkian's most important paintings which he has generously placed on loan here for a considerable period.

The great pictures of the world are gradually being absorbed into public or permanent collections, and in the future few private collectors, whatever their resources, will be able to put together a series of pictures which will do honour to the National Gallery. Mr Gulbenkian's collection not only enriches the Gallery as a whole, but strengthens it at points where it is weak.

We have nothing by Guardi, Boucher or Fragonard comparable to the superlative works by these painters in the Gulbenkian collection; Hubert Robert, La Tour and Monet, each of whom is now seen at his best, were not previously represented in the Gallery at all; and rich as it is in Gainsborough, the Gallery has always lacked a full-length portrait of a woman of the quality of Mrs Lowndes-Stone.'

Even before the Second World War, the Gulbenkian pictures were the finest private collection in the world. Afterwards, no other man, either side of the Atlantic, owned a collection to touch it—in quality or in value.

His masterpieces are now conservatively valued for probate at £4,500,000. If they were put separately on the market, they would certainly fetch two or three times that figure—owing to inflation and the uncertainties of the international situation. Great pictures are among the few gilt-edged securities left and a sure investment for those with knowledge and taste—and the funds to wait for profit-taking. Gulbenkian was one of the first to recognize this trend.

Yet the crowds who have admired these wonderful works of art during the last twenty years know but a fraction of Gulbenkian the collector. His friend, Sir Kenneth Clark, has recorded that pictures were not even Gulbenkian's strongest suit.

Apart from 150 paintings, French furniture and Oriental carpets, all of the first quality already mentioned, Gulbenkian possessed sculpture, jade, silver, coins, *vermeil*, books, manuscripts—all stored in 51 Avenue d'Iéna, the grandest private house in Paris.

This miscellaneous treasure trove—paintings and No. 51 apart— was also conservatively valued for probate at £1,500,000 and is also probably worth two or three times its estimated figure.

Nor was Gulbenkian what the art world calls an "accumulator". His collections are not very large and contain little or no rubbish. He always threw out comparatively inferior pieces as soon as he could get something better to take their place. Consequently his collections reached the highest level through and through. 'Only the very best is nearly good enough for me,' was one of his sayings.

2. Brainwork

How did he come by these great possessions?

It was not merely a matter of money, although he was ready to pay record prices for what he wanted, if necessary.

He inherited, of course, the Armenian genius for textiles; then he studied diligently under the leading French professors of art. Sir Kenneth Clark says: 'Gulbenkian developed a phenomenal sales resistance in later life. It was colossal, although earlier he was a sucker for dealers' sales-talk. For example, he paid £25,000 for Nicolas Lancret's "A Fête Galante"—a pleasant, gay open-air scene—but winced at parting with £5,000 for a Cezanne or a Renoir. I had great difficulty in persuading him to buy Edgar Degas's "L'Homme et le

Pantin" and Renoir's "Madame Claude Monet Lying on a Sofa" for £5,000 each. The values have now been reversed.

'He also went to almost incredible pains to see that he wasn't cheated. He was a man of the most violent suspicions. I've never met anybody who went to such extremes. He always had people spying for him.

'This was his strength—and also one of his weaknesses. He would send me to look at a picture, which I was advising him to buy, and check up on what I'd said about it in his absence. Check, check, check was his rule in life.

'Mountains of painful correspondence accumulated between us when he imagined, quite wrongly, that I was in league with his son —or possibly with people putting up money for Nubar—when father and son had their case.

'Once he thought I'd lost two *famille noire* Chinese vases, which he had lent. There was correspondence a foot high because there was some delay in returning them. He insisted on the packing-case being opened in his presence. I had to prove that substitutes had not been packed in place of his own vases. Finally they had to be tested by independent experts. And I was supposed to be his friend!

'Yet, we never quarrelled. He quarrelled with many people, including his own family, but not with me—nor John Walker, another friend, who is the Curator of the National Gallery in Washington (D.C.), nor his confidant and lawyer, Lord Radcliffe, who also discussed art with him.

'I used to talk with him for hours and I loved to listen to him. He had the most marvellous mind I have ever met: the most powerful I have ever encountered. You could almost see it wrestling with a problem and working out the solution. I grew genuinely fond of him.'

That was another explanation of Mr Five Per Cent's success as a connoisseur, as well as in business. He was highly selective in his friendships. It is quite wrong to suppose he was utterly unsociable. As Nubar says: 'Father simply couldn't be bothered with duds. He preferred pitting his brains against the very best in everything which interested him. He was never "anti" anybody. But he hadn't got time for anybody or anything except essentials.' In fact he picked the finest brains in the world.

Cyril Radcliffe, for instance, whom he first met in the Chambers of that famous K.C., the late Wilfrid Greene, who joined with the future Lord Chancellors, Simon and Hailsham, in giving him their advice over the Foreign Office "usurpation" of 1914.

Or Mr E. S. G. Robinson, former Keeper of Coins at the British Museum and Gulbenkian's adviser on numismatics, which was the start of the collections.

John Walker, brother-in-law of the Duke of Norfolk as well as Curator of the National Gallery, Washington (D.C.), who was as close to Gulbenkian as Kenneth Clark, is still known as the great Bernard ("BB") Berensen's "pet bi-ped".

Gulbenkian's admiration was reciprocated.

Lord Radcliffe told me: 'Mr Gulbenkian educated himself to be an expert in artistic taste during a long lifetime.'

Dr Robinson also told me: 'Mr Gulbenkian had remarkably good judgement. He was not a hoarder. When he obtained one coin which was a better example than another of the same type already in his possession, he threw the latter out. He was one of the first to whom we appealed when we needed funds for a new acquisition and we were not disappointed.'

Nubar, like many of his father's chivvied staff, was "fed up with antiques", and, if he'd had any say in the matter, would "Bung 'em in the National Gallery and forget about them."

His home was a museum and he was repeatedly being roped in by Father to help in the more stealthy art deals. Willy-nilly, therefore, Nubar observed his father's methods from the inside and it is interesting to hear that the experts' summing-up of the old man tallies with the son's more Philistine opinion.

Nubar says: 'Quality, not quantity, was Mr Five Per Cent's principle as a collector. He was surrounded by dealers when he began, but he educated his taste and bought his experience. He became a shrewd buyer. Consequently, his collections were not particularly large but they reached a very high standard. He always got rid of inferior stuff when he found something better.'

3. Arts and Craft

In time Mr Five Per Cent was up to all the tricks of the art dealer. He even taught them a trick or two. Nubar says: 'Papa's passion for negotiation also found an outlet in his art-collecting. He would never go to an auction himself, in case—despite his anonymity—he should be recognized and so send the prices up. Instead he would send three or even more people, who were even less known, in order to bid for him.

'Usually I was one, before my beard and orchid became known. Hacobian, the slightly built and inconspicuous Armenian, who was one of Pa's henchmen for forty years, was another of us who used to be sent to Christie's and Sotheby's.

'Only Hacobian or I would know the maximum Pa was prepared to bid. The others did the actual nodding and were unknown to each other, so there was no chance of their getting together.

'When Pa's maximum was reached, Hacobian or I would give a secret sign to our man. I would take out my pocket handkerchief or adjust my spectacles . . . and our men would stop bidding. It was all most carefully rehearsed and Papa took the utmost glee in laying on the pantomime. It worked splendidly. That is how we got some very fine bargains.'

Gulbenkian was one of the few collectors who ever got the better of the greatest of all art dealers, the late "Joe" Duveen (later Sir Joseph, later still Lord, Duveen)—the man who taught American millionaires how to buy immortality by buying masterpieces and bequeathing them to the nation; the man who thus brought culture to the United States; and the man who added the great hall to the Tate Gallery and persuaded the late Andrew Mellon to give the National Gallery to Washington (D.C.).

There was a time before the First World War when you could get a sculpture by Catherine the Great's protégé, Houdon, for £5,000. By 1912, Houdon's had so advanced—owing to Duveen's creating a corner in them and bidding them up—that you couldn't get one for £10,000. Duveen owned more than a dozen and paid nearly £20,000 for the bust of Houdon's ten-months-old-daughter, Sabine. It was always his policy to bid anything of which he owned a lot to the ceiling, or beyond. As a result, Edward S. Harkness paid almost £50,000 for little Sabine just after the war.

This astronomical rise in Houdons and other art treasures—largely due to Duveen's salesmanship—did not escape the notice of the Soviets, who badly needed ready money to repair the tatters of the lost war and the Revolution and had little credit. The Bolsheviks accordingly put the art treasures of the Tsar's palaces, the cathedrals and the mansions of the aristocracy up for international auction.

Duveen and his client, Gulbenkian, discussed The Hermitage sales in Leningrad, before the start, as man to man and old friends. Naturally having a hoard of Houdons, Duveen tried to interest Gulbenkian in the sculptor's finest work, the Diana. He judged this would appeal to his client's oriental and erotic taste and anticipated a handsome deal.

Gulbenkian did not disappoint his friend. He too expressed a strong desire to accommodate the provocative Diana in the seclusion of his mansion. But there was a snag. Gulbenkian proposed to bid for it himself. 'You go past a million and I'll begin to think,' he jested. when Duveen revealed that he was authorized to go up to $750,000 dollars by the Sacramento storekeeper, Collis P. Huntington. So Duveen left, imagining he might still do a deal with the Armenian and, anyway, looking forward to a fight after his own heart.

Realizing that the parvenu Bolsheviks were rather shy of selling the Russian national art treasures and sensing that they'd welcome as little publicity as possible, Gulbenkian approached the Soviet Embassy in Paris ahead of the sale. Or rather, he sent a representative to act for him, unknown to the Russians—and, of course, Duveen.

This man was Aucocq, the famous jeweller in the Rue de la Paix. He pitched the yarn it would be far better to sell Diana privately than to let her go to some American millionaire, with the certainty of maximum publicity on arrival in New York.

'And it worked,' Nubar says. His father obtained Diana for only $30,000. It was almost giving her away.

Mr Five Per Cent took elaborate precautions to see that this under-the-counter deal didn't fall through at the last moment—either through some masterly counterstroke by Duveen or a Soviet change of mind. Aucocq was instructed to pay only half the price when Diana arrived safely in Berlin, half-way to Paris from Leningrad, and the other half when she reached Paris.

So, when the representatives of Duveen, Andrew Mellon, Solly Joel and other multi-millionaires arrived at The Hermitage for the opening of the sales—each with cheques for at least £1,000,000— they found that the *chef-d'œuvre* was gone. Diana was by then installed in 51 Avenue d'Iéna and has never left there during the last thirty-five years. After the Second World War Gulbenkian refused $1,000,000 for her.

Nor was the Houdon the only piece "missing" when The Hermitage sales opened. The finest old French silver in the world, the eighteenth-century service by Germain, which had escaped melting-down by Napoleon during his wars, had gone secretly to Gulbenkian for £50,000. Only a little comparable silver now exists, in Portugal, which Napoleon never occupied, and it's now all worth ten times as much.

One of Gulbenkian's pictures is of Germain and his wife and

shows a fine piece of silver by the master which is owned by Ricardo Spirito Santo, head of the Banco Spirito Santo et Commercial, the leading Portuguese bank. For years after Gulbenkian fled to Lisbon to to live, the banker tried to persuade him to sell the picture. And Gulbenkian tried to buy the silver. When Ricardo died Gulbenkian continued the argument with the executors but the deal never came off.

The finest examples of rare *vermeil* also went to Gulbenkian under the counter from Leningrad. So did Marie Antoinette's table and Talmar's magnificent French furniture. So, too, did Rembrandt's "Pallas Athene" and his "An Old Man Seated" from Catherine II's Collection, Rubens's "Portrait of a Young Woman", Hubert Robert's "Felling Trees at Versailles" and Dierick Bouts's "The Annunciation".

'It was a package deal,' says Nubar. Some package! It was the finest art coup of all time.

Another time, Gulbenkian met Duveen in the lift of the Paris Ritz and was able to tip him off that Almina, Lady Carnarvon, wanted to sell a Gainsborough, a Reynolds and a Lawrence in one lot. As a reward, Gulbenkian suggested that Duveen should buy them and give him the choice of one of the three. Duveen was to fix his own prices and the total was not to exceed what he had paid the owner plus 10 per cent profit.

Naturally Duveen tried to guess which one Gulbenkian wanted. The finest painting, although the least spectacular, was Gainsborough's "Portrait of Mrs Lowndes-Stone". The Lawrence had the more obvious charm, and, after much deliberation, Duveen decided this would appeal most to his Oriental client, whose judgement was usually warped by a pretty face or a pleasing motif. He accordingly priced the Lawrence high and the Gainsborough low.

Gulbenkian did not know the prices, when he came to take his choice, and Duveen waited anxiously, although he was well-acquainted with the art-hungry millionaires. He was confounded. Gulbenkian chose the low-priced Gainsborough. Duveen had not realized he was dealing with another expert of his own calibre.

Gulbenkian was less successful trying to obtain two Rembrandts through Duveen in 1921. They were "Portrait of a Lady with an Ostrich-Feather Fan" and "Portrait of a Gentleman with a Tall Hat and Gloves", two masterpieces even by Rembrandt. They belonged to Prince Felix Youssoupoff, the patriot who helped to kill Rasputin, the evil genius of the Romanovs who imposed on the last Tsarina. The Prince had escaped with the pictures from the Russian Revolution. Youssoupoff was in need of funds and offered to lend them to the

American multi-millionaire racehorse-owner, Joseph E. Widener, as collateral for a loan of £100,000.

Not being a money-lender, Widener made a counter-proposal—to buy the Rembrandts for £100,000 on the condition that he would sell them back at the same price, plus 8 per cent interest if, by 1st January, 1924, a restoration of the Old Régime in Russia made it possible for the Prince "to keep and personally enjoy these wonderful works of art".

Duveen informed Gulbenkian of this strange transaction and Gulbenkian's appetite was whetted. £100,000 for the two masterpieces seemed cheap to Gulbenkian after Duveen had talked to him. £200,000 was more like it. The dealer saw that this intelligence reached the refugee Prince, who thereupon asked Widener to return the pictures. But the Tsar had not returned to Russia, and Widener saw no reason for obliging the Prince.

The consequent lawsuit in the New York Supreme Court in 1925 was savage. Youssoupoff's lawyers maintained that he had only mortgaged the pictures to Widener, whom they called a "pawnbroker", "perjurer" and a "thief", who was "taking advantage of a gentleman".

But, since Widener was one of Duveen's best pupil-customers, the dealer's evidence in the witness-box was less uncomplimentary. 'Widener's name on my books is good enough for me,' declared Duveen for the defence.

Another witness described how Youssoupoff's friends had tried to handle Widener's cheque before the contract was signed and made the Prince look grasping.

Gulbenkian's counsel argued that he had merely advanced the money to Youssoupoff as a gesture, because he thought the Prince ought to have the pictures back, and that his client had only been offered a claim on them as a matter of courtesy.

Widener's counsel maintained that Gulbenkian wanted the pictures for himself and not so that Youssoupoff could 'keep and personally enjoy them'.

Then Widener made a false move. He said the Prince had cabled confirming the deal, but he could not produce the telegram. Nor could the telegraph company. Widener, now on the defensive, seemed to have invented the telegram. In fact it did not turn up until a year later, after the case, and it dropped out of his stud-book.

But Youssoupoff (and Gulbenkian) had lost. Widener continued to enjoy the pictures. Duveen kept his friendship. Gulbenkian had to make do without the "Fan and Gloves" or the "Tall Hat".

4. *"My Children"*

His pictures were the only thing over which Gulbenkian—tycoon, patriarch—was sentimental. "My children" he called them, and devoted at least as much time and loving care to them as Nubar or Rita. 'My children,' he used often to say, 'must have privacy.' Like him, they had to have protection from vulgar stares, immunity from idle chatter and 'a home fit for Gulbenkians to live in'.

That was why he built 51 Avenue d'Iéna for them, with the thirty-foot barricade, the burglar alarms, the watchdogs and his own secret service. Lock, stock and barrel the place must have been worth at least £10,000,000.

'My children must not be disturbed' and 'They must be happy' were two more of his maudlin slogans, which drove his family wild. He would spend hours at a stretch revelling and gloating alone over "the children". It was his nearest approach to miserliness; at such moments "The Meanest Man in the World" jibe rang true.

As each additional masterpiece fell into his clutches and he perfected his collection, he obtained tangible proof of his own merit, which made public acclaim superfluous. Not for him titles or decorations, the common or garden baubles of success; Gulbenkian's baubles were unique—the approbation of his "children" was enough. He basked in their presence as other men bask in the company of Royalty or savour the adulation of the mob.

These "children" were harder to get than his own progeny—and more reliable. They were harder to get than money, which other men could gain. They were unique. They satisfied all his fiercest urges—his competitive instinct, his acquisitive instinct, his need for beauty, his yearning for self-esteem. They did not chatter or answer back. They were intellectual company at the highest level. What more could a man want? They made him sufficient unto himself: beholden to nobody: a sovereign personality.

For ten years he allowed no intrusion to disturb this megalomania. A large slice of the cultural heritage of mankind was jealously kept for the enjoyment of his private eye alone. No. 51 has never yet been opened to the public. The marvellous contents were rarely, if ever, released on loan. They might as well have not existed. Only the experts remembered where they were or what the world was missing. All attempts to prise the art treasures out of their solitary confinement were met with a blank refusal or stony silence. "My children mustn't be disturbed."

Over his private possessions, as in business, Mr Five Per Cent was, in the words of the *Financial Times*, "harder to squeeze than granite".

But water was being dropped, drip by drip, upon the stone. Lord Radcliffe, John Walker, Dr Robinson, Sir Kenneth Clark and other experts, whom Gulbenkian knew and respected, were at him one after another. In the long run the attrition was irresistible. The stone cracked.

One day Nubar arrived unexpectedly with a newspaper parcel under his arm at the office of the head of the Egyptian Department at the British Museum. After some delay, while he made himself known, he was ushered in. And out popped the head of "The King of Kings".

The curator, too, was old; he nearly fainted. When he recovered, he gasped: 'Don't you know this is the finest head of sculpture which ever came out of Ancient Egypt? This is the finest moment of my life!'

And the head, with other items from the Gulbenkian Egyptian Collection, went on loan to the British Museum for several years.

Sir Kenneth Clark relates: 'I was in bed one night—in 1934, shortly after I'd gone to the National Gallery and made Gulbenkian's acquaintance—when the telephone rang and I was astonished to find him on the line. I didn't know him very well then but was aware how jealously he guarded his works of art. To my amazement he asked if I'd like to borrow his pictures and which I would choose.

'I thought it wisest to say I left the choice to him. In due course twenty-four arrived (later increased to thirty-one) and they stayed until after the war.'

What had happened? Mr Five Per Cent's reasoning was this, according to Nubar: 'I have only let "the children" out of my sight for a few years. The mob can have its stare at them. Afterwards nobody can say I haven't given the public its chance. Then my children can return home and live in peace.'

Sir Kenneth Clark regarded this attitude as tantamount to sending them to Coventry. Gulbenkian was sixty-five and Clark tactfully began to suggest that something ought to be done about "the children" for posterity. This line of thought coincided with the first years of commercial oil production in Iraq and an increase in Mr Five Per Cent's income (and responsibilities) by millions.

Sir Kenneth says: 'His grand design for keeping the framework of his business intact and building a great gallery for his collections after his death began to take shape about 1934. He engaged the great

American architect, Willie Delano, to draw up plans. A fifteen-foot model was made and a contract was prepared.

'The original idea was to present the collections to the National Gallery. But this was killed by the Second World War.'

That is another story.

At this stage it remains to register astonishment that, amid all his business worries, responsibilities, arguments and detail, Mr Five Per Cent ever had the time, inclination or acquisitiveness to accumulate one great art collection—let alone ten.

Among Gulbenkian's pictures, unmentioned by name in this book so far, were: Boucher's "Cupid and the Graces" (1917); Carpaccio's "The Virgin and Two Donors Adoring the Child" (1924); Cima's "The Rest of the Flight" (1923); Corot's "The Bridge at Mantes" (1913) and his "Venice from Dogana" (1924); Sir Anthony Van Dyck's "Portrait of a Man" (1927); Fragonard's "A Fete at Rambouillet" (1928), from the Kaiser's Collection; Ghirlandaio's "Portrait of a Woman" (1929); Guardi's "S. Pietro di Castello, Venice" (1921), "A Regatta on the Grand Canal" (1919) and "A Fete on the Piazza di San Marco" (1919); Frans Hals' "Portrait of Sara Andriedr, Hessix" (1924); de La Tour's "Mlle Sallé" (1928); Lochner's "The Presentation in the Temple" (1921); Manet's "The Boy with the Cherries" (1910); Monet's "The Break-up of the Ice" (1925) and his "Still Life" (1924); Rubens' his "Portrait of My Wife". The bracketed years refer to Gulbenkian's purchase dates. His heaviest period of buying was between 1919 and 1930, when the Iraq Petroleum Company came to life in approximately its present form.

Besides the National Galleries in London and Washington (D.C.) and the British Museum, the few other places where he exhibited were the Petit Palais, Galerie Georges Petit, Galerie Rosenberg, and the Monet and Manet Exhibitions in Paris and the National Museum in Lisbon.

23

CHURCHMAN

THEN there was Calouste Sarkis Gulbenkian, the churchman. Strange as it may seem, Croesus, Casanova and Conoisseur also feared God. All his life he was an active, knowledgeable and generous—if not devout—member of the Armenian Church, in which he was born and bred.

It would be easy enough to misrepresent him as a sinner, who repented: a craven creature fearing it was easier for a camel to pass through the eye of a needle than a rich man to enter the Kingdom of Heaven: another frightened millionaire, who woke up with a jolt to the fact that you can't take your mammon with you, a wary realist, expiating his earthly crimes and taking out an insurance policy against the hereafter. But it wouldn't be true.

Puritans and prudes may scoff and argue that his licentiousness could never be redeemed. But Mr Five Per Cent did not regard his philandering as sin. It was natural "rhythm"—an aid to the fulfilment of his personality—a contribution towards the achievement of his life-work. In fact, he had his own morality, which he practised with no qualms of conscience. For him, it was not what you did but the way that you did it, which counted. He did not feel damned.

Levellers-down, equalizers and "fair shares" socialists may bridle. They may fling slogans—"monopoly", "exploitation" and "big business"—at his memory and hold him up to obloquy. But Mr Five Per Cent was not ashamed of his wealth. He regarded the creation of wealth as a token of a man's true worth, a proof of the fulfilment of his purpose in life and a contribution to the progress of mankind— the bigger, the better. That is why he hated waste and extravagance in any form and counted every penny. It is also why he hated idleness and worked so hard, long past the modern age for retirement, until he was more than eighty-five: why he despised frivolity and ostentation and quarrelled with his only son. He had his principles.

Out of them developed his tactics, for instance his avoidance of publicity. Coincidentally, privacy happened to be convenient. The virtues of outward modesty and self-effacement were part of his being and did not connote fear, let alone shame. His associates, such as

Henri Deterding, J. D. Rockefeller, Junior, or Joseph E. Widener, were terrified of Marxism and made a fetish out of "simplicity" and false modesty. Having lost a million as a youth, J. D. Rockefeller, Junior, spent a lifetime giving away his father's cash. Deterding, having made his own millions, saw the Red Bogy everywhere and ended by recommending penal death duties.

Fear, wrapped up in noble sentiments, was in each case the underlying motive. Not so with Gulbenkian. His insistence on privacy was merely part of his stock-in-trade. He had no inferiority complex about the "monolithic state", "Wall Street adventurers", "bloated millionaires" or "grinding the faces of the poor". He had worked with Russians since boyhood and knew their limitations. He had no hesitation about matching his wits with the Bolsheviks and doing a £1,000,000 art deal with them under the counter. To the end of his life he was urging another package deal with the Russians over Near East oil. It did not seem in the least strange to him to bequeath £143,000 ($400,000) for the restoration of a cathedral in "godless" Russia. The inverted inferiority complexes of "McCarthyism" were outside his philosophy. Oil men, capitalist or Communist, were alike creating wealth, work and a better life for millions, including himself, and he saw no wrong in that. Why not do a deal? Great possessions and Christian principles were not incompatible to Mr Five Per Cent. Nor was Communism.

Therefore his church-going was not necessarily a sham. It was possible for him to believe in the Christian Church, as a stabilizing institution, a creative force, a power for good, a discipline and even as a focus for his own "divine spark". The most ruthless millionaire is not entirely oblivious of salvation.

The Armenian Church has a beautiful liturgy, which appealed to the connoisseur in him. His association with the Armenian faithful also gave him a feeling of "belonging" somewhere, which is the yearning of all ex-patriates. Through centuries of persecution the Armenian Church has been the link, inspiration and consolation which has maintained the moral, individuality and aspirations of this keen but pitiable race. The piety and austerity of his father, Sarkis, were exemplary. The philanthropy of his father, his in-laws and "Uncle" Nubar Pasha was famous. It would have been a breach with tradition and upbringing if Calouse Gulbenkian had turned his back on his mother church.

A test of his sincerity is the impression he made on lowly and exalted fellow church-goers. I have yet to find one member of the regular congregation of two hundred at St Sarkis, the Armenian Church in Iverna Gardens, Kensington, W.8. who was not convinced of his piety. He himself built and endowed this beautiful church, modelled on an old Armenian church in Trans-Caucasia, in 1922, in memory of his father and mother. Since the Second World War the maximum congregation has increased from 500 to 1,500 Armenians, owing to reinforcement by refugees from the Persia of the nationalist Prime Minister, Dr M. Mossadeg; students from Iraq; and businessmen from India. This movement led to an Armenian bishopric being established in London in 1955. The first holder of this office is the former Vicar of St Sarkis, Father Besak Toumayan, who is also the Gulbenkian family chaplain. Before the Second World War, the main centre of Armenian life in Britain was in Manchester, where the bishopric was situated. Nearly a thousand Armenians then lived there, mostly engaged in the textile trade, but the community has now dwindled to about five hundred.

Nor did Gulbenkian merely impose himself on a grateful and well-meaning congregation. He also convinced that shrewd Anglican Churchman, Dr Geoffrey Fisher, Archbishop of Canterbury, of his sincerity. Dr Fisher has twice gone out of his way to preach at St Sarkis, and his words are worth quoting at some length: not only for the tributes to Gulbenkian, but for an understanding of the importance of the Armenian Church to Western civilization.

On 7th October, 1951, Dr Fisher said:

'In expressing the gratitude which Anglicans feel for the opportunities of mutual friendship and understanding afforded to them by the existence of this church and parish here in London, I would also join with you in acknowledging the generosity of Mr Gulbenkian, who built and maintains this church.

I have seen evidence of this generosity in other connections, and rejoice to see by his actions what importance he attaches to the place of Christian faith and Christian worship and Christian values at the centre of the Armenian community in this country.

I am happy to take this occasion of saying that we and others outside his own church appreciate his care for this church and the benefit it brings to us as well as its great spiritual benefit to you.'

The occasion for that tribute was the 1500th anniversary of one of the decisive battles of the world—at Vardanantz, where the Armenians stopped the invasion of Europe by Persian hordes of Zoroastrian pagans.

The point of the Archbishop's address was that Armenians are still holding the Christian fort at the cross-roads of Europe and Asia against paganism in the form of Soviet Communism, whose founder,

Lenin, called religion "the opium of the masses". Dr Fisher identified England with the Armenian struggle in the most political terms possible at divine service:

'The Armenian Church in its close identification with the Armenian nation and people has kept alive and vigorous among them the Christian faith. . . . We do not forget that the Kingdom of Armenia was the first state in the world to adopt Christianity as its official religion, and that King Tiridates III in the year of Our Lord 303 set an example, which was to be followed ten years later by the Emperor Constantine. Thus the Armenian Church stood early in the forefront of the Christian Church. . . .

I welcome the understanding and fellowship which happily prevails between that Church and the Anglican Communion. Nowhere is this more evident than in Jerusalem, where the happiest relations exist between our Anglican Bishop and the (Armenian) Brotherhood of St James, as is most strikingly revealed in the part which our Bishop of Jerusalem is invited to take part in the solemn ceremonies of the Washing of the Feet at the Armenian Cathedral of St James in Jerusalem on Maundy Thursday. . . .

Today we celebrate an event which symbolizes and expresses the devotion of the Armenian people to the Christian Faith. While the Persian rulers respected the Christian Faith, all was well. But when they attempted to interfere with it, the Armenians resisted.

As a result of an appeal from the clergy, the whole of Armenia rose. The Roman Emperor could not help and the Armenians were left to their own resources. They fought well and valiantly, but were eventually overwhelmed by the superior numbers and discipline of the Persian army. But the defeat of St Vardan Mamikonian on the battlefield of Avarair, with more than a thousand of his followers, was a spiritual victory. From a political point of view all was lost. But the advance of paganism was stayed, and the Persians were persuaded to revert to a policy of toleration towards the Armenian Church.

Throughout history, Armenia has stood at the crossroads of Europe and the East. The Armenian people have often been defeated and overrun, yet their historic role of constant resistance to invasion has played a vital and self-sacrificing part in saving Europe.

Yet more again, we see in this battle the victory of Armenian Christianity. The death of the body was the victory of the soul. . . . It is for this that we honour today, 1,500 years later, the heroes of the battle, and pray God will ever keep the Armenian people faithful to that example.'

We thus begin to grasp the hold their Church has on Armenians—Gulbenkian included—in their perpetual struggle.

Bishop Toumayan quoted the ringing words of the Armenian faithful as they hurled defiance at the Persians: 'From this Faith no one can move us, neither angels nor men, neither sword nor fire. For our torments our endurance, for your sword our necks!'

Against the Seljuk Turks, the Armenians were the spearhead of the Crusaders. In the First World War, half the nation perished in the struggle against the Ottoman Turks and helped to save Suez. In 1917–20 Armenia briefly held Bolshevik barbarism at bay and has ever since been a thorn in the flesh of the Kremlin materialists. In the Second World War, the remnant of the race helped to halt the Wagnerian Nazis on the threshold of the Caucasian oilfields, which were the key to Soviet (and Western) survival. The Armenian Church survives and the struggle is not over yet.

The martyrdom of the Hungarian, Polish and Czech Churches today is no more remarkable than the sacrifices the Armenian Church has made even in this century. It is a fighting church—no wonder it appealed to Mr Five Per Cent and inspired him. He, too, fought against great odds and never gave up.

Not only did he acknowledge his debt to the Armenian faith by building and supporting St Sarkis. He presented a great library building to the Armenian Cathedral of St James in Jerusalem, to which the Archbishop of Canterbury referred. Gulbenkian also bequeathed a substantial legacy to the Yedi-Kule Hospital in Istanbul—the Armenian old folks' home, where his parents were buried—in order that Mass might be said for them at prescribed intervals.

He even took the trouble to have his son born at Chalcedon, where the historic Fourth Council of Christendom was held in 451, the Great Schism began and the Armenian Church acquired its individuality.

The point has not been lost on the *enfant terrible*. Nor has Nubar forsaken the paths of righteousness. He, too, is religious. He could not have mourned his father more punctiliously. Three memorial services were held for Mr Five Per Cent at St Sarkis at monthly intervals and there was another on the first anniversary of his death. Nubar and Marie attended. Both wore black and used black-edged notepaper for six months. They interrupted their hunting—foxes in Buckinghamshire and hares in Portugal.

When Lord Radcliffe arrived on the blazing hot Lisbon aerodrome in September, three months after Mr Five Per Cent's death, he was in brown tweeds. But Nubar was *de rigueur* to meet him: in a black suit, black kid gloves, black suéde shoes, Eden hat and his black Rolls-Royce.

At the Palacio Hotel, Estoril, he and Marie were taking their meals in retirement in their suite and avoiding the public restaurant.

Mr Five Per Cent seems to have instilled the forms of devotion into his volatile offspring. Knowing Nubar, I may say that is a considerable achievement.

As I have mentioned, Mr Five Per Cent also left £143,000 to the restoration of Etchmiadzin Cathedral, Erevan: a sum far beyond the alms of the faithful in the U.S.S.R., since the churches are allowed no revenues.

This had an electric effect on the atheist authorities of the Kremlin. They put up the money required for the restoration. When Bishop Toumayan arrived at Etchmiadzin, fifteen months after the publication of Gulbenkian's will, he found the cathedral had been renovated for the first time since the Revolution in 1917. The ancient frescoes had been newly restored to their mediaeval glory in silver and gold. The roof had been repaired with precious copper. The walls had been shored up and assurances given that the work would soon be completed so as to last.

The occasion of Bishop Toumayan's visit was the consecration of the new Catholicos, Vazgen I. The utmost publicity was given to the cathedral services by the State. Two thousand Armenians packed the building and 10,000 more listened to the relay into the close.

The Soviet Embassy in London suddenly produced visas for Nubar (and his valet) to visit Erevan, which he had to refuse, as it turned out, because he was genuinely ill in bed for weeks and his doctors did not think the long journey (over Moscow) would be wise.

On Bishop Toumayan's return, it was learned that the Soviet Armenian authorities had earmarked the £143,000 for new municipal drainage. So perhaps it was just as well Nubar could not accept the invitation.

But the Etchmiadzin incident just showed what one tough and realistic little man like Mr Five Per Cent could achieve by standing up for his beliefs against the mighty Marxist machine of the Soviet Union. He did not take an artificial view of history. He understood that Armenian and Near East history is continuous and cannot be divided into closed chapters by an event of even such magnitude as the Russian Revolution.

Mr Five Per Cent supported his Church and fought for it. No doubt he also believed in it, after his fashion. But he never made his peace with his Maker. As Nubar says: 'He could never face death. That is why he never made a proper will.'

24

PHILANTHROPIST

YEARLY from 1920 to 1929, the Council or the General Assembly of the League of Nations drew attention to the scandalous Armenian refugee problem. But little or nothing was achieved in or outside Turkey and the Soviet Union for them. (Shades of Lake Success and the Hungarians of 1956.)

By 1920 Armenian independence was in its death throes and the final obliteration of the Armenian race in Anatolia in 1925–9 was at hand—as a result of the abortive Treaty of Sèvres. The refugees from the slaughter in the Caucasus and the New Turkey by 1920 numbered a million, 115,000 in Europe, 125,000 in Syria-Lebanon and the rest in Russia proper.

Until the Treaty of Sèvres on 10th August, 1920, the Armenian cause was placed in the aged hands of Boghos Nubar Pasha, son of Calouste Gulbenkian's "Uncle" Nubar Pasha, the Egyptian elder statesman; but he utterly failed to measure up to great historical events. The Armenian tragedy was as much due to his incapacity and the chronic inability of Armenians to co-operate as to the power politics of the Allies.

Boghos Pasha was a brilliant architect; his name nevertheless hypnotized the Armenian people, and they wanted him at any price at the head of the Armenian Delegation at the Versailles Peace Conference. He wished to decline the invitation, but—mainly because there was nobody else of equal prestige—he was prevailed upon to accept the post.

Living in Egypt and dealing exclusively with British and Egyptians, Boghos had disregarded everything to do with Armenia; he had even forgotten his own language. He worked at his mother tongue and prepared to do his best; but he had no talent in choosing his advisers —who displayed the traditional Armenian inability to pull together. He was a benevolent Girondin, admirable in theory, useless in practice.

Too late the Armenians turned to the unlovable but competent Calouste Gulbenkian. They invited him to head their cause, instead of Boghos, in order to try and save something from the wreck of the Treaty of Sèvres and get something done for the million refugee survivors of the race. He refused any political appointment, 'I'll rub people up the wrong way and get shot,' he said.

Nubar explains: 'He didn't believe in an independent Armenia at any time during his life. He thought independence was detrimental to the best interests of the race. He considered Armenian talents were best adapted to making a livelihood and carving out a position in the world at large.' (To cite a parallel: if he had been a Jew, he would not have been a Zionist, wanting a State of Israel, but would have remained an assimilator.)

'He also realized—especially after the massacres of the First World War—that there were not enough Armenians left to form a workable, free Armenian state.' That was indeed the sad but realistic state of affairs in 1920, and it remains so today.

It is unfair to suggest, as his enemies do, that he let his fellow countrymen down in their hour of destiny and avoided political entanglements with the Soviets because of past and future financial interests in Russian oil.

It is true that he had just been expropriated from the Ural-Caspian and North Caucasian oil companies. He had lost the expected benefits from a deal he was negotiating for Deterding with the Grosnyi (tsarist) oil producers. He had also lost the Mantachoff business.

It is also true that he always looked forward to a rapprochement between Soviet and Western oil interests. But he held that the oil interests of the world (and his own) would be better served by abandoning an impossible Armenian independence movement than by pressing this outworn and artificial policy.

He avoided contact as far as possible with the leaders of the emigré "White" Russians, Armenian interventionists and their Western backers.

But he was not deaf to the humanitarian appeal. For three years, amid all his other labours, he took on the Chairmanship of the Armenian General Benevolent Union, and it was a huge job. The Union had and has two purposes: to help refugees, when necessary, and to invest the millions at its disposal against the unknown day when a free Armenia may once more become possible.

As Chairman, he was brought into contact with the great Norwegian explorer, author, scientist, king-maker, ambassador and humanitarian, Fridtjof Nansen. In 1924, Nansen and the International Labour Office at Geneva were charged the study of the possibility of settling substantial numbers of Armenian refugees in the Caucasus and elsewhere. This measure followed the appointment of a League Committee in 1920 to investigate the problem after Lord Robert Cecil had demanded proposals for 'averting the danger which now threatens the remnants of the Armenian race'.

At the same time Nansen had gone straight to the point, suggesting 'an expedition of at least 60,000 men should be sent at once to save the Armenians from the Kemalists'.

Again in 1921, Professor Gilbert Murray hoped it would be possible 'to discharge that debt which has been owed, not indeed by the League of Nations, but by all the Western Powers of Europe for so many years, and, indeed, for so many generations, to that much-suffering people'.

Nansen's findings were published in his *Scheme for the Settlement of Armenian Refugees* (Geneva, 1927) and in his *Armenia and the Near East* (London, 1928). He and four experts, including the original Vidkun Quisling, went via Constantinople and Batum to Erevan in mid-1924.

Nansen submitted his report to the Sixth Assembly of the League of Nations in 1925 and suggested drainage and irrigation of 90,000 acres at a cost of £900,000, which would settle 15,000 refugees.

But Nansen did not get his £900,000. Mr Five Per Cent, as Chairman of the Armenian General Benevolent Union, had a whip-round his rich friends and contributed privately. But it was not enough.

In 1926, Nansen appealed once more to the Assembly in vain.

Again Mr Five Per Cent put his hand in his pocket. But few responded to his appeals or to Nansen. For two more years Nansen continued appealing eloquently, in vain. By the Tenth Assembly in 1929 he at last gave up. The opportunity of continuing international relief work inside the most sensitive frontiers of the Soviet Union was lost. Stalinism and the iron curtain were to come. But the wrongs live on, both sides of the borders, and will fester again or be righted. Mr Five Per Cent had done his bit.

By 1926 he had realized nothing much could be achieved through the Armenian General Benevolent Union and resigned the chair.

A Joint Armenian Committee was appointed, with Nansen as Chairman, to help Armenian refugees outside Russia. Some success was achieved in Syria, where some 90,000 were gathered in overcrowded camps at Alexandretta, Aleppo and Beirut. By the end of 1929 there were still 32,000 in the camps, which developed malaria, although sanitation, food and clothing were supplied. Settlements in town and country were made in Syria and Lebanon for about 60,000 Armenians—the last tiny colonies in their ancestral Levantine homes. Many of them migrated to the Soviet Union after the Second World War under the influence of elaborate propaganda by the Armenian Soviet Republic and out of fear of rampant Arab nationalism.

Although he no longer held an official post in Armenian organizations, Mr Five Per Cent continued to subscribe to the cause.

His wizened little henchman, Avetoom P. Hacobian[1] says: 'All his life, including the Second World War and afterwards, Mr Gulbenkian sent great benefactions to Armenian charities everywhere—to almost every country in the world, including the countries behind the iron curtain. The Treasury made special arrangements for him to transfer the necessary currency. It was a great labour keeping up with his wishes and the files on this one branch of his activity became enormous.'

But among Armenians Mr Five Per Cent is not considered to have been a great philanthropist. His brother-in-law, Atvarte Essayan, says: 'Compared to the Essayans, Nubar Pasha and even Mantachoff, Calouste Gulbenkian was small fry.

'There is a tradition among wealthy Armenians that they should leave nine-tenths of their money to Armenian charities, as my father and Uncle Meguerditch did.

'Calouste built his church in London, the library in Jerusalem and subscribed to Armenian charities during his life, it's true, but he left almost his entire fortune and all his possessions to the Gulbenkian Foundation. Armenians got practically nothing. For instance, his two brothers' wives only got £1 a day each for life! He didn't even carry out my sister's wish to endow an Armenian orphanage, when it came to making his will. He was primarily interested in preserving his business, his life-work, intact.'

Atvarte still cannot get over the fact that his adored sister never had many jewels beyond the Empress Eugénie pink diamond (now Rita's). One piece is, I know, valued at £56,000. But Atvarte says his sister once told him that some of her jewels were in reality paste.

[1] Director of Gulbenkian's subsidiary companies and go-between in art deals, originated in the wealthy old Armenian community in Calcutta. Served as a Cadet in the Calcutta Volunteer Rifles at the start of the First World War. At the end of 1914 came to London and met Gulbenkian socially. One of his chief employees for the last twenty-four years, mainly in philanthropy.

The Armenian Croesus of Calcutta was Galstaun, who dealt in real estate and built the well-known Galstaun Mansions. One story about him concerns the Armenian nuns who used to drive round the offices collecting (very successfully) for charity in a phaeton. One day their old nag dropped dead outside their church and a few minutes later a magnificent horse cantered up riderless. There seemed to have been a miracle. The horse was harnessed to the carriage and off charged the nuns, who were soon out of control. The alarm spread and a groom caught the carriage, explaining to the terrified nuns that their new horse was one of Galstaun's thoroughbreds which had just escaped from the racecourse! Galstaun replaced it with a quieter animal.

Another story concerns the Armenian millionaire, Gubbay, who presented a zoo to Calcutta. Inspecting the monkey house, a visitor asked the keeper innocently: 'And who's Gubbay?' The keeper is said to have answered: 'I never know. Down in the Armenian quarter they all look like monkeys.'

Evidently, Armenians in India are no more popular than elsewhere.

Nubar sums up his father's attitude towards giving in these terms: 'If you watch every penny, every £1 and every £100, you have more millions to give away—and I agree.'

The point arose after an incident at the Mikael Essayan-Geraldine Guinness society wedding at St Margaret's, Westminster, in 1956. The three-tier wedding-cake weighed only twenty-six pounds and had to do for 600 guests at the reception at the Hyde Park Hotel. Afterwards there was a heated discussion about it. The Essayans objected to the manufacturers charging 1s. 6d. for sending off each little souvenir box of cake to absent guests. Eventually the price was beaten down to 9d. a box, thus saving £3. Finally, the manufacturers, fed up with the whole argument, closed it by saying they would send the bits of cake off for nothing.

I told Nubar I thought that once in a lifetime one could forget about such trifles, especially on such a magnificent and happy occasion. 'Life is too short,' I remarked. 'I don't think so,' Nubar replied. 'I think the Essayans were quite right. So would my father.' I was surprised.

What finally seems to have persuaded the former private secretary, David Young, that Mr Five Per Cent was "The Meanest Man in the World" was their parting in the middle of the First World War.

Young had been engaged twenty-six years earlier, straight from school at 30s.-a-week. He complains: 'During the war when he was plotting his greatest coup, I left him to answer the bigger call of duty —to fight for my country.

'For the first two years he paid me my full salary of just over £8 a week. Then, as a sergeant in uniform, I called on him one day at the Ritz Hotel in Paris.

'His greeting was: "Times are getting hard, Young. I can't go on paying you".'

Young adds: 'His obsession was to make millions—and to avoid spending a single unnecessary shilling.'

So he and Nubar Gulbenkian seem to be largely in agreement as to the old man's thrift.

Whether or not Mr Five Per Cent was "The Meanest Man in the World", I suppose depends on what importance one attaches to the spirit and motives behind the giving, the worthiness of the cause and the proportion of the wealth with which the donor parted.

If one wasn't at the receiving end, I suppose it must have been rather galling.

Anyway, in the end Mr Five Per Cent gave all his possessions, the bulk of his £25,000,000 cash fortune and £5,000,000-a-year (rising fast to £10,000,000) to the world.

25

ARABIAN NIGHTMARE

ULBENKIAN'S real hard-luck story was Arabia. That is what his stern struggle for the self-denying "Red Line" Agreement of 1928 was really all about. There was more to it than merely preventing internecine competition between the Iraq Petroleum Company partners within the borders of the Iraq concession.

Gulbenkian (and his partners) already had their eye on the neighbouring Arabian lands of the former Ottoman Empire, where petroleum had yet to be discovered, but which might very well appear at any moment.

He, with his minority shareholding of 5 per cent, was determined to be "in" on any finds which his more powerful partners might make there—and the Red Line bound them all together. They, led by the Americans, who still hankered after the Open Door, wanted to be free to go ahead individually and, of course, squeeze Gulbenkian out. Hence the Red Line chafed them, while it reassured Gulbenkian.

Gulbenkian had insisted on the self-denying clause ever since he founded the Company with Babington-Smith, Cassel and Revelstoke in 1911. But the restrictions were largely theoretical until 1927, when the great strike was made at the Baba Gurgur "Burning Fiery Furnace", near Kirkuk, in fields geologically separate from the proven possibilities of neighbouring Persia and the offshoot at Naftkhana.

Baba Gurgur immediately raised hopes to the south, right the way down the Persian Gulf. Hence the bitterness with which the Red Line agreements were debated.

Not that the Arabian Peninsular had been entirely neglected.

The name of Major Frank Holmes, the New Zealander, has already cropped up in this story: in the many-sided competition for the Mosul concession for instance. The main object in his forming Eastern and General Concessions as far back as 1920 was, however, the acquisition of Arabian oil rights. He did not have much luck. Progress was bound to be slow when he began. The authority of the Sultan was moribund. The Arab parts of the Ottoman Empire were undefined and as yet had no recognized sovereign rights to award concessions. Arabia was still steeped in mediaevalism and even the local sheikhs—let alone the Bedouin—could not conceive the importance of any petroleum, which might lie beneath their sands. Their wealth was counted in camels, goats, slaves, jewels and Maria Theresa dollars. Life was cheap, and based on an endless series of raids and counter-raids. The mentality of the area was ignorant, suspicious and greedy.

Exploration was therefore difficult, dangerous, expensive and speculative. Agreements were shaky. In the beginning Holmes met with little competition from the big oil companies and the Great Powers behind them. In 1920 he turned first to what was to become the Kingdom of Saudi Arabia. But the future monarch, Ibn Saud, was still only the Sultan of Nejd in Southern Arabia, whence he expelled the rival Hashemite dynasty from the Holy Places, and the extent of his suzerainty to the north was uncertain.

One of the disputed frontiers was the desert area between Nejd and Kuwait, near Iraq and the head of the Persian Gulf. The Sheikh of Kuwait claimed to be independent and did not acknowledge the suzerainty of the Sublime Porte. But he in turn was regarded by the emerging kingdom of Iraq as an apanage. Furthermore, Kuwait had long been in treaty with Britain.

In 1922 the British Commissioner in Baghdad, Sir Percy Cox, resolved the intricate frontier dispute by creating a Neutral Zone between Kuwait and Nejd (Saudi Arabia) and joint Saudi-Kuwait sovereignty was established.

In 1922 Ibn Saud also granted Holmes a two-year licence for Al-Hasa, on the verge of the Neutral Zone but inside Saudi Arabia proper. Later on he obtained rights for Kuwait proper.

In 1923 Ibn Saud granted Holmes an exploration permit for the Neutral Zone, which of course had to be confirmed by the Sheikh of Kuwait to be any use. In 1924 Holmes had his rights in the Zone confirmed by *both* rulers. (But his rights did *not* extend into Kuwait proper, where the Sheikh reserved the concession.)

In 1925 Holmes extended his interests to the island of Bahrain, half-way down the Arabian side of the Persian Gulf, where the Sheikh gave him exclusive rights. But these were not transferable without permission of the British Government under an old agreement between the two countries.

By 1927 Holmes therefore had his foot in what we now know to be four oil-bearing districts—the Saudi-Kuwait Neutral Zone, Al-Hasa (Saudi Arabia), Kuwait and Bahrain. Baba Gurgur immediately focused world-wide attention on all these and, naturally enough, the lands beyond them.

Old and new frontiers and agreements merely infuriated the

Americans, who wanted to press on and grab the expected oil, but to Gulbenkian the complex details were vital. In a free-for-all he would have been helpless. With the Iraq Petroleum Company bound to him he had a fighting chance in Arabia. The "Red Line" was his ultimate weapon.

2. Bahrain

In 1927, *before* the Red Line Agreement, the Gulf Corporation of Pennsylvania (an Iraq Petroleum Company constituent) took an option on Holmes's island and mainland rights at Bahrain.

Behind the Gulf Corporation stood five other great American oil companies: Standard Oil of New Jersey; Standard Oil of New York; Atlantic Refining Company; and Pan-American Petroleum & Transport Company—all of which were to bind themselves by the Red Line the following year,[1] under duress by Gulbenkian—and the (Sinclair) Consolidated Oil Corporation.

Behind them all stood the State Department, urging the Open Door policy.

The immediate issue at Bahrain was the 1914 "nationality clause", forbidding the Sheikh to transfer oil rights without the consent of the British Government. After much argument, His Majesty's Government was compelled by heavy pressure from the State Department to give way in the alleged interest of Anglo-American relations. Consequently the Gulf got Holmes's concession and, in the absence of an agreed Red Line, which was still being argued, was able to pass the Bahrain rights on to Standard Oil of California.

The (non-Iraq Petroleum Company) Standard Oil Company of California formed the Bahrain Petroleum Company in 1929, in order to exploit the concession, and (to save British "face" over the nationality clause) registered Bapco in Canada.

With a view to this deal, the Texas Oil Corporation had in 1925 secured 50 per cent interest in the embryo Bapco—in return for surrendering 50 per cent of Texas Eastern (including European) marketing facilities to Standard Oil Company of California.

So Caltex was born: and Britain, the Iraq Petroleum Company and Gulbenkian lost the Bahrain oilfields in all but name. The production is now shared 50-50 by the all-American Caltex partners.

[1] Later they were reduced to Standard Oil Company of New Jersey and Socony-Vacuum.

Three years after this victory for the Open Door, came the noteworthy strike at Bahrain in 1932, which confirmed the infinite possibilities of Arabia (1955 production, 1,500,000 tons).

3. Kuwait

Also, before the Red Line, the Gulf and Anglo-Persian (both Iraq Petroleum Company constituents) had intervened to prejudice Holmes's rights in Kuwait proper. Hence the heated argument as to whether this Sheikhdom owed allegiance to the Ottoman Sultan, or was part of Iraq, or was independent. If part of Iraq, it would be bound by the Red Line. Then the Gulf and Anglo-Persian Oil Company would have been bound to pool Kuwait oil rights with their Iraq Petroleum Company partners, including Gulbenkian.

But Gulbenkian, in order to prevent a complete breakdown of the 1928 negotiations and the disruption of the Iraq Petroleum Company, was obliged to draw the "Red Line" outside Kuwait. So he missed out on Kuwait as well as Bahrain.

The Gulf and Anglo-Persian were freed to proceed with muscling Holmes out and in 1934 they formed the Kuwait Oil Company on a basis of 50-50 American and British capital. The Sheikh conceded 6,000 square miles on his mainland and in 1938 was rewarded with the first colossal oil strike in his tiny territory—at Burgan, fourteen miles inland. This was destined to prove the richest oilfield in the world, with petroleum spouting at nearly 250 times the rate of the average American well. By 1956, it was yielding the Sheikh, Sir Abdullah al Salim al Sabah, £50,000,000 a year for his personal account and another £50,000,000 for public works. The equivalent £100,000,000 was shared by the two oil companies.

Britain did at least get half this prodigious output and income. But Gulbenkian again got nothing. He and the Iraq Petroleum Company were beaten right on their own doorstep.

4. A Little Matter of £20,000

Again before the Red Line, the Anglo-Persian had in 1925 started trying to explore Al-Hasa (Saudi Arabia) in defiance of Holmes's rights there. But this time the Iraq Petroleum Company and Gulbenkian intervened and sent an intermediary to enter into private negotiations with

Holmes. They succeeded in obtaining first claim on the latter's option and Al-Hasa seemed as good as in the bag. All King Ibn Saud wanted was £20,000 in gold sovereigns. The Company, persuaded by Gulbenkian and the French, immediately approached the British Treasury.

Nubar Gulbenkian relates the sequel: 'The authorities categorically refused to release any gold. Britain had just gone off the Gold Standard and the Treasury refused to allow the Iraq Petroleum Company to enter into any Contract involving gold. It was argued that desert monarchs didn't understand paper money and had always been paid in gold. But the Treasury insisted that if an exception were made in this case, it would "reflect on the stability of British currency". The special interests of His Majesty's Government in Arabia were pleaded, but all to no avail. So the option lapsed and Britain lost all the oil of Saudi Arabia. This was Papa's real hard-luck story. "The fools," he raged.'

Nor did the Anglo-Persian get the concession. Britain was frozen out.

While efforts were made to talk sense into the Labour Government's Chancellor of the Exchequer, Philip Snowden, the Arabians lost interest. The (non-Iraq Petroleum Company) Standard Oil Company of California intervened energetically and in 1933 secured the Al-Hasa concession, covering the whole east coast of Saudi Arabia.

The Americans immediately formed the Californian Arabian Standard Oil Company (Casco) to exploit their success. In 1939 they struck a great oilfield at Dhahran in Al-Hasa and by 1954 Saudi Arabian production was practically 50,000,000 tons a year, worth £130,000,000, divided equally between the King and the Company.

But for that little matter of £20,000, the Company's £65,000,000 would have been going to the Iraq Petroleum Company and 5 per cent of that would have meant another £3,500,000 a year for Gulbenkian. But he didn't think like that.

(In 1943, Casco became the Arabian-American Oil Company (Aramco), which the Iraq Petroleum Company's Standard Oil of New Jersey and Socony-Vacuum wanted to join, but were temporarily prevented by the Red Line. But that is a later contest.)

5. Neutral Zone

Gulbenkian was also done down in the Saudi-Kuwait Neutral Zone.

Frank Holmes passed his option on the Saudi half-share, which Ibn Saud had confirmed in 1924, to Standard Oil Company of California.

The Americans sat on it until 1933, when the strike at Bahrain awoke them to the possibilities. But the Sheikh of Kuwait stalled and so operations were held upt until after the Second World War.

The zone was much coveted, since it lay astride the line of the Persian Gulf oil discoveries, and in 1946 the Sheikh of Kuwait adopted the time-honoured Oriental course of putting his wares up for auction.

Again the (non-Iraq Petroleum Company) Americans won, but on terrific terms. By 1953, Aminoil and John Paul Getty's Pacific Western had spent no less than £12,000,000 on concessions and operations without achieving major production or even proving the existence of major oil deposits. Mr Five Per Cent as he lay dying in 1955, may well have thought he and the Iraq Petroleum Company were well out of the Neutral Zone.[1]

But in March 1957 the Wafra field suddenly gushed 50,000 barrels a day, revealing estimated reserves of 5 billion barrels, thus thrusting Getty on to Gulbenkian's two-years' vacant throne—the sole great independent oil king in the world. If sixty-four-years-old, five-times married Getty lives long enough, he is also certain to be the richest man in the world.

Like Gulbenkian, Getty is a rich man's son, semi-recluse, habitué of the swagger hotel suites of Europe and art-fancier (Gainsborough, Rubens, Titian, Louis XV and XVI furniture and a Santa Monica museum of a mansion). In preference to Gulbenkian's exotic Japanese pheasants and Birds of Paradise, Getty goes in for buffalo, bears and Abyssinian mountain goats.

6. Consolation Prize

Gulbenkian's Arabian consolation prize was Qatar.

In 1924 the Anglo-Persian sent geologists to Oman, on the borders of the promontory and Sheikhdom of Qatar, midway down the Persian Gulf; and a geological survey of Oman and Qatar was completed in 1933.

Throughout, the Anglo-Persian Oil Company acted on behalf of its Iraq Petroleum Company partners, with full Red Line agreement, so as not to confuse the senile Sheikh Abdulla, who could not follow the transformations of oil companies.

[1] A second Neutral Zone, between Saudi Arabia and Iraq, which is so far unproductive, was allotted in equal shares in 1938–9 to Casco (Saudi half) and the Iraq Petroleum Company (Iraq half).

Abdulla extended the Anglo-Persian exploration permit from 1933 to 1935, when he signed an exclusive agreement for seventy-five years, covering 4,000 square miles. Whereupon Anglo-Persian assigned the concession, as previously agreed under the Red Line, to the Iraq Petroleum Company, which then formed, as a subsidiary, Qatar Development Company.

In 1939 the Iraq Petroleum Company struck oil at 5,500 feet at Dukhan. At last Gulbenkian's Arabian nightmares turned to sweet dreams and fulfilment. The first well and shipment were completed in 1940. His famous Red Line paid off.

But, after two more wells had been drilled, the British Government panicked over a hypothetical Japanese invasion. The wells were plugged. The equipment was moved to Basra in Southern Iraq or Bombay. Operations in all-British Qatar and in half-British Kuwait were suspended.

Meanwhile the Americans, with no such inhibitions about Saudi Arabia, forged ahead.

Drilling did not start again in Qatar until late 1947, partly because the Americans held out on equipment, and shipments were not resumed until 1949. In 1952 a new and retrospective agreement was reached with Sheikh Ali, in whose favour Abdulla had abdicated.

By 1955 Gulbenkian and the Iraq Petroleum Company were getting 5,400,000 tons a year from Qatar mainland, with the early expectation of 8,000,000 tons. The Sheikh and his chieftains entered the solid gold pistol and platinum camera class and could choose fleets of limousines in different colours to suit each mood. For they were drawing £13,000,000 a year in royalties. The Iraq Petroleum Company, too, was drawing £13,000,000 a year, of which Mr Five Per Cent pocketed £650,000 a year.

That Red Line battle proved worth while—even if there is a difference between an annual income of £650,000 and £3,500,000.

7. Qatar Complications

There is always plenty to think about in the oil business.

In 1945 the U.S.A. claimed that a seaside state exercised authority not only over its territorial waters (as Gulbenkian had carefully defined in 1928) but also over its off-shore "Continental Shelf" beyond.

The oil companies with mainland concessions, covering "territorial islands and waters" or "exclusive rights", naturally claimed the new submerged territories as theirs already by virtue of the original grant.

Competitive companies and the rulers (with visions of new concessions to sell) naturally argued the opposite.

Taking advantage of this doctrine, Aramco surrendered the Saudi Arabian half-share in the Saudi-Kuwait Neutral Zone in 1948, thus enabling Getty to complete his 1946 purchase of the Kuwait half-share, and in exchange accepted the Saudi Arabian "Continental Shelf".

In 1949 the Foreign Office also encouraged rulers along the Persian Gulf to proclaim such rights for themselves (in the hope of relieving the British taxpayer of commitments in the sheikhly Protectorates). Thus the rulers acquired huge new areas of "submerged land".

Accordingly, Qatar granted a separate, new oil concession for its "Continental Shelf" to the Superior Oil Company (associated with the Central Mining Corporation of London and the International Marine Company of Canada) in 1949.

Gulbenkian and the Iraq Petroleum Company—jealous of their hard-won Qatar concession of 1935—took legal action. But this test case was lost, by arbitration, in 1950, before Lord Radcliffe, of whom more anon.

An Iraq Petroleum Company subsidiary, Petroleum Development Trucial States, also lost a similar case over the submerged land belonging to the Sheikh of Abu Dhabi.

Thus a concession was limited to the territory under the authority of the ruler at the time of the original grant. Mr Five Per Cent had evidently slipped up in 1928. He had not looked as far as continental shelves.

This did not seem to matter much until 1957.

In 1952 Superior withdrew from the Qatar "Continental Shelf", after discouraging results. Superior was succeeded by a new company, Shell Overseas Exploration Company, which acquired rights over 10,000 square miles of sea for seventy-five years at an initial cost of £260,000 and a 50-50 share of the proceeds for the Sheikh.

By then the Red Line had snapped and this was the first concession taken by an Iraq Petroleum Company partner independently inside the limits of the former Ottoman Empire, which, incongruously, was not considered to have included its "Continental Shelf".

This was a bitter pill for Mr Five Per Cent in his eighty-third year.

But so long as he lived, Shell Overseas had no luck "offshore". And in 1957 it lost one of its £900,000 "oil islands", while drilling in the Persian Gulf.

The "Continental Shelf" however paid-off outside the Saudi Arabian Coast in 1957, when the first big oilfield under the waters of the Arabian Peninsular was discovered by the Americans.

Meanwhile development forged ahead in Qatar.

At hitherto uninhabited Dukhan, jetties, a transit yard, offices and residential and industrial areas were created. Tankage and loading capacity were built up. A deep-water channel was dredged to lead in-shore at Umm Said, where previously there had only been a primitive point of call for small craft. Thither the oil was pumped seventy-three miles and parallel with the road, the Company built the first surfaced road and telegraph line in the principality.

At Dukhan and Umm Said, electric power and lighting, hospitals, airfields and (most important in a desert country) drinking water were laid on. The effete population was given medical services, vocational training, transport all the week (including holidays and days of prayer). Sturdy housing was provided in place of the ancestral tents or shacks for the 3,000 workers.

A small Police Force, under a British officer, was set up. Since 1949 there has also been a British Adviser to help the Sheikh adapt the entirely patriarchal administration to modern life and his stupendous, sudden fortune.

The Qatar workers received unprecedentedly high pay (holidays included), good food and undreamed amenities. Their physique improved. But they remained the least effectual workers in Arabia, which is a considerable achievement, and had to be eked out with Indians, Pakistanis, Jordanians, Iraqis and other assorted Arabs. Idleness, thieving and trouble-making continue.

Apart from Arab nationalism, Cairo Radio, Russian intrigue and Arab character, Qatar has its peculiar and unsettling political diffi-culties. Non-existent frontiers have had to be established across the paths of nomads. The mountainous hinterland of Oman is still unde-fined. So is the interior of the Trucial Coast. The Saudis claim the east coast of Qatar and—less forcibly—Qatar itself. In 1950 a Saudi Arabian armed escort conducted an Aramco reconnaissance unit into Southern Qatar. With American encouragement, the Saudis also temporarily occupied the Buraimi Oasis, looking for oil at the junction of Saudi Arabia, Oman and the Trucial Coast. With the Saudis spending billions of dollars on their armed forces and the Americans relentlessly grabbing every concession and business opportunity in the Middle East (regardless of British interests), the future of Qatar remains peculiarly uncertain.

26

EXILED

WHEN the Second World War broke out in 1939, Mr Five
Per Cent was in Paris, where he intended to remain—as in
1914–18—at the hub of affairs. He was seventy, but still
active in mind and body, and—if the First World War was any guide
—his ingenuity would be needed to save the Iraq Petroleum Company.

The Company now had concessions for the whole of Iraq. Production was running at more than 4,000,000 tons a year. Exploration
was being pushed ahead. Plans were afoot for doubling the existing
pipelines to the Mediterranean at Tripoli and Haifa. His fifty-year-
old dreams were being realized. But they were short-lived.

In June 1940 Italy entered the war. France fell. Shipping became
unsafe in the Eastern Mediterranean and for three months had to be
suspended. The collapse brought pumping on the northern branch-
pipeline to Tripoli in the French Mandate of Syria to a stop. Lebanon
also fell under the collaborationist control of the Pétain Government.
By the end of the year production was back to 1,400,000 tons: less than
1934. British staff began to melt away from the Iraq Petroleum
Company organization in Iraq to join the Forces. The Nazi juggernaut
was rolling towards the Caucasian oilfields and the approaches to Iraq.
The Axis was going from strength to strength and it was only a
question of time until Tokio came in and the pressure was to start
from the east, across the Indian Ocean. The meeting-place was to be
in the Near East, as ever the crossroads of the world.

In anticipation of the Axis powers joining up in Mesopotamia, the
Iraq Quisling, Rashid Ali al-Gailani, and his generals, seized power in
Baghdad. They sabotaged many of the Company's installations and
plundered its records. Each British member of the Company staff was
put under house-arrest with an Iraqi soldier in charge. Then the
Germans arrived and the guards were doubled. The British Minister,
six-foot-six Sir Kinahan Cornwallis—record-holder for the 'Varsity
Sports half-mile and a famous Arabist—was besieged. Eventually he
and the Iraq Petroleum Company staff were rescued by a brilliant
desert operation by Glubb Pasha's small, but élite and mobile, Arab
Legion, operating from Jordan, whose King Abdulla was then

Britain's only effective ally. Meanwhile, the Japanese—anticipating the kill—came in. In a panic the newly installed British oil equipment at Qatar and Kuwait was removed out of harm's way to Basra in Southern Iraq.

But Hitler's mistake in going for a prestige conquest of Moscow, instead of putting all he had into the Caucasus, prevented the junction of the Axis pincers. The Russians, aided by the North African Campaign, turned the tide. Iraq became a huge Allied Military base and the Iraq Petroleum Company did its bit.

The needs of the Armed Forces were paramount. To supply them locally became the Company's main function. Kerosene was piped from Naftkhana across the border to the forces in Persia and another pipeline was laid from Abadan to the R.A.F. base at Shaiba. Kirkuk was adapted to produce refined petrol for the Army. Fuel for the Royal Navy was "slugged" to Tripoli. A four-inch pipeline was laid from Kirkuk to the forces in Mosul. The Company greatly helped the forces' commissariat, telecommunications and technicians.

But in 1942 the German-Japanese threats from north and east increased. All Iraq Petroleum Company wells were closed, except one at Quaiyara, and the equipment joined the stuff from Qatar and Kuwait in Basra. A slightly more acute Japanese threat and the British Commanders might have lit, or otherwise wrecked the wells, and the Iraq Petroleum Company would have been out of business for many years. As an act of faith, the Company, which was losing money, lent the Iraq Government £500,000 interest-free and promised another £1,000,000 at the Armistice.

Not until 1943-5 did Gulbenkian's fortunes in Iraq begin to look up again, with the end of the Axis pincers movement and the discomfiture of Iraq Quislings. Production was 3,780,000 tons in 1943, 4,250,000 in 1944 and 4,620,000 in 1945, of which he should of course have had his 5 per cent.

But it didn't work out like that.

2. On the Run

History seldom repeats itself in detail and it compelled Mr Five Per Cent to take the fateful step, which conditioned the rest of his life and still governs the destiny of his gigantic fortune. He had to drop his plan to stay in France. His son tells the story thus:

'At the outbreak he meant to remain headquartered in Paris, as he did—so successfully—during most of the first war. In the spring of 1940 he was still there, hovering between No. 51 and the Ritz; he took a villa at Deauville for the summer.

'Then came the French collapse in June and—sticking to his plan —he followed the French Government to Bordeaux, Biarritz and finally Vichy.

'There he became legally "an Enemy under the Act", according to British war-time legislation. This not only wounded him—after half a century of service to British oil interests—it also led to the confiscation of his 5 per cent in the Iraq Petroleum Company by the British Custodian for Enemy Property.

'He could not—or would not—follow the argument that the British authorities declared him to be "an enemy" in order to protect him from actions he might be compelled to take under duress while he remained at Vichy.

'He was convinced that the Anglo-Dutch-American groups of the Iraq Petroleum Company seized the opportunity to prevail on the British Government to squeeze him (and the French) out of the Company and steal his oil, which was sold at a price fixed by an American oil-broker, without his or French consent. None of the profits were marked up to him or the French.

'The Royal Navy was refueling with his oil at Tripoli and the British Forces were using his oil and facilities in Iraq. Yet he was treated in this way! He could not understand it.

'One of the consequences of this apparent ingratitude was that he began to reconsider seriously whether he would, after all, leave his pictures to the National Gallery.

'Another consequence was that he decided to make use of Persian citizenship. He had been a Commercial Counseller of the Persian Diplomatic Service for many years (keeping an eye on his bugbear,[1] the Anglo-Persian Oil Company). So long as Persia remained neutral, Persian status somewhat improved his position at Vichy. Another point arises here. . . .

'There has been some doubt whether Pa *formally* renounced his British citizenship and became Persian instead. But I am satisfied that was the case.

'If so, the renunciation has a fundamental bearing on his subsequent will. For he certainly never *formally* re-applied for British citizenship.

---

[1] The *Memoirs* go out of their way to say in fairness that in 1923–8 Lord Cadman, the Anglo-Persian's Chairman, and the Company 'adopted the fairest attitude' and that 'their methods were well above those of the other groups over my personal negotiations'.

And British Law stipulates that if a person obtains another nationality his British citizenship is lost permanently. In that case, Mr Five Per Cent died a Persian, domiciled in Portugal.

'The basis of the present Portuguese claim to his fortune—that he was a British subject and so could dispose of his estate as he liked—therefore goes by the board.

'The estate may not only have been subject to Portuguese Law governing Death Duties, but also Persian Duties (if he was Persian) or British Duties (if it could be proved that he never formally lost British citizenship).

'But the Persians would have to "come and get it". The Portuguese hold the vital documents. However, Persians are not exactly backward about money, and something may yet come out of this tangle.

'To get back to Vichy. . . . When Persia was occupied by the Russians and British and in 1942 declared war on the Axis, Mr Five Per Cent (as a Persian diplomat) had to leave Vichy with the Persian Legation.

'At first he intended to go to Switzerland, where he asked his distinguished old legal friend, Dr Henggeler,[1] to prepare for him.

'I pointed out that Switzerland was hemmed in, whereas Portugal —which I knew, and father didn't—had access to America, an ideal climate, excellent food, an hospitable people and a stable government. For once he accepted my advice and he went there.

'He never left. He died there thirteen years later.'

3. "A Very High-Tone Hotel"

In Lisbon Mr Five Per Cent repeated himself, setting up in the Hotel Aviz, the local equivalent of a Ritz. Some guests believe the small and select Aviz is the best hotel in the world, despite its proximity to the trams, noise and dust of Lisbon's boulevards.

This was to be his last home—garish enough for the most oriental taste and, indeed originally built for a film magnate. It might be a set for an exotic church, a museum or a Ruritanian palace. There is wrought ironwork, heavily carved furniture, an array of coats of arms, tapestries, statuary and chandeliers. The silence is sepulchral, the servants slipping by soft-footed on thick baronial carpets. It is so

[1] Henggeler acted for Persia and Gulbenkian from 1922 in their relations with the Anglo-Persian Company. He died in 1951, aged seventy-five.

exclusive that even the Iberian sunbeams only reach the ornate tiles one or two at a time, as if by stealth. The lift is a golden palanquin upholstered in satin.

Pictures, armorial bearings and notice-boards, like an exclusive Public School's Honours List, leave visitors in no doubt that the Portuguese have been to sea. Solemnly listed are the Portuguese discoverers from 1418 to 1542.

Perhaps the most comforting entry on the "honours list" was the Portuguese perpetual alliance with England, dating back to 1386. Nobody could now accuse him of being "an Enemy under the Act"—and at the end of 1943 he was "reinstated". But he did not take out another British passport. He continued to use his Persian diplomatic status.

Other distinguished guests have shared Gulbenkian's fondness for the Aviz. William Saroyan, another Armenian, wrote in the Visitors' Book:

'A very high-tone hotel. There are flies in the room. They are very plain and apparently do not know they are at the Aviz. Bravo.' W. Somerset Maugham added, more cornily: 'I have only one thing against the Aviz. I hate leaving it.' Alan Lennox-Boyd, the Tory Colonial Secretary, went one better: 'We like it better than any hotel we have stayed in in Europe yet.'

Nevarte would have climbed into her social heaven if she had been at the Aviz, which was seldom. Here are some of the guests of Gulbenkian's time in their brackets. Banking: Hambro, Lazard, Rothschild and Cameron Cobbold, Governor of the Bank of England. Royalty: The Duke and Duchess of Windsor, the Princes Alexander and Nicholas of Yugoslavia, the Queen Mother Elizabeth of the Belgians, Crown Prince Umberto of Italy, ex-King Carol of Rumania and King Faisal of Iraq. Soldiers and statesmen: Clement R. Attlee, Lord Louis and Lady Mountbatten, General Alfred Gruenther and General A. Juin of NATO. Miscellaneous: Gracie Fields, Yehudi Menuhin, Elsa Schiaparelli, H. R. Knickerbocker, Charles Boyer, André Maurois and Madame Lupescu.

In this gilded cage Gulbenkian had a bedroom, bathroom and sitting-room for himself (Suite 42), on the first-floor balcony, overlooking the entrance hall. He also had a suite for his devoted private secretary, "Madame Theiss" (who originated in Alsace and was married to a Monsieur Riehl). His valet had a room too. That was all until the last two years of his life, when nurses moved in. He would have had no room for any of his lovely things, even if he had missed them. Apparently he didn't, although they were his "children". He seems to have accustomed himself to hotel life after 1925, when he quit London and built No. 51 in Paris. He never bothered to rent a summer residence outside Lisbon. He didn't even set up an office. By 1943 he seems to have become completely self-centred, living his own life, wrapped up in his own brain, no matter where or in what surroundings.

Having ceased to be "an Enemy under the Act" in 1943, he re-established contact with his London office, his Iraq Petroleum Company partners and the financial world. He also kept an eye on the Axis and Vichy through his window on to Franco's Spain. If the worst came to the worst, he could always bolt to America. True to form, he kept a foot in all possible camps. That was the basis of his business.

But there is no doubt where his sympathy lay. As the last paragraph of his *Memoirs* says: 'It has been a source of vivid satisfaction to me that as a result of the events and developments, which I have outlined, Iraq oil was made available to the Allies during the Second World War at a point of such vital strategic importance as the Eastern Mediterranean.'

Whitehall was not so certain about him. Sir Kenneth Clark has told me: 'He could never get over the way he was treated by the British Government. His suite was searched in the Aviz, on instructions from the Secret Service, and in Portugal he was actually arrested.'

Thus, in the Second World War, as in the First, he was treated as a spy by his adopted country, which he had served so well—again as a result of the machinations of his business rivals, whose object was to blacken his reputation and grab his oil interests.

Sir Kenneth continued, as we drove to his ITV office: 'I went right up to the top, when Anthony Eden was Foreign Secretary in the Coalition Government, to try and get an apology. But I didn't succeed. Gulbenkian never got over that either. That may have been a contributory reason why he finally decided not to bequeath his pictures to the National Gallery.

'I don't believe the story that he changed his mind because a Labour Cabinet Minister was said to have insulted him with an allegation that he was pro-Nazi. Such a charge would have been too ridiculous to be taken seriously. Gulbenkian would have been expropriated immediately, if Hitler had won the war (in the same way as the Deutsche Bank was pushed out of the future Iraq Petroleum Company after the First World War).

'Nor yet do I believe the latest theory—that Gulbenkian believed he would live to be a hundred, like his grandmother, who reached 106; that he could not face death or making a proper will.

'I believe he had made up his mind, back in 1934, when his huge fortune started rolling in from Iraq, that he would try and keep all his possessions and his business organization together in some shape or form after he'd gone.

'Besides, Portuguese taxes are comparatively low and British death duties are penal. After the way Britain treated him, he naturally began to consider domiciling himself in Portugal and making arrangements for his affairs to be carried on from there.'

Some belated effort was, however, made at restitution. Nubar says: 'In 1953 the Conservative Government offered him a K.B.E. Perhaps they hoped to appease the affronts to his British citizenship and revive his idea of leaving his pictures to the British nation. But Father replied: "Thank you. It's not my cup of tea."' He never set foot in England again after 1940.

4. The Lost Half-Million

Once reinstated, Gulbenkian's first concern was to get compensated. His Five Per Cent had been appropriated by his Anglo-Dutch and American partners and he reckoned that since no Iraq Petroleum Company signatory had been free "to act independently directly or indirectly in production or manufacture of crude oil" since 1914, he was entitled to compensation. In 1943 he was owed for 95,000 tons, 1944 for 112,750 tons and 1945 for 115,500 tons.

The Lisbon-London radio-telegraph hummed for months, as he bombarded Freshfields, his lawyers, and the British authorities with protests and arguments against his injustice.

The fact that he had founded, shaped and organized the Iraq Petroleum Company seemed to be forgotten and the fact that the British Armed Forces were using his oil seemed to be taken for granted. In the stress of war, he got little satisfaction.

His case was complicated by his early war-time contact with Vichy and the Vichy-controlled Compagnie Française des Pétroles. London insisted that he and the Compagnie Française des Pétroles were in the same boat.

It was many months before he and his eminent Counsel managed to persuade His Majesty's Government and the Iraq Petroleum Company to regard the two cases as distinct and separate, as they were.

The Compagnie Française des Pétroles, he argued, was under

enemy control and maybe was rightly treated as enemy property, subject to the jurisdiction of the Custodian for Enemy Property.

His own case, he maintained, was entirely different. He had personally always been a free agent and had never been under enemy duress— as was proved by his unimpeded exodus to Portugal. Either as a British citizen at large or as a Persian diplomat, it was an error (as well as a grave injustice) to condemn him as "an Enemy under the Act" and to confiscate his property.

Anyway, he ceased to be an "enemy under the Act" in neutral Portugal in 1943 and in May 1945 as soon as VE-Day dawned, his claim was recognized and he was compensated by 1948: almost £500,000. At seventy-six he was still a fighter.

The Compagnie Française des Pétroles did not settle their more controversial case until 1950.

5. The Last Battle: a Master Stroke

From 1944 to 1948 Mr Five Per Cent waged the bitterest and most important battle of his long life (with the possible exception of San Remo in 1920) and mopping-up operations were not completed until 1954. He had lost none of his tenacity and he needed all of it. It was again a lone battle, fought by one man against the world, Governments and vast oil combines, from a hotel room.

Away back in 1927 Socony-Vacuum and Standard Oil of New Jersey had together formed Near Eastern Development Corporation for the express purpose of breaking into Arabian oilfields, following the revealing oil strike near Iraq's Burning Fiery Furnace that year.

They were only prevented from carrying out their designs by Gulbenkian's insistence on the self-denying Red Line Agreement when he engineered their entry into the Iraq Petroleum Company at San Remo.

Gulf (a participant in Near Eastern Development Corporation) was able to pass Bahrain to Standard Oil of California in 1929, but had to abandon its own claim in the same year owing to the newly drawn Red Line. Similarly, in 1943, Near Eastern Development Corporation was prevented by the Red Line from joining Casco (the future Aramco) in the tremendous Saudi Arabian developments (Chapter 26).

Arabia was a nightmare to Near Eastern Development Corporation (Gulbenkian's American partners) as well as to him. While the Red

Line was his sheet anchor, it was a hangman's noose to the Americans and they hated it: and Mr Five Per Cent, who invented it and introduced it, used it implacably and profited by it at their expense.

Such a restriction went entirely against the grain of the go-getting American oil men and the Congress oil lobby prevailed on every Administration, Democratic or Republican, to fight it from start to finish at the highest diplomatic level.

The Roosevelt Administration took advantage of Britain's war-time toils in the Middle East to handicap expansion in the British Protectorates, Qatar and Kuwait, as well as Iraq, and to forge ahead in Saudi Arabia. The United States held out on equipment, steel for pipelines and capital for investment in British-owned or partly owned oilfields, while pouring men, money and equipment into their own concessions. While the British were forced to close down completely in Qatar until 1947, partially in Kuwait and temporarily in Iraq, in order to deprive the Japanese of possible oil spoils, the United States transformed Saudi Arabia to serve as a forward oil source against the common enemy.

In 1944 the California and Texas Companies agreed with the United States Petroleum Reserve Corporation to build a Saudi Arabian pipeline to the Mediterranean for about £50,000,000. Aramco was to supply the oil and maintain a large U.S. Government reserve. The cost was to be repaid by the Company over twenty-five years, thus securing the concern from the Government for itself.

But the Senate and U.S. oil industry as a whole objected to such serious State interference with private enterprise and the scheme temporarily died.

However, the continuation of the war in the Far East eventually gained Casco-Aramco permission to build the huge (210,000 barrels daily) refinery at Ras Tanura at its own expense, with a high military priority. In 1946 the U.S. Air Force obtained its base at Dhahran (in the heart of the great al-Hasa oilfield), which King Saud has recently re-endorsed.

From 1932 to 1939 Gulbenkian had successfully fought Near Eastern Development Corporation, the Anglo-Persian and Shell attempts to break the Red Line and enter Bahrain; so Near Eastern Development Corporation knew the score. Near Eastern Development Corporation therefore ignored him when they wanted to join up with Casco-Aramco in Saudi Arabia in 1946–7.

In defiance of the Red Line, Socony-Vacuum acquired 10 per cent and Standard Oil Company of New Jersey 30 per cent (making a Near Eastern Development Corporation holding of 40 per cent) in

Aramco and its twin company, Tapline, which owned the new pipe-line.

Near Eastern Development Corporation flatly told Gulbenkian the Red Line was dead, that he could "do as he damned well liked", but they were going ahead. And the State Department, regardless of their lip-service to the rights of minorities, gave Near Eastern Development Corporation its full support.

The Americans may have reckoned that Gulbenkian was getting feeble: that he was discredited as a former "Enemy under the Act": and that Britain, in need of dollar aid and world-wide diplomatic support, would let him down.

They still didn't know their Mr Five Per Cent: and of course any gratitude for his having long ago, in 1920, first introduced the Americans in Mid-east oil had evaporated. "Oil friendships are slippery."

He fought like an old tiger.

What seemed a mortal blow hit him in 1947. British Counsel advised that the effect of the German Occupation of France, where the Compagnie Française des Pétroles was incorporated and Gulbenkian was resident, was to dissolve the 1928 Red Line Agreement.

But he rallied. Counsel also advised that the corporate existence of the Iraq Petroleum Company partners' holdings and stock was not affected. He still had an outside chance of saving his interests. Near Eastern Development Corporation, the Royal Dutch-Shell, Anglo-Persian and the Compagnie Française des Pétroles remained unable to act without his consent in Iraq and Qatar.

The Compagnie Française des Pétroles, his old allies and the partners most indebted to him of all, had alone been supporting him. But now the Red Line had finally snapped. They saw compensation for their war-time losses coming up (following Gulbenkian's reim-bursement in 1945). After the French had received their compensation in 1948 they and Gulbenkian temporarily parted company. They joined with the Anglo-Dutch-American groups in letting Near Eastern Development Corporation into Saudi Arabia.

He was even more completely alone than he had been at San Remo, after the First World War. Then he did have the French Government on his side and the original 1914 "joint action" clause in the Foreign Office Agreement. Now he had no card except Counsel's opinion that the Iraq Petroleum Company was still "corpo-rate". It was a small card. But he turned it into the decisive trump.

The Gulbenkians, father and son, played it for all it was worth. Nubar relates: 'Even the British Government backed the American

in the interest of Anglo-American relations. Father stuck to his last
surviving rights in the 1928 Agreement.

'He was then involved in the prospect of a huge international
lawsuit, although he entered his eightieth year in 1948.

'He offered to grant his permission for Near Eastern Development
Corporation to enter Saudi Arabia in return for their surrendering
their right to limit production in Iraq. Rather than face long, costly,
and possibly damaging international litigation, the Americans agreed.
Thus he secured for himself a vastly increased income from Iraq,
with the prospect of further growth on a gigantic scale as the world
demand for oil expanded.

'His main objection was overcome—the certainty that his American
partners would otherwise have restricted production in Iraq in order
to expand more rapidly, in collaboration with their countrymen, in
all-American Saudi Arabia.

'By 1955 Iraq accordingly became the sixth greatest oil-producing
country in the world, providing Father with an income, from this
source alone, of at least £5,000,000 a year and the early prospect
of £10,000,000, with the intended doubling of the Iraq Petroleum
Company pipelines.'

Gulbenkian was also compensated for his losses under the former
Red Line Agreement in Bahrain, where Caltex had been introduced
by the Iraq Petroleum Company's Gulf partners and were obtaining
1,500,000 tons of oil annually by 1955.

A specific development programme, a price formula and a price
for Iraq Petroleum Company inter-group sales were laid down in
annexes to the new 1948 Group Agreement, which became known as
"The Stroke 54 Documents" because the negotiations lingered on
from 1948 to 1954.

"/54" now governs Iraq oil production and protects the Gulbenkian
5 per cent interest as securely as once did the famous Red Line.

Again one pauses to boggle at the temerity of this little wizened
recluse in his two hotel rooms away in Portugal, in the extremities
of Europe—practically alone, just thinking—fighting to the last
ditch.

Now that one petty Middle East country, at present personified
by Colonel Nasser, has got away with expropriation of a great international business enterprise in the shape of the Suez Canal, it remains
to be seen if "/54" will last as long as the twenty-year-old Red Line.

Gulbenkian, the realist, always pinned his faith on the determination
of the Great Powers to protect their vital, legitimate interests (notably
Britain) in the long run. He also counted on the self-interest of the

oil-producing and oil-transit countries outweighing their hysteria in the long run.

But within eighteen months of his death, both premises collapsed. What next?

He did not have long to cash in. And one may ask: Was one million to five million a year for twelve years a disproportionate reward, late in life, for sixty-five-year-long herculean effort?

The American strong-arm methods of 1944–8 make nonsense of the Federal Trade Commissioner's 1952 Report, condemning the Iraq Petroleum Company as an international oil cartel and the Red Line 1928 Agreement as 'a sad case of wrongful cartelization'. The Red Line was in fact, as S. L. Longrigg suggests in *Oil in the Middle East*, 'an enlightened example of international co-operation and fair-sharing'.

The Commission, however, chose to ignore Gulbenkian's *Memoirs*, which it subpoenaed and didn't like when it read his true exposure of grasping American oil policy.

It will be interesting to see if the latest examples of selfish and short-sighted United States policy, playing off Britain's fear for her Mid-east oil and communications against the Communist bogy, pay in the long run. (It did in Abadan, where America cashed in on Mossadeg's Leftist coup and horned in on the hitherto all-British Anglo-Iranian Oil Company in 1954.)

Would it not pay the Americans to support the British, as Gulbenkian supported the entry of American partners into Iraq, and serve the common interest of the two Powers in maintaining orderly production and a sound Western economy?

By 1957, Gulbenkian could have gone beyond 'I ha'e ma doots . . .' about American oil policy. His "doots" of 1945 were confirmed.

He did not miss the opportunity of celebrating his victorious "/54" counter-attack. Nubar describes the closing scenes:

'The twelve signatories were assembled at the Aviz for a week. Every day Father thought up some possible new snag. Three days in seven I had to fly between Lisbon and London for documents or advice.

'Finally, at the end of June 1948, the last detail seemed to have been thrashed out. The signing was fixed for 7 p.m. But a few minutes before the twelve were to put pen to paper, Mr Five Per Cent thought up yet another snag.

'The party sat down to dinner and you never saw such a dull show in your life. We sat round the table with long faces and hardly exchanged a word. Everybody was thinking how the others might be trying to steal a march and was trying to keep a clear head.

'When I came to pay the bill, guess how many bottles of champagne we had drunk—exactly one! And when we *did* eventually sign—at three in the morning—the cellars were closed!

'Although Pa was seventy-nine, he wasn't even drowsy. He kept his wits about him right up to that late hour—after a week of intense concentration. His associates were terrified he'd pull a fast one over them at the last moment and didn't dare take a drink.'

6. Curtains

Having introduced the Anglo-Dutch, German, French and American interests into the Middle East oilfields (and pushed the Germans out again), Gulbenkian's last ambition was to add his old friends, the Russians. It didn't matter whether they were Communists or Capitalists. To him they were oil men.

His basic principle was to come to terms with powerful competitive interests, rather than antagonize and have to fight them and leave bitterness on both sides. From a long-term business viewpoint he regarded Soviet admission as the only possible peaceful solution for the area which could last. The 1920 Near Eastern frontiers seemed to him artificial and uneconomic and in need of overall, rational adjustment. The 1945 triumph of the Grand Alliance between the Western Powers and Russia also seemed to him a unique chance of putting his dream into practice.

Three years of fighting simultaneously on the Eastern and North African Fronts had likewise saved the Caucasian and Middle East oilfields. This was fresh in everybody's mind and the physical occupation of oil-bearing Persia by Anglo-Russian Forces was living witness of the joint interest of the Western and Eastern Powers in this area. The converging of the Japanese and Germans on the Middle East had also demonstrated that the area was still the focal point of world interests, as always. The war-time American build-up in Saudi Arabia was evidence in bricks and mortar of a similar convergence of United States interests in the Middle East, with its two-thirds of the world's proven oil reserves.

To Mr Five Per Cent, thinking alone and dispassionately in Lisbon, with his unrivalled fifty-five years inside knowledge of the Middle East and the oil industry of the world, 1945 seemed the obvious moment to

bring the Russians into partnership. They were allies, victorious and on
the spot. For a hundred years the Great Powers had been fighting over
Mid-east spoils. The First and Second World Wars were economically
as much about oil as they were popularly about The Kaiser and Adolf
Hitler—who to Mr Five Per Cent seemed mere slogans cloaking the
real causes of both struggles: the imperative need for raw materials;
above all, oil. Now that Russia had again risen to her natural position
as an effective Great Power, it seemed to Mr Five Per Cent essential to
prevent a Third World War by doing an oil deal with her. Otherwise,
sooner or later, there was bound to be a fight and that to him was
stupid, wasteful, unbusinesslike and avoidable. His magic word was
"consortium"—the solution to all major oil problems, the foundation
of prosperity and the guarantee of peace.

He never, so far as I know, went to the length of recommending a
World Oil Authority—a pooling of resources—but that, logically,
was where his reasoning was leading; and others were feeling their
way along the same line.

In 1957 such thinking seems traitorous to Capitalism and
Communism alike—wrong and/or Utopian—and (in the thick
of the Cold War) ridiculous. But is it? Is there any other
solution to the problems of the Middle East—short of atomic
warfare?

In 1945-6, when Roosevelt imagined he alone could "manage"
Joe Stalin and the United Nations Organization was born, these ideas
were not so far-fetched. There was a fleeting moment in history when
the common victory, the complementary basic interests of industrialized
America and agricultural Russia, and the universal longing for peace
made such great schemes of human partnership thinkable. The follies
of the Versailles Peace Conference were still writ large in the minds of
statesmen (and Mr Five Per Cent). The chance was at hand to loosen
the bonds which had tied the Great Powers for a quarter of a century
and produced six years of unprecedented destruction. Mr Five Per Cent
seized the moment and the chance.

Nubar Gulbenkian recalls: 'Father proposed that the Soviet Union
should be admitted to the Western Powers' Middle East oilfields in
1945. He put the case up to Mr Harold Ickes, who was then Chairman
of the American Delegation at the Anglo-American Oil Treaty
Negotiations in London. It was in September, when Mr Ickes was in
Lisbon and was also Secretary of the Interior in the Democratic
Administration, Solid Fuel and Petroleum Administrator, and
Chairman of the National Power Policy Committee.

'But the Grand Alliance was already drifting into the Cold War.

The proposal soon became politically impracticable. But maybe it held the clue to some future settlement of the Middle East problem.'

I understand that Mr Five Per Cent visualized the re-admission of the Western Powers to their expropriated oilfields in Southern Russia, in exchange for concessions to the Soviets.

If that were so, it would have been pointless and impracticable for Russia or the Western Powers to maintain large armed forces on either side of the Caucasian iron curtain, and a new era of international co-operation might have been introduced at the hub of the world. It was Mr Five Per Cent's Columbus Egg—very suitably laid in his Aviz nest of seafaring souvenirs.

It was not Gulbenkian's fault that the egg never hatched. Stalin, the cuckoo in the nest at Potsdam, was already thinking in terms of Two Worlds and expansion.

So were the Americans. Their expansion in Saudi Arabia and simultaneous victimization of European interests in neighbouring Mid-east oilfields has been noted.

Two attempts were made to regulate Anglo-American oil interests: in 1944 by Harold Ickes and Lord Beaverbrook: and in 1945–7 by Ickes and Emanuel Shinwell.

But both proved abortive. S. L. Longrigg's *Oil in the Middle East* states: 'Such agreement, blessed by the American Government, might, indeed, have had value in the better definition of functions and spheres as between companies, and in the admission that such arrangements, instead of being denounced as "cartel", were in fact desirable.

'But the attempt was twice thwarted finally by the uprising of American devotion, in the industry and outside it, to unrestricted free enterprise and dislike of government intervention.'

Philip Graves in *A Record of the War: the twentieth quarter,* adds: 'The United States and Great Britain signed agreement on August 8th, 1945, on the broad principles governing international trade in petroleum to assure adequate petroleum supplies to all peaceful countries at fair prices and on a non-discriminatory basis, the development of producing centres, the recognition of the principle of equal opportunity in acquiring concessions, respect for valid concessionary contracts and the liberation of production and distribution from unnecessary restrictions.

'An International Petroleum Commission was to be established to estimate the world demand for petroleum and to recommend how this might best be met. Unfortunately for the prospects of the Agreement, it began at once to encounter such strong opposition from the principal oil companies of the United States that the President post-poned its submission to Congress.' So it foundered.

At no level were the Americans prepared to co-operate with the British—let alone the Russians—in any such universal oil panacea as Gulbenkian envisaged.

But the seed he planted with Harold Ickes may not be dead yet.

7. Full Circle

An apt turn of history rounded off Gulbenkian's oil career to perfection. The wheel swung right back to Persia—Persia where he had secured his first oil concession in 1897-8—Persia where he made his great mistake in abandoning the concession—Persia where he learned his lesson, "never give up an oil concession"—Persia whence the Anglo-Persian reached out to gatecrash his own Iraq Petroleum Company—Persia, whose oil company nearly always thwarted him and provoked some of his few regrets—Persia, which gave him diplomatic status and, in affording him liberty, unwittingly shaped his final destiny.

In no phase of Gulbenkian's long life is the importance of the continuity of history in the Middle East more evident.

To recapitulate. In 1828 Persia ceded Erevan, the spiritual focus of Armenian life, to Russia. A large and influential Persian colony remained in Russia and was steadily reinforced by immigrants from Persia-proper to the south, until the Russian Revolution. The Caspian remained, until Stalin, the natural channel of communication between the two countries and the outlet for their trade, north and south, to Euro-Asia for the Persians, to South-East Asia for the Russians. The five Northern Provinces of Persia were indeed such a sensitive area that they were omitted from William Knox D'Arcy's Anglo-Persian concession in 1901 and have remained unallotted ever since. Persia dared not let one Great Power in there for fear of offending another.

Came the Second World War and the German-Japanese pincers movement on the Middle East, the German penetration of Armenia and the Quisling rising in Iraq. The Russians were obliged to occupy North Persia, the British the South.

From their arrival in 1941, the Russians got busy oil-prospecting and organizing the crypto-Communist Persian "Tudeh" Party. In

September 1944 Sergei Kavtaradze, Soviet Vice-Commissar for Foreign Affairs, arrived in Teheran, where he was promptly nicknamed "Keftarzadeh" ("Son of an hyena"). His brief: to demand full freedom to explore North Persia for five years and the assurance of a concession afterwards. His pretext: shallow drillings during the Soviet Occupation.

The admission of Russians into the heart of the country for years after the war, under cover of industrial activity, with the victorious Red Army across the border in Azerbaijan, was too much for the Persians. British and American negotiators withdrew from other parts of the country and in October the "hyena" also withdrew, empty-handed. There were strong Soviet press reactions, Tudeh demonstrations and Red Army parades. But eventually the Red Army withdrew, having hung on to the last moment and outstayed the British.

In 1947 the Persian Government quietly passed a law requiring the Anglo-Persian to 'take such measures as are necessary to regain national rights'. In 1948–9 the Anglo-Persian volunteered what Longrigg calls 'the most favourable terms enjoyed at any time by any Middle East government': eighteen months before any profit-sharing offer had been made to any other government in the Middle East.

But nationalization was in the wind and the Company was not allowed to advertise its generosity. The terms were submitted to an oil committee under the nationalist, Dr Mossadeg, whose backers were the Tudeh. Then, in 1950, Aramco proposed a 50–50 new agreement for Saudi Arabia. Mossadeg was given a handle against the Anglo-Persian and in December pronounced the Company's terms were "unacceptable". In April 1951 the Anglo-Persian was nationalized—i.e. expropriated—losing its entire rights, status and assets.

As nationalization and the Abadan grab loomed up in 1950, and the Anglo-Persian was also trying to negotiate a 50–50 agreement, the Shah secretly sent his Paris Ambassador, Ali Soheily, to seek the advice of Mr Five Per Cent in Lisbon. Gulbenkian still enjoyed the rank of Persian Commercial Counsellor, but Soheily said he came to see him as 'the greatest living expert on oil'.

What was the Shah to do? Should he acquiesce in his Government's nationalization policy? Or, oppose it and possibly lose his throne?

This was more than a multi-millions quarrel between Persia and the British Government-controlled Anglo-Persian. It was a test case for all

great Western interests in the Middle East. It was also the parting of
the neutral way Persia had managed to follow for thirty years between
the Soviet Union and the Western Powers. Being wise after the event,
this was the recent date (if any) of the real start of the 1956–7 Middle
East Crisis. Glubb Pasha put it to me as 1946, when Britain gave way to
the Jews over a State of Israel in Palestine. In fact one could take
almost any year during the last century as a starting-point. But 1950–1
was when the rot really set in.

One would have expected Mr Five Per Cent to compromise:
to suggest a "consortium" with the Tudeh's Russian friends:
anything rather than back the Anglo-Persian monopoly, of which
he had never approved in principle and personally detested. But
back the Anglo-Persian he did: with the full weight of his unique
experience.

Nubar Gulbenkian, who is himself Hon. Commercial Attaché
of the Persian Embassy in London, reveals: 'Mr Five Per Cent told
Soheily to tell the Shah to accept the Anglo-Persian's offer. Father
pointed out it was the best ever proposed by an oil company in the
Middle East and ended by declaring bluntly, "Our country is not yet
qualified to take over the oil industry." Soheily found this opinion
very embarrassing. The British authorities offered to put a special
'plane at the disposal of Father and me (and our suite of five persons)
so as we could fly to Teheran to give the Shah our views personally.
But Mr Five Per Cent refused to move. Soheily himself had to report
back the unpleasant news.

When Mossadeg became Prime Minister in 1951 and set about
expropriating the Anglo-Persian Oil Company, Papa's advice came
to his attention. Whereupon Mossadeg took it into his head that
Persia had been insulted and Papa and I were both sacked from our
diplomatic posts. I was not reinstated until after Father's death,
although Mossadeg was disgraced and imprisoned earlier. I felt it
would have been invidious to accept reinstatement while Father was
still smarting from his curt dismissal, after twenty years' service to
Persia. So I had my built-in C.D. plate cut out of my Rolls.

'But there is no ill-feeling now. Soheily is Ambassador in London
and we work together well. Events have proved Father was right. If
the Shah had taken his advice the Abadan Crisis might have been
avoided. Persia would not have lost her oil markets and would be
richer. And a fashion for expropriation might not have been set in the
Middle East.'

Mr Five Per Cent lived just long enough to be able to say to the
Anglo-Persian: 'I told you so.' In 1954, after three years of economic

sanctions (or boycott), Persia was obliged to de-nationalize the Company. And the Anglo-Persian itself was obliged to adopt his own policy, which the Company had so often opposed. It became an international "consortium".

British Petroleum	40 per cent
Royal Dutch-Shell	14 per cent
Compagnie Française des Pétroles	6 per cent
Gulf, Socony, Mobil, Standard Oil of New Jersey, Standard Oil of California and Texas, 7 per cent each	35 per cent
Eight "Independent" American Companies ..	5 per cent
	100 per cent

If imitation is the sincerest form of flattery, Mr Five Per Cent must have died very highly flattered. There were his foreign associates, whom he had first introduced to the Middle East oil riches—the Royal Dutch-Shell, the Compagnie Française des Pétroles and Standard Oil of New Jersey.

It seems odd not to see the Five Per Cent Gulbenkian Interest included. But by now the Red Line had fizzled out. All the same he was doing very nicely with his Stroke 54 Documents.

Now even the Soviets are coming round to his way of thinking. As I end this book, I notice that Persia and the U.S.S.R. have agreed on free, two-way trade transit rights across the Caucasian Isthmus and the Caspian.

The Germans and Italians are bidding for the unallotted Persian provinces, where Teheran would never dare grant oil rights to Russia, America or Britain. The crossroads of the world are getting congested. Perhaps the day when Mr Five Per Cent's last dream of a truly international oil consortium of Great Powers in the Middle East is not so distant after all.

It is extraordinary how people eventually came round to his way of thinking, whether they liked it or not—and they usually didn't.

*   *   *   *   *

I have reserved Mr Five Per Cent's parting dig at the final (1925) compostion of the Iraq Petroleum Company for this point: 'The final setting was Anglo-Persian Oil Company, Royal Dutch-Shell, Near East Development Corporation and Compagnie Française des Pétroles

23¾ per cent, Pandi (Gulbenkian) 5 per cent, with Anglo-Persian Oil Company getting 10 per cent free oil in consideration of reducing its shareholding from 50 per cent to 23¾ per cent. This architecture has not changed. And one cannot refrain from remarking that this 10 per cent royalty, although granted "in compensation", was in reality a gift, because none of the Companies had any rights or concessions in Mesopotamia (at all).'

That is so. In each case the Companies were presented by Mr Five Per Cent with a slice of the Iraq Petroleum Company cake. It could be argued that he was the most generous man of all time.

27

THE EDIFICE: 1955

'MR FIVE PER CENT took no part in the welfare work of the Iraq Petroleum Company,' says his son, Nubar. 'He approved of it, but he simply hadn't the time to cope with the detail. That was work for experts: and he believed he had the best in the world. It wasn't that he didn't care. Contentment among his employees and in Iraq was obviously a good investment.

'Away back in the 1880s he had seen with his own eyes the horrors of Baku and the inefficiency. He also saw the advantages of the Nobels' pioneer social welfare there. Humanitarianism was one of the great developments of his day and he often used to say, "You can't put the clock back." He recognized that the Iraqis had a claim to benefits since the oil is in their territory. So far as the Government co-operates with the Company and the Iraqis work for it, they deserve a generous deal. But Father had no illusions about buying gratitude with "good works".

'The Iraqis never made any secret about their intention to increase their take as soon as they could run it. They told Father (and me) more than once that it's "their" oil and that they're going to take it, bit by bit—that eventually the Iraq Petroleum Company will merely become well-paid contractors to the Iraq Government. There is no real love lost between the Iraqis and the Company.

'But, as Father used to say, "The Iraqis have the good sense to realize they can't run the show yet." Consequently the relations between the Iraq Petroleum Company and Iraq have been good.'

The time has now come to take a look at the "whole show"— or the "architecture" of the Iraq Petroleum Company, as Mr Five Per Cent called it.

2. Financial

Calouste Gulbenkian, the architect-in-chief of the Iraq Petroleum Company, left a mighty edifice at its peak.

In 1955 the authorized capital of the Company was £125,000,000.

If those shares had been sold on the pre-Suez open market, they might have realized fifteen to twenty-five times their nominal value—something like two to three thousand million pounds.

Of the authorized capital, Gulbenkian subscribed his Five Per Cent, namely £5,250,000, which might have been worth £100,000,000 to £150,000,000 pre-Suez.

Thanks to Iraq Petroleum Company operations, Iraq had become the sixth largest oil-producer in the world. Only the United States, Venezuela, Russia, Kuwait and Saudi Arabia produced more.

From 1952 Iraq production rose steadily from 20,000,000 tons a year to 34,000,000 in 1955. World production in 1955 was 786,000,000 tons, of which the U.S.A. contributed 325,000,000, Venezuela 111,000,000, Russia and satellites 80,000,000, Kuwait 55,000,000 and Saudia Arabia, 48,000,000.

Under the 1951 profit-sharing agreement, Iraq was guaranteed minimum oil royalties of £25,000,000 a year and in an emergency £5,000,000 for two years. Actually Iraq received £33,000,000 in 1952, £51,000,000 in 1953 and £67,000,000 in 1954. In 1955 it was £80,000,000 ($223,400,000).

Equivalent half-shares accrued to Royal Dutch-Shell, Compagnie Française des Pétroles, the Americans' Near Eastern Development Corporation and the remaining 5 per cent went to Gulbenkian. In 1955 his share amounted to £4,000,000 and he got another £1,000,000 from the Company's Qatar fields.

The Iraq Government's half-share provided the bulk of the national revenue. With indirect cash benefits in the form of wages, purchases, public services and utilities, the Iraq Petroleum Company provided a quarter of the total national income.

3. Productive

By 1955 1,250,000 feet had been drilled in Iraq, each well varying in cost between £20,000 and £1,000,000, with only a one-in-five chance of success.

Kirkuk had forty-four wells, each about two miles in depth, yielding some 29,000,000 tons of oil and filling the 30-inch pipeline to Banias in Syria to capacity. Basra had eighteen wells, including five beneath the surface level of Lake Hor al-Hamar, and was yielding some 3,000,000 tons yearly. Mosul, the least successful field, had only four wells yielding about 1,275,000 tons, although a hundred test wells were drilled in a single year and the great depth of 11,367 feet was reached.

Besides the huge, intricate plant and local pipelines linking the scattered units, the Company had 12-inch and 24-inch pipelines running up to sixty-five miles to Fao, the terminal at the head of the Persian Gulf, with four tanker jetties and twenty-two storage tanks.

Even more impressive were the Mediterranean pipelines:

1. The 12-inch pipeline running from Kirkuk 532 miles to Tripoli in Syria and forking 620 miles to Haifa in Israel, each capable of taking 2,000,000 tons a year. This double line and its twelve pumping stations required 200,000 tons of building material. It was completed in 1934, when it was one of the engineering wonders of the world, and it was reconditioned in 1948.

Ten 93,000-barrel tanks were erected at Haifa and fifteen at Tripoli. For more than a year 2,600 Syrians and Lebanese, 4,250 Palestinians and 4,250 Transjordanians were employed on the job.

This was one of the few technical matters in which Mr Five Per Cent intervened.

Unfortunately the Haifa branch remained unused after April 1948, owing to a continual state of war between Israel and the surrounding Arabs.

2. The 16-inch pipeline from Kirkuk to Tripoli and Haifa, following the 1934 alignment, was completed in 1949–51 to bring Kirkuk capacity up to 13,000,000 tons. Two-thirds of the 180,000 tons of pipe was supplied by Britain, the remainder by France. At that time sterling area manufacturers could not supply bigger than 16-inch piping. The cost was £40,000,000. Five countries supplied 15,000 workers for the job. The Haifa branch of this pipeline also remained unused from April 1948, owing to the Palestinian situation.

The quickest, flattest and easiest route was from Kirkuk across French Mandated Syria to Tripoli. The Haifa route was longer and over unblastable lava country. For prestige and political reasons the French insisted on the former, the British on the latter. Each advanced a multitude of technical reasons in making out its case. Says Nubar: 'Mr Five Per Cent listened, Then, when there was deadlock and the whole project stalled, he cut through the impasse with characteristic precision. 'Why not have a pipeline through *both* countries?' he asked. Thereupon it was decided to divide the pipeline at Haditha, on the Iraq side of the Syrian border, and branches were taken through the French and the British Mandates. Both sides were satisfied and the political quarrel ended.

3. The 30–32-inch pipeline from Kirkuk to Banias in Syria was

completed by American contractors in 1951–2, also four pumping
stations. The distance was 555 miles, requiring 165,000 tons of piping
and costing another £40,000,000. Seven thousand Iraquis and Syrians,
300 Britons and 90 Americans were employed on the job. Kirkuk
capacity was raised to 25,000,000 tons a year.

The original pipeline route to Tripoli and Haifa crossed 267 miles
of Syria, 17 of Lebanon and 40 of Palestine. A tax-free and Customs-
free transit agreement was reached by Gulbenkian's old associate,
J. Skliros. In January 1955 the Iraq Petroleum Company entered into
a revised agreement with Syria and Lebanon, undertaking to go 50–50
on the profits of transit and loading operations in each country.

4. Economic

Thanks to the majesty of the great Iraq Petroleum Company
international "consortium", which Gulbenkian had created, and the
stupendous tangible benefits which the Company brought to the
6,000,000 population, Iraq did not suffer a bad attack of the worst of
all Middle East diseases, "economic nationalism": "worst" because it
permeates every phase of public and private life and the cure can only
take place in the slow and mysterious processes of the human mind.

An unusually enlightened government was able to curb the
hysterics of its budding intelligentsia and younger army officers. In
1955, under the veteran Premier Nuri es-Said, who dropped the title
of Pasha in deference to "progressive" slogans, and the young ex-
Harrovian King, Faisal II, Iraq seemed a bulwark of stability and a
pattern for progress in the Middle East.

A statutory non-political Development Board was established in
1950, which was entitled to 70 per cent of the oil receipts. With the
70 per cent rising to £50,000,000 a year, there was reasonable hope
that Iraq might be transformed into a modern state in a generation.
Schools, hospitals, housing, town and village planning, irrigation and
flood-prevention, better food and clothing, could all forge ahead so
long as the precious oil flowed and sensible relations continued
between the Company and the Government.

The besetting dilemma of Iraq was always too much water in the
wrong place at the wrong time. The Development Board accordingly
set out to apply the new capital to linking the country's alluvial soil
to its abundant waters. Much planning was required. Iraq was not too

proud to take the advice of Lord Salter. The 1955–9 plan was expanded to £500,000,000 to be derived from the Iraq Petroleum Company.

The Tigris and Euphrates send down enormous useless floods and the emphasis of the plan was to control and conserve them. Two major flood relief schemes were embarked upon: one, a barrage across the Tigris at Samarra to divert surplus water to the Wadi Tharthar Depression, another to turn the Euphrates into Habbaniyah Lake. Both works were completed and opened in 1956 and immediately proved their worth by preventing the usual disastrous floods.

Both schemes were later intended to generate power and conserve water for irrigation. A group of dams on the Tigris was started with similar objects.

Those enterprises are among the biggest of their kind in the world and are basic to the future development of Iraq as a modern state. But that is far from all.

Iraq's roads are being rebuilt, together with numerous bridges and railways, in order to provide east-west communications in addition to the classical north-south routes dictated by the great rivers of the country.

The 6,000,000 population is not enough for widespread industrialization. Industries which are being developed by the Board concentrate on utilizing existing raw materials, such as cement and cotton, which will supply material for projects in hand or local requirements.

But already spectacular items are coming out of Iraq's windfall: the first television station in the Middle East; a "Viscount" airline; an oil refinery; a bitumen plant; and all manner of modern conveniences, such as running water supplies, air-conditioning, refrigerators, efficient cable and telegraph services, and fleets of private cars.

All that would have been inconceivable but for the vision, patience and ingenuity of Gulbenkian and the herculean efforts of his company.

5. Educational

What the Iraq Petroleum Company provided from its own resources, apart from oil, is an example (and education) for the nation:

(a) *Training in Britain*. Fifty technical and scientific students are brought every year by the Iraq Petroleum Company for training at British universities and colleges at the Company's expense. Twelve students are also maintained at Industrial Training Centres in Britain for specialized trades. In any year about 300 young Iraqis come under this scheme. At the personal level it is supervised by the Iraq Embassy in London.

(*b*) *Apprentice Training Scheme*. After six years in Iraq Government schools, fifteen- and sixteen-year-olds are selected for five-year courses by a board under the chairmanship of an Iraqui. The intake is about sixty youths a year and in any year about 300 are being trained at Iraq Petroleum Company expense. The subjects include English, Arabic, mathematics, science, engineering (mechanical, electrical and civil) and commerce. The passing-out standard is equivalent to the British National Certificate.

(*c*) *Artisan Course*. This lasts for two years and caters for twenty youths a year between the ages of seventeen and twenty. The first six months are spent at English, mathematics and in the workshop, the remaining eighteen months in gaining industrial and general knowledge. In any year about fifty youths benefit, at the Company's expense, from this scheme.

(*d*) *Commercial Course*. For this there are vacancies for twenty young men a year and it lasts nine months. Subjects include Arabic, English, general knowledge, industrial knowledge, typing, book-keeping and office methods.

(*e*) *"Training Within Industry" Course*. For twenty-four foremen, supervisors and executives. Weekly. Instruction is provided on how to give orders, work methods and human relations.

(*f*) *Background Evening Classes*. Three hours five evenings a week. For about 500 volunteers. Instruction is provided in English, shorthand, typing, book-keeping, office methods and organization, chemistry, physics, mathematics and practical aspects of oil production such as hydraulics, vehicle and diesel fitting, instrument fitting, plumbing, welding and workshop techniques.

Apart from Arabic lessons for the foreign staff, the Iraq Petroleum Company provides education and vocational training for about 1,200 of its 10,000 to 20,000 employees. Sixteen out of seventeen of the employees, who vary according to developments, are Iraqi.

The overall object is to generate modern technology in a backward country in order to overcome Nature and turn the uncontrollable water and barren desert to human benefit. Incidentally, the Company too benefits from its considerable investment of time, trouble and money in the education of its staff, which seems fair.

The only reason for the relative scarcity of Iraqis in the higher spheres of the Company is the lack of trained men willing to join and serve the Company in its out-stations. Few have been willing to leave

Baghdad, the capital, and Kirkuk, with its 85,000 inhabitants. Consequently the Company insists that students for whom it had paid courses in Britain shall guarantee to serve double the time with the Iraq Petroleum Company in Iraq. That also seems fair.

6. Welfare

The list of amenities, provided at Iraq Petroleum Company's expense, is not exhausted.

In Kirkuk the Company maintains a hospital of 125 beds, with a senior medical officer, one surgeon, two doctors, a matron, seven sisters and four nurses. Two pharmacists, one radiographer, and three laboratorists are also on the Company's staff. Three dispensaries four more doctors and two dentists are also maintained for outlying districts. TAB and inoculation injections are provided for the entire staff. The equipment is modern. So is the water supply, an important factor in a primitive desert country. A sanitary inspector supervises general sanitation, anti-malarial measures, sewage, rat control and town cleansing in the Company estates.

A large modern canteen for 750 workers is maintained at Kirkuk and smaller premises at other oil centres. Good meals, subsidized by the Company, are served for 7d. each.

Working clothes, including overalls, boiler suits and protective wear, are provided by the Company.

There is a Company bus service to and from work.

The Kirkuk Recreation Centre has 450 members, paying 3s. a month. It has facilities for cricket, lawn tennis, basket ball and athletics; taps providing fifteen tons of iced water a day; a cinema for 300, with seats at 2s. each; a library with books, magazines and newspapers in comfortable quarters. Smaller centres are provided at outlying oilfields and pumping stations. Throughout the country the Company has built a series of swimming baths.

A school is run by the Company, under Iraq Government auspices, for employees' children.

The Company also runs a "home ownership" scheme, contributing 10 per cent of the estimated cost of land and building as an advance, repayable over ten to twenty years; offering free advice on design and construction. Applicants may choose their own sites and building contractors. Floods, storms and other catastrophes not intervening,

100 houses a year are built under this scheme in the Kirkuk area. There are 1,000 applicants, whose needs could be satisfied in another ten years of orderly development. The Company runs similar schemes at its outlying stations.

It also provides houses for its employees everywhere: 700 in the Kirkuk area at rents varying from £4 16s. a month for one bedroom, one living room, kitchen, w.c. and shower, to £9 12s. a month for larger houses. The Company's brickworks is the best in the country.

Wages average £450 a year. Seventy-five per cent of the staff contribute 10 per cent of their income to the Kirkuk Savings Group, organized by the Company. In 1953 3,600 Kirkuk employees saved £150,000.

The staff get holidays with pay. In place of a contributory provident fund, the Company has substituted substantial benefits on retirement.

Joint Consultative Meetings, under Iraqui chairmen, are encouraged by the Company in order to discuss all problems and grievances between staff and management which are not covered by the Government Labour Law. A strike in 1946, a general strike in 1951 and another abortive general strike in 1952 showed that conventional Western trade union practice was not ideally suited to the Iraquis in the current state of their industrial experience.

7. The Contrast

Contrast Iraq with neighbouring Saudi Arabia and the difference is one between modern and mediaeval. The Saudi Arabian Government royalties are now based on a 25 per cent greater output than Iraq and exceed £100,000,000 a year. Saudi Arabian production did not catch up on Iraq until 1948 and the needs are infinitely greater in the Arabian Desert than along the banks of the Tigris and Euphrates.

Yet there is no Saudi Arabian Development Board. Only 16 per cent of the royalties or £16,000,000 a year are devoted to public works. Only 8 per cent or £8,000,000 is devoted to Social Services. No less than 35 per cent goes to the Armed Forces, namely £35,000,000. The remaining 41 per cent, amounting to £41,000,000, is pocketed by the royal family. Large sums are not easy for small countries with a population of 5,000,000, like Saudi Arabia, to spend productively. But the disproportion between productive and wasteful expenditure in this feudal backwater is staggering.

Saudi Arabia has achieved little of worth with its riches beyond a 350-mile railway from Riyadh, the desert capital, to the Persian Gulf; some improvements to the old Hedjaz Railway of Lawrence's day; a sprinkling of schools and hospitals, mostly for the new-rich aristocracy; a few model farms, for the same clique; and the beginnings of modern communications. Miles of new motor road serve only for the sheikhs' fleets of American limousines.

No proper accounts are published. The money simply pours into the royal coffers, as in feudal England, with no parliamentary control. Yet the royal family has already overdrawn its royalties for several years. Until twelve years ago the only notable source of revenue was about £10,000,000 from pilgrims to Mecca and the Holy Places. The royal family has since been swamped with "liquid gold" and has yet to prove capable of handling it with a sense of responsibility.

Agriculture and education each get less than a tenth of what is squandered on the armed forces or the royal palaces in the reigning family's settlement at Riyadh. Even the mosques and pilgrims of this self-styled "pure" Mohammedan country get less than a quarter of what goes to the army and palaces.

Little of the wealth trickles down to the common people, who live in illiterate poverty and disease, herding their sheep and goats, as they have for centuries.

How the royal family and its multitude of dependants and retainers manages to get rid of its new riches is a mystery. Many millions go to subversion throughout the Middle East (as in Jordan and Egypt, where Arabian gold has done much to turn the people against their long-standing British friends). Many more millions go to providing arms for surrounding tribesmen to make a nuisance of themselves to the British in Aden and to the British-protected sheikhs of the Trucial Coast in Southern Arabia and at the headwaters of the Persian Gulf. Some goes on luxurious new mansions in Egypt.

Even so, the most lavish estimates for such wanton activities leave a wide surplus. The royal family cannot be mopping up the outstanding millions with fresh supplies of slaves and concubines, jewels, limousines, solid gold revolvers and gold cameras. There is a limit even to such monumental extravagance and stupidity. The only explanation is that the King and his innumerable Emirs (Princes) are salting away fortunes in foreign banks against the day when they get thrown out.

All administrative, technical and specialized operations are in the hands of the 2,500 to 3,500 Americans at work in Saudi Arabia. They have done an extraordinary job in a few years making themselves comfortable and introducing "the American way of life" into the primitive desert.

They have done something, despite the indifference of the Saudi Arabian régime and the conservatism of the priesthood, for the 16,000–20,000 employees of the two operating companies, Aramco and Tapline. Housing and training are provided. New piers, jetties, breakwaters and causeways have been constructed where only sailing craft could land recently. New aerodromes have been laid out. A wireless network has been installed. Railway-building has triumphed over unprecedented difficulties with shifting sand. Water has been piped to towns and wells have been dug in the desert. The elements of irrigation have been introduced and a start has been made with a pilot scheme for model farms.

Yet the contrast between progress in Iraq and backwardness in Saudi Arabia is staggering. Immense wealth can build one nation and ruin the morale of another. Iraqis are the wise virgins, Saudi Arabians the prodigal sons.

Gulbenkian and the company he founded have been a blessing to Iraq. It remains to be seen whether Frank Holmes and his American successors have been a curse to Saudi Arabia.

*   *   *   *   *

The edifice which Gulbenkian visualized, founded and left behind in Iraq is his memorial. No statue is necessary. Anyway, it would one day be pulled down—like Ferdinand de Lesseps' at Port Said.

PHASE III

1955 . . .

28

EIGHTY-SIX: OUT

NOT until May, 1950, when he was eighty-one, did Mr Five Per
Cent consider the time was ripe to draw up a will.

His mind was still keen, his vision unimpeded. His control
over his business empire was unrelaxed and his advice was still sought
by governments. But there was no escaping the fact—he was getting
old. Not many of his generation were left. Nevarte was seventy-five
and had been ailing since 1943. His brother, Vahan,[1] and sister-in-law
were still alive in Algeria. But Karnig was gone, leaving his aged
widow in Paris. His own in-laws, Anna Frenkian and Atvarte Essayan
(still only fifty-eight), were also in Paris. Otherwise the Gulbenkians
and Essayans of his own time were departed. He had only to look at
his own children, the bearded Nubar, aged fifty-four, and Rita, aged
fifty, to know that time was running out.

He was the last of the mighty magnates, who emerged both
sides of the Atlantic in about the 1880's to forge the First Industrial
Revolution, and the only one of the four founders of the Iraq Petroleum
Company from back in 1911. New oil men had come to the fore, who
knew Gulbenkian only as a legend, a sender of sharp messages or a
ghost, who suddenly came to life and gave everybody a shock with
some forgotten clause in an old contract or with a visionary new idea.

He was not ill, nor ailing. But his daily "constitutional" was
reduced to a toddle and he had to be coaxed into a spin in his old
hired car. His eau-de-Cologne massage no longer revived him in
the same old way. His Swedish drill had become perfunctory. His
days of "rhythm" were over. But he still worked ten hours a day,
employing not only his faithful "Madame Theiss", who had by this
time been with him thirty years, but a second secretary. It was an
increasing struggle to get him to sleep. He had always fasted one day a
month, but now he sometimes lived on mineral water for several
days at a time, lest he should put on weight or get drowsy. Not even
the special chocolate éclairs of the Hotel Aviz tempted him during
these periods of self-denial. The "Hellfire Jack" of the old Carlton
Restaurant days had become almost as austere as his father, Sarkis,
with his luncheons of bread, cheese and grapes.

[1] He died in 1953.

He saw practically nobody, except his personal staff—not even Premier Salazar, with whom he had so much in common—self-effacement, austerity, financial genius, religious convictions and auto-cratic methods. He had got so big that Salazar couldn't be useful to him.

One of the few Portuguese seen by Gulbenkian was his brilliant and fashionable lawyer, Dr José de Azeredo Perdigao. Other, less frequent visitors were Mr Five Per Cent's cultural friends, Lord Radcliffe, Sir Kenneth Clark and John Walker, with whom he never quarrelled. Either Nubar and Marie or Rita and Kvork were in almost constant attendance, but only rarely the other surviving members of the two families.

He was more difficult than ever. Anna Frenkian says with a smile: 'I tried to interest Calouste in pictures painted by my son, Aram. But I never got anywhere, although Calouste professed to be interested in art.'

As for his own treasures, the "children", Mr Five Per Cent seemed to have grown away from them. The pictures had been in the National Gallery in Washington (D.C.) since 1949, commemorating George Washington's death and recognizing American war efforts, and he had not seen them since he was last in England in 1940. Nor had he enjoyed more than fleeting glances at his other collections since fleeing from Paris with the French Government in 1940.

Clark and Walker each discussed with the old man how the pictures should be left. Cyril Radcliffe also discussed with him what to do with his possessions.

So, on 6th May, 1950, Mr Five Per Cent took the plunge and made a will. By no means princely sums were provided for the maintenance of his dependants, including 1,000,000 dollars in trust for Nubar and 650,000 dollars for Rita. Nubar was also guaranteed the same annual sum as he was then drawing through his father and it was stated that this should never be less than 70,000 dollars a year.

If the family did not wish to continue living at 51, Avenue d'Iéna, it was to be offered to the United States as an Embassy, or, if it was not required for this purpose, should be used "for educational purposes"—a clear indication of the philanthropic lines along which his brain had been working for some years.

His "children", the art treasures, were not to be sold, because, as the will explained later on, he had additional provisions in mind.

The fortune was to remain "under the administration of the family for five years". Thereafter, unless all were in accord, it was to be divided "as indicated in a new will".

He pointed out that this first will was "drawn up quickly" and for that reason "might possibly contain errors". But, he "relied on the family to realize the spirit of his wishes".

He wanted, he said, his son, son-in-law and grandson "always to keep working" and "trusted to divine clemency to guide them".

When the family and trusted friends, such as Sir Kenneth Clark and John Walker, pressed Mr Five Per Cent for details of the arrangements, he replied with such phrases as "Cyril Radcliffe knows what I want", "Cyril Radcliffe will look after that" or "Leave it to Radcliffe".

Nubar is convinced that his father "could not face death" and believed he would live, like his grandfather, to at least 106. For this reason, Nubar thinks, his father was acting on the assumption that he had another twenty-five years to run and did not bother to put the details of his charitable intentions into writing.

Three reasons are also given by Nubar for his father's abandonment of the idea of leaving the pictures to England:

1. Mr Five Per Cent felt sore over being treated as an enemy during the Second World War;

2. Sir Philip Hendy, Director of the National Gallery after Sir Kenneth Clark, adopted a "technically right" attitude—insisting that the pictures should be split up among others in the Gallery, according to periods—although Gulbenkian wanted them in one gallery (which he was ready to provide), and under his own name. And this made difficulties over lighting and hanging, over which Mr Five Per Cent was "undoubtedly troublesome"—so much so that Sir Philip, "not knowing his man", lost patience.

3. In 1949 John Walker flew specially from Washington to see Mr Five Per Cent in Lisbon, where the American Ambassador invited them and Nubar to dinner. With him Walker brought a beautiful colour film, indicating exactly "the artistic and handsome manner" in which he could accommodate "the children". And off the treasure trove went from London to Washington, where it has remained pending arrangements for its ultimate disposal.

Sir Kenneth Clark, who discussed the destiny of the pictures and the will with Gulbenkian, does not wholly agree with Nubar's explanations.

He told me: 'I often talked to Gulbenkian about his will and what was going to happen to the masterpieces. I think he hoped to control what happened to his possessions after his death. Rich men have been trying to dictate from the grave for thousands of years. But it never works. The only hope is to dispose of things during one's lifetime, without strings, and hope that the recipients will take one's advice and respect one's wishes.

'Gulbenkian should have built a gallery and seen, while he was alive, that all the arrangements were carried out; then hoped for the best. I told him so. He never saw his treasures anyway. They were in Paris and he was in Lisbon, or they were lent to museums, while he lived in an hotel. But he was afraid of what his family would say. So his plans were never completed. Rather than part with his possessions in his own lifetime, I am sure he would have burned the whole lot!'

As Sir Kenneth pointed out earlier, when Iraq oil started flowing on a huge scale in 1934, Mr Five Per Cent had already visualized a Gulbenkian Foundation for his money and treasures. He had even had the model built by the American architect, Delano.

This shows that sixteen years earlier Gulbenkian was anxious to preserve the "architecture" of his affairs and that he was beginning to doubt the ability of private individuals (his son included) to carry on.

In 1950, when his I.P.C. income was already running into millions each year, the case for a Foundation was even stronger.

Lord Radcliffe told me: 'He wanted above all to preserve the structure of the great organization he had built up during his life. But he could not face death and hated to talk about it. Consequently he did not like to go into detail.'

The chances of the pictures going to Britain or any other single nation were therefore remote in 1950. The conception of centralizing his Five Per Cent and treasure in a truly international organization, headquartered under Lord Radcliffe in Lisbon, had taken shape. But only in outline. The will was very vague.

Then Nevarte died at 51 Avenue d'Iéna, Paris, in 1952, aged seventy-seven.

Calouste, at the Normandie Deauville, was overcome when the news was broken to him by Nubar and he never recovered.

Nevarte alone shared his whole extraordinary background from the Sublime Porte to London, Paris and (occasionally) Lisbon. Whole chapters of history and the evolution of a mighty international industry were personified in their union. Together they had come through the finale of their Armenian race in Anatolia and in exile they epitomized its qualities, good and bad. They shared, in their different ways, the same sturdy Christian faith. She had saved his business and provided a shopwindow for his achievements. She had borne him two children of character and intelligence and through Mikael, the grandson, the Gulbenkian-Essayan line from the shacks of the Levant to the great corporations and salons of the world was prolonged. When the frequent crises with their volatile children arose, Nevarte had been the peacemaker and kept the family together, despite the fissile influences of great wealth. She ran his homes with charm and efficiency and had the wisdom to take his peccadillos for what they were, shallow distractions.

In his peculiar way he loved her, as he loved nobody else. To him she was both a good wife and an asset. She had become part of his routine, a habit, a fixture. They had been married sixty years and, somehow, it had worked. It seemed to him they would go on together indefinitely, like his grandfather, to be centenarians. She was part of the illusion which prevented him from facing death: an incalculable event, quite outside his highly organized existence.

Then she departed. It struck not only at his heart, but at his fundamental attitude of mind, which made him a genius—his determination to have everything and everybody under his own control. Something snapped in him. He found himself suddenly alone, as he had never really been, for all his hiding: completely alone. Suddenly he realized he too was mortal and it was more than he could bear. He was never the same man again. His grip and his health began to slip very fast.

He was stricken too low to go to Paris for the funeral or to the interment at Nice, in the sunshine and surroundings they both loved. The shadow of death passed over him and never left.

That was the disillusioned and distraught condition of the father whom Nubar was obliged to tackle about Nevarte's ten-year-old last wish—the Armenian orphanage she wanted to build and endow with the proceeds of her £9,500 dowry, which had saved and, in a way, made the family fortune.

Nubar elicited the fact that there was no provision for the orphanage in his father's 1950 will. But Nevarte's letter in her Paris safe left her wishes in no doubt and Nubar asked that they should be respected. As we know, she included in the letter some very outspoken things about one of her husband's women friends and Nubar refused to show such a painful document to his father. As he says, 'this went down very badly.'

Next year (1953) Mr Five Per Cent altered his will and "Perdi" advised him on the alterations.

Soon he was bedridden. The solitary nurse was reinforced by a night nurse and, towards the end, by two more, making four in all. Occasionally they got him out for a drive, but by Christmas, 1954, he had left the hotel for the last time.

On 14th April, next year, Nubar came to see him for his eighty-sixth birthday and they mentioned the centenarian grandparent. 'I can't equal that,' Mr Five Per Cent confessed. At last he admitted he was beaten. The family established a death watch. But in July he seemed to rally. Nubar and Marie seized the chance to slip away for his annual cure at the Baden-Baden spa. Rita drove 120 miles to Coimbra in North Portugal, where Salazar's sisters live, for a change. Kvork was left behind, holding the fort.

After breakfast on 20th July, 1955, the day nurse had taken over from the night nurse and straightened up Mr Five Per Cent. Kvork strolled out of the Hotel Aviz to buy a packet of cigarettes.

When the nurse returned to the room at 10.20 a.m. to give an injection, Mr Five Per Cent did not respond and stopped breathing: alone, but for the nurse and his faithful secretary, "Madame Thiess", in a plush hotel: a characteristic and fitting end.

The era when one man could build a business big enough to finance a whole country was over.

CHRONOLOGY

The creation of the Iraq Petroleum Company by Calouste Gulbenkian and the growth of this unique international business under his guidance into its present form covers sixty-five years of violent history. The reader may therefore find it useful to refer to this

Summary of the Main Stages in

The EVOLUTION OF THE IRAQ PETROLEUM CO.

1890   Gulbenkian reported on Mesopotamian oil prospects for the Sultan. Oil territories transferred from the Ministry of Finance to the Privy Purse. (In 1899 the transference completed.)

1909   The Young Turks restore the oil lands to the Ministry of Finance.

1910   Sir Ernest Cassel, Lord Farringdon and Lord Revelstoke formed the *National Bank of Turkey* with Gulbenkian as Executive Director.

1911   *African & Eastern Concessions Ltd.* formed. Capital £80,000 in £1 shares, of which the National Bank and Cassel held 28,000, Gulbenkian 32,000 and *the Germans* 20,000 (free).

1912   African & Eastern Concessions was transformed into the *Turkish Petroleum Co.*, in which the National Bank and Cassel retained 28,000 shares and the Germans 20,000. Gulbenkian retained only 12,000 shares, passing 20,000 to Anglo-Saxon (*Royal Dutch-Shell*).

1914   *Foreign Office Agreement*. The D'Arcy Exploration Co.
(March)   (*Anglo-Persian*) came into the Tuakish Petroleum Company with 50 per cent interest. The Germans and Royal Dutch-Shell each obtained 25 per cent. Gulbenkian's rights usurped. He became a "beneficiary with *5 per cent interest*", but without voting rights. (No signatory to act independently "directly or indirectly in production or manufacture of crude oil within the Ottoman Empire".)

1914   *Grand Vizier Sa'id Halim's promise* in a letter to the British
(June)   and German Ambassadors in Constantinople to lease

petroleum deposits "discovered or to be discovered in the Vilayets of Mosul and Baghdad".

1914–15   British Government backed Anglo-Persian claim to the whole Mesopotamian concession.

1915–16   *Long-Berenger Agreement* that France shall succeed to the German share in the concession. Sykes-Picot Agreement promised Mosul to France "without prejudice to British oil rights".

1918   Lloyd George-Clemenceau Agreement that Mosul shall form part of a British-controlled Iraq.

1918–20   U.S.A. demands share of Iraq oil as "An Allied and Associated Power" and in accordance with a policy of "Equal opportunities for all in the Mandates" and the "Open Door".

1920   *San Remo Oil Convention.* Lloyd George rejects American claims and abandons exclusive Anglo-Persian claims to Iraq. *France* gets the 25 per cent German share in the Turkish Petroleum Co. Anglo-Persian retains 47½ per cent and Anglo-Saxon (Royal Dutch-Shell) 22½ per cent, each surrendering 2½ per cent to give Gulbenkian 5 per cent in his own right, with voting power.

1921–2   Gulbenkian alone supports U.S. claims to a share in the Turkish Petroleum Company.

1922   *Provisional Agreement* gives U.S. 25 per cent at the expense of the Anglo-Persian Oil Company, which is compensated with a 10 per cent royalty on all oil produced by the Company.

1923   First "commercial" oil strike in Iraq: at Naftkhana in "Transferred Territory", where the Anglo-Persian Oil Company held oil rights.
          Iraq became a British Mandate under the Lausanne Treaty.

1925   *Pre-Final Settlement:* Anglo-Persian Oil Company, Royal
(March)   Dutch-Shell and the French reduce their shareholdings to 23·75 per cent each in order to let *the Americans* into the Turkish Petroleum Company with 23·75 per cent as well. Gulbenkian retains his 5 per cent. But the Turkish Petroleum Company is bound by the Open Door to auction half its concession after choosing "Plots" for its own use. Iraq Council of Ministers ratifies Turkish Petroleum Company concession for "the whole of Iraq, covering the provinces of Mosul and Baghdad, except Transferred Territory and

the Basra area". League of Nations Frontier Commission awards Mosul to Iraq. Turkey is compensated (December).

1928   *Definitive "Red Line" Group Agreement.* The "self-denying"
(June)   1914 clause, forbidding participants in the Turkish Petroleum Company to act independently within the borders of the former Ottoman Empire, is reaffirmed. The Open Door is closed. A marketing arrangement, whereby each participant obtained a proportionate share of the Company's crude oil at cost price plus a 1s. royalty per ton.

1929   *Turkish Petroleum Company renamed Iraq Petroleum Company.*
1931   Gulbenkian, wanting cash and not crude oil, arranged for the French to market his oil at the mean market price ruling on 1st January and 30th June each year, this price to apply to deliveries during the ensuing year.

1932   British Oil Development Limited obtained the concession for Iraq west of the Tigris.

1934   Iraq Petroleum Company into production.

1938   Iraq Petroleum Company buys out British Oil Development Limited and is granted the latter's Mosul concession (in 1941). The Iraq Petroleum Company also secured the Basra concession in Southern Iraq thus completing its rights for the whole country (except the Iraq share in the Iraq-Saudi Arabia Neutral Zone).

1940   Gulbenkian, resident in German-occupied "Vichy" France, is declared to be "An Enemy Under the Act" and his Five Per Cent is confiscated by the Custodian for Enemy Property. The Anglo-Dutch-American partners in the Iraq Petroleum Company appropriate the Gulbenkian and French shares of the oil and sell it.

1943   Gulbenkian, resident in Portugal, is reinstated as a British citizen.

1947   British Counsel advised that the effect of German occupation of France, where the French Company was incorporated and Gulbenkian was resident, dissolved the 1928 Red Line Agreement but did not affect the corporate existence of the Iraq Petroleum Company partners. U.S. partners sought freedom to participate with other Companies within the Red Line, specifically with Aramco in Arabia.

1947
(June)

The four Groups agreed to the American partners participating in Arabia. But Gulbenkian objects. Operations in Qatar (started in October 1938 and suspended in May 1942) are resumed.

1948–54

The "Stroke 54" Documents laid down a specific course of increased development in Iraq and a price formula for inter-Group sales. Gulbenkian was also compensated for his losses under the abrogation of the Red Line Agreement. His rights under the acquisition or reacquisition of concession within the former Red Line are safeguarded. He and the French are reimbursed the value of their oil sold during the war.

1955

Thus he secured an income from the Iraq Petroleum Company of at least £5,000,000 a year, with the prospect of £10,000,000 a year on the doubling of the Iraq Petroleum Company pipelines capacity by 1958.

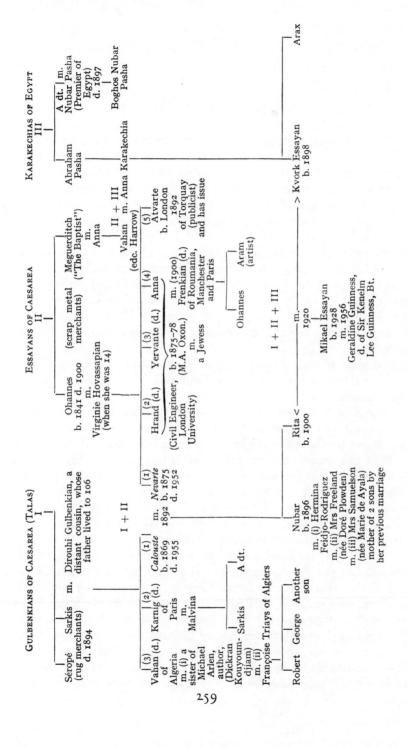

GULBENKIANS OF CAESAREA (TALAS)
I

ESSAYANS OF CAESAREA
II

KARAKECHIAS OF EGYPT
III

Séropé   Sarkis   m.   Dirouhi Gulbenkian, a distant cousin, whose father lived to 106
(rug merchants)
d. 1894

I + II

Ohannes   (scrap metal   Meguerditch
b. 1841 d. 1900   merchants)   ("The Baptist")
m.   m.
Virginie Hovassapian   Anna
(when she was 14)   (edc. Harrow)

Abraham   A dt.   m.
Pasha   Nubar Pasha
                       (Premier of
                       Egypt)
                       d. 1897

Boghos Nubar
Pasha

(1)   (2)   (3)   (4)   (5)
Calouste   m.   Nevarte   Hrand (d.)   Yervante (d.),   Anna   Atvarte
b. 1869   1892 b. 1875   (Civil Engineer, b. 1875–78   b. London
d. 1955   d. 1952   London   (M.A. Oxon.) m. (1900)   1892
                           University)   m.   Frenkian (d.), of Torquay
                                            a Jewess   of Roumania,   (publicist)
                                                         Manchester   and has issue
                                                         and Paris

II + III
Vahan m. Anna Karakechia

(3)   (2)
Vahan (d.) Karnig (d.)   A dt.
of   of Paris
Algeria   m.
m. (i) a   Malvina
sister of
Michael
Arlen,
author,
(Dickran
Kouyoum-   Sarkis
djian)
m. (ii)
Françoise Triays of Algiers

Ohannes   Aram
            (artist)

Nubar   Rita <   > Kvork Essayan   Arax
b. 1896   b. 1900   b. 1898
m. (i) Hermina
Feidjo-Rodriguez   m.
m. (ii) Mrs Freeland   1920
(née Doré Plowden)
m. (iii) Mrs Samuelson   I + II + III
(née Marie de Ayala)
mother of 2 sons by   Mikael Essayan
her previous marriage   b. 1928
                          m. 1956
Robert   George   Another   Geraldine Guinness,
                  son   d. of Sir Kenelm
                            Lee Guinness, Bt.

ACKNOWLEDGEMENTS

Among many scattered and assorted contacts of Mr Five Per Cent, who have generously helped me with first-hand information, photographs and opinions, I am primarily indebted to his only son, Nubar S. Gulbenkian. In frequent interviews in London and Lisbon in the last eighteen months, during which he has racked his brains unmercifully, he has not held back (for good or ill) wherever he could contribute to an objective and accurate picture of his incredible father. He has moreover made the collaboration a pleasure, with his humour and humanity. It is time I said thank you for those zealously warmed glasses of precious Armenian brandy, the carefully poured cups of coffee and the deftly punctured long cigars at the London Ritz. A profile of Nubar Gulbenkian has to be included in this book in order to explain how he came to quarrel with his father and be left with little or no say in the vast estate—and I trust he will overcome his first dismay at what he smilingly calls "the slant of the book". I am also indebted to his wife, Marie Gulbenkian, and private secretary, Mrs. Lyons.

Mr Five Per Cent's unique *Memoirs* enable me to present the greatest oil man Europe has yet produced in his own downright terms, which expose the ways of great combines, both sides of the Atlantic, in their nakedness—for the first time. It is a *continuous* inside history of the events of the last sixty-five years, with no arbitrary or preconceived notions of when the present crisis originated and what the remedy should be. It is an utterly realistic document by the last survivor of the great men who went through it all and should encourage Governments and oil magnates to think again.

Secondly I am indebted to Mr Five Per Cent's brother-in-law, Atvarte Essayan, for his frankness and boon companionship in London and Paris; also Madame Anna Frenkian (sister-in-law) and Aram H. Frenkian (nephew) of Paris, for family history, photographs and personal impressions of their elusive relative. Doré Gulbenkian (former daughter-in-law) has helped me charmingly in the same way.

Many friends, acquaintances and associates of Mr Five Per Cent have contributed to the picture which I have formed of him, but they are in no way responsible for my conclusions. I am specifically grateful permission to reproduce their map of the "Red Line".

Since this book was completed against time in order to coincide with the 1956–7 Middle East Crisis, I must beg the indulgence of my numerous kind contacts for any unintentional errors or misinterpretations, for which I, of course, accept responsibility.

Finally my thanks are due to my elder sister, Eleanor Carver, and to my childhood friend, Dulcie Parker, for ministering unto me during my labours.

RALPH HEWINS

Quarry House, Liphook, Hants